STUDIES IN GANDHISM

STUDIES IN GANDHISM

NIRMAL KUMAR BOSE

SECOND EDITION
July, 1947

Published through the courtesy of
THE NAVAJIVAN TRUST
Ahmedabad

INDIAN ASSOCIATED PUBLISHING CO., LTD.
BOOKSELLERS & PUBLISHERS
8-C, RAMANATH MAZUMDAR STREET,
CALCUTTA

Published by
NARENDRANATH CHATTERJEE,
8-C, Ramanath Mazumdar St.,
Calcutta.

Rs. 7/8/-

Ten shillings.

Printed by
TRIDIBESH BASU, B.A.
THE K. P. BASU PRINTING WORKS,
11, Mahendra Gossain Lane, Calcutta.

PREFACE

TO THE FIRST EDITION

These essays were published in various journals at different periods ; so there has been some amount of unavoidable repetition here and there. I have been chiefly interested in the economic and political ideas of Mahatma Gandhi. This has naturally led to an emphasis on certain aspects of his teachings at the expense of others. Many may not like this ; but the purpose of the publication will be served if it succeeds in stimulating those interested in the subject into an ampler reading and a more correct appreciation of what Gandhiji really stands for.

My thanks are due to the Editors of *The Visvabharati Quarterly*, *The Modern Review* and the *Forward* for kind permission to reprint the articles from their journals. I owe a special debt of gratitude to my friend Sj. Krishna Kripalani, for it was mainly due to his enthusiasm and encouragement that many of the present studies were undertaken.

Calcutta, 15-9-1940   NIRMAL KUMAR BOSE

TO THE SECOND EDITION

The book has been entirely revised, and practically rewritten. My thanks are due to the Navajivan Trust of Ahmedabad, who now hold the copyright of Gandhiji's writings, for kind permission to use quotations extensively.

20th June, 1947
37, Bosepara Lane
Calcutta-3   NIRMAL KUMAR BOSE

CONTENTS

AN INTRODUCTION TO GANDHISM

I have tried to study Gandhi's writings with reverence ; and have endeavoured to keep my mind, as far as possible, free from personal preconceptions, so that the meaning of what he has written may come clearly to me. But in offering the present introduction to Gandhism I may perhaps be excused if I place along with Gandhi's views, a few personal observations by way of comment or criticism. The reader will then be able to understand the mind of one with whom he is about to undertake a long and perhaps tiresome journey.

Philosophy of History

Let us first begin with what might be termed Gandhi's philosophy of history, *i.e.* the lesson which he has drawn from the succession of historical events. Gandhi is one of those who have come to the conclusion that in spite of temporary setbacks, the human race is on the whole marching forward. In other words, the spirit of brotherhood or the sense of human unity has grown steadily in course of time. He has written :

> I subscribe to the belief or the philosophy that all life in its essence is one, and that the humans are working consciously or unconsciously towards

the realisation of that identity. This belief requires
a faith in a living God who is ultimately the Arbiter
of our fate. Without Him not a blade of grass
moves.—(*GC*, 88.)

We shall try to discuss this opinion a little while
later. But before doing so, it is necessary to deal
with a similar opinion shared by another class
of social scientists. Many of my Marxian friends
entertain the opinion, like Gandhi, that human
society is steadily progressing forward ; this being
the result of the operation of some natural law
which can also be traced in biological, and even
physical evolution. Where Gandhi speaks of God,
the Marxian speaks of History, or of Nature.

When we observe the entire range of mankind's
past, a steady and considerable measure of progress
begins to impress us whatever may be the standard
which we choose for purposes of comparison. But the
progress has not, apparently, penetrated very deeply ;
it has not substantially altered the inborn capacities
of the human individual. For instance, a child of
today in an Asiatic home does not seem to be born
with a different fund of instincts from another born
of highly cultured West European parents. But the
manner in which their respective conducts are
shaped by the social environment differs markedly
from one another from the moment of their birth.
The result is that the mind which has to adapt itself
to a wider range of social relations and individual
situations, *i.e.* to cultural stimuli, shows a greater
amount of flexibility and richness than another set
to a narrower range of collective experiences.

From this, it is not unreasonable to conclude that the mind of modern man, who has inherited a vast store of cultural materials, would be superior to the mind of a man belonging to prehistoric times when such accumulations were few. But this is not the same thing as believing in the inborn superiority of modern over primitive men. The observed progress has only been due to the piling up of culture and of subjective adaptation to it. As a matter of fact, what is more is that the large majority of mankind today is denied the privilege of sharing in that culture on account of social inequalities, and their mind consequently remains no more developed than the mind of a primitive man. And even where sharing has been possible, the degree of mental development often remains at a superficial level ; for, when passions are roused, even so-called civilized people do not take long to revert to an animal-like behaviour. Individuals can, and sometimes do show restraint even under such circumstances, if they are already accustomed to guide their actions in conformity with a higher purpose in life, and not that of self-interest or the interest of the herd. But then progress becomes a matter of education instead of heredity.

In spite of this reservation, we should not fail to admit that, on the whole, history can be made to show a change for the better in human nature when a sufficiently long view is taken of things. This has, as we have said, been partly due to the mechanical growth of culture and of subjective adaptation to it. But it has also been, I believe, due to the influence of men who have been born from time to time with

more love and more sympathy than was stamped
upon them by the social circumstances under which
they happened to be born and reared. Thus Bakunin
or Marx held a larger view of human unity than their
surrounding conditions justified. It was the same
with Buddha, and it is the same with Gandhi today.
This love, or sense of human unity, may have been
in them from the beginning ; or, it may have had
small normal beginnings, from which it was developed to an extraordinary extent by later application.
In any case, what is relevant, is that the leadership
of men like these, seems to have been more responsible for the progress of civilization than any other
single factor which I can think of.

A Marxian will legitimately object and say : 'Yes,
you are right. But the mental make-up of these men
has nothing supernatural about it ; all can be explained
in terms of personal history. And, moreover, such
men can occupy positions of leadership in society
only if the objective conditions are favourable. It is
the latter which plant the germs of victory in human
breasts ; among the leaders the tendency only finds
heightened expression. So the importance which
you assign to leadership is overdone. It is the
material conditions, evolving by dialectic steps
towards the final emancipation of labouring
humanity, which are at the root of everything.'

While admitting the soundness of this criticism to
some extent, I cannot unfortunately subscribe to the
Marxian faith that freedom is the goal towards which
history is inevitably leading mankind, or that progress
is itself an undeniable causal law. If it were so, more

of it should have been in evidence in surrounding life than actually happens to be the case. Large masses of men so often permit themselves to be led by narrow sectional interests. Where is again the reason to suppose that all counter-revolutionary forces will surely lose in the long run, and the unity and freedom of the toilers of today will inevitably be vindicated by their final victory ? If there is, it lies in our determination to see that it shall not be otherwise.

A man of faith in God will say that the presence of such a determination in individual minds, and of adequate leadership to give proper expression to the growing victorious tendencies, or the fact that there has been an unbroken succession of thinkers and prophets who have led mankind forward, is itself proof of the operation of a Higher Law which rules human destiny. In many of Gandhi's writings, such a belief is clearly implied. But personally, let me confess, I have not yet come across any sure evidence on which I can depend for the formation of such an opinion. For me, the existence of a Higher Purpose has neither been proved nor disproved. And so long as it remains so, I shall prefer to continue in my belief that the observed progress in human history (though it is not deep in quality), has been brought about by the operation of intelligent love. Men inspired by a sense of human brotherhood, pained by the sufferings of their fellowmen brought about through maladjustment between technical progress and the mental state of social groups, gave a new lead to society and changed circumstances to suit the needs of common human welfare, and thus brought about what little improvement we see in man's mind today. That is how, I would say, it actually happens. But if someone were to ask me why it so happens, when it actually does ; and if the mental progress is not caused by technological progress or not, I would prefer to say that I have not yet been able to frame any decisive opinion on that point ; and I would leave the matter at that. I have seen enough of antiquated mental tendencies blocking the path of progress to be optimistic enough to believe that such obstruction will surely vanish in the course of time due to some historical necessity.

Subject and Object

In the above discussion there is an implication that the Marxian Communist subscribes to a form of superorganic theory of culture. He believes that human civilization proceeds along its own line of evolution, and this process will eventually lead to the complete emancipation of labouring humanity all over the world : this movement being comparable in its inevitability to that of the river's progress towards the sea.

The comparison might be continued a little further. We know that every river is confined within its own banks, and the form of the banks is determined, to a considerable extent, by the force and direction of the water's current. In the same way, the stream of culture creates the mentality of the subjects in whose midst it operates. Each phase of civilization is attended by a conditioned form of the desires in the subjects' mind, and this expresses itself in the shape of thoughts and of values, all of which are consistent to, and a result of, the movement of culture at that particular moment. The object and the subject do not however play an exclusively active and passive role, but they also act and react upon one another. It cannot, however, be denied that the Marxian places more emphasis upon the object rather than the subject. Thus, if some of the subjects are ready for progress and the object is not, there can be no forward movement. But if the objective conditions are ripe and even a handful of the subjects are ready, the rest not being so, then a step forward can be taken in anticipation of coming events. The likelihood is that the rest of the subjects will fall in line in due course.

What is then the role of the revolutionary according to the Communist ? He believes that the true revolutionary has the gift of perceiving beforehand which way civilization's car is moving. All that he is called upon to do is to remove the impediments in the way of the car's movement, which he thus succeeds in quickening to a certain extent. Once he and a few more like him feel that the objective conditions have become ripe for an advance, the subjective role of the remaining masses of men involved in the process, becomes of comparatively little moment. Their feelings may create a slight noise while the car is in motion ; they may cause some amount of friction, which could have been avoided with greater care. But that is not the business of the revolutionary. His task is to speed up the change in objective conditions as fast as possible. Men will soon learn to adjust themselves to the new order. If they resist, they will suffer. If they fall in line, their life would be smooth and happy ; and revolution will bear fruit more quickly than otherwise.

This theoretical attitude of the Communist leads him to a very interesting position in practical life. His aim, as we have said, is to bring about a transformation in the objective conditions as fast as possible. In this, he finds justification for the use of violence. Not that he has any special liking for violence as such, he hates it as much as any other lover of peace. He wants to free the world from the bane of war as much as any pacifist. But with him, as this is the quickest way, it is therefore the most desirable one.

Personally, I find it hard to accept the super-organic theory, even in its modified form, as the last word in describing the relation between man and his culture. Nor do I accept the practical deductions which a Communist usually draws from it. There is no doubt that most men generally function in a passive manner ; this saves them from the expenditure of a large store of nervous energy. But they can behave in a different way also. There have been moments in history when the active element has asserted itself in individuals, as well as in large masses of mankind, and given culture, including the course of economic events an unexpected turn. That such occasions are rare, is due to the fact that men like to avoid the sufferings consequent upon every change, and thus conserve their nervous energy.

And it is their inner acquiescence, born out of conservatism which gives culture its apparent power to rule over the lives of men.

Taking up the simile of the river and its banks, we may say with the Marxian that although we admit that the current of the river is largely responsible for the nature of the banks, yet, we cannot overlook the fact that it is the land, of which the bank forms a part, which determines, to a considerable extent, the nature of the current itself. Land-forms are continually evolving ; but, unlike the river which must find its way to the sea, there is no particular goal towards which land-forms are destined to proceed in course of time. In a similar manner in social evolution, the direction is discontinuous and unpredictable, and set largely by the momentary choice of the subjects, whether they function in the active or the passive manner.

This being so, unlike my Communist friend, I would prefer to place more importance upon the subjective element in revolution than he is prepared to admit. Whatever the circumstances may be, a Satyagrahi should not suffer from a sense of defeat ; but should be able to find some way to carry him out of the wood towards his desired goal. In other words, the subject, while working within the possibilities offered by the objective framework, should himself be able to contribute the decisive element in the whole situation. The Marxian will, I am sure, make a similar claim for himself. But then the subject becomes of more importance in his scheme of revolution than he is generally prepared to admit in theory.

The Means Contrasted

The above is also the reason why the means employed by the Communist and by the Non-violent man for effecting social change, are so unlike one another. The Marxian plan is to capture the citadel of social power, in the form of the State, from the present ruling classes. Then it shall be placed under the dictatorship of the proletariat, which will remodel all things in such a manner as to render all exploitation impossible. Old institutions will disappear ; old habits and values of life will be set aside, and their place taken by new ones in conformity with the new purpose of the social institutions. The Communist hopes that the majority of men, who prefer a passive mental attitude, will fall in line with the new order. But if they do not, he will probably rush to bring about the desired transformation by means of heavy punishment. Unfortunately, the chain of violence thus grows longer and longer as new difficulties crop up in the way, many of them being, in fact, the product of violence employed in the previous step.

Gandhi, on the other hand, relies more upon a basic change in the present mental organization of mankind brought about through the corporate activity of the Constructive Programme and of Non-violent Non-cooperation. The idea behind the first is to create a new mode of production in place of the existing one by means of intelligent voluntary effort, even in the teeth of opposition of the present ruling classes and of the State. Its purpose is to convert all men into toilers, and distribute the wealth of society equitably if not equally. And the idea behind Non-violent Non-cooperation is not to oust the present rulers anyhow from power, but to convert them by means of self-suffering, so that they will ultimately join hands with their erstwhile victims in building up a new economic and social system based on freedom and equality. In Satyagraha, the personality of the exploiter is given due respect ; its successful termination leaves no stigma of defeat, nor the pride of conquest. It thus blesses him who uses it, and also him against whom it is used. And, on the whole, it thus makes for the establishment of a more stable social order than can be brought about by violent means.

But can depraved human nature be set right by the method of love ? In poetic language Gandhi once wrote :

> When I was a little child, there used to be two blind performers in Rajkot. One of them was a musician. When he played on his instrument, his fingers swept the strings with an unerring instinct and everybody listened spell-bound to his playing. Similarly there are chords in every human heart. If we only know how to strike the right chord, we bring out the music.—(*H*, 27-5-39, 136.)

Explaining why he prefers the method of self-purification, instead of exterminating the exploiters of today by means of violence, he once wrote :

> It is because the rulers, if they are bad, are so, not necessarily or wholly by reason of birth, but largely because of their environment, that I have hopes of altering their course. It is perfectly true

that the rulers cannot alter their course themselves. If they are dominated by their environment, they do not surely deserve to be killed, but should be changed by a change of environment. But the environment are we—the people who make the rulers what they are. They are thus an exaggerated edition of what we are in the aggregate. If my argument is sound, any violence done to the rulers would be violence done to ourselves. It would be suicide. And since I do not want to commit suicide, nor encourage any neighbours to do so, I become non-violent myself and invite my neighbours to do likewise.

Moreover, violence may destroy one or more bad rulers, but like Ravana's head, others will pop up in their places, for, the root lies elsewhere. It lies in us. If we reform ourselves, the rulers will automatically do so.—(*H*, 21-9-34, 250.)

Exploitation of the poor can be extinguished not by effecting the destruction of a few millionaires, but by removing the ignorance of the poor and teaching them to non-cooperate with their exploiters. That will convert the exploiters also. —(*H*, 28-7-40, 219.)

The end of non-violent 'war' is always an agreement, never dictation, much less humiliation, of the opponent.—(*H*, 23-3-40, 53.)

Thus, I wholly accept Gandhi's plan of effecting social change through conversion, both of the ruling classes, as well as of the ruled ; I am prepared to work for it assiduously, and give it a fair trial on a large scale ; for, in many respect, it seems to me superior to all other methods of social change which have so far been tried in history. The Marxian way seems to me to be based upon an undue depreciation of the individual's role in history. It also betrays a serious lack of faith in man's capacity to change except under the influence of compulsion or fear. An unseemly reliance is also placed by Communists on the mechanical process of drilling in necessary habits of either action or of thought by means of repeated and skilful propaganda. The best in individual nature can hardly spring forth from such a barren soil unwatered as it is by the joy of inner conviction.

Other, and more gentle methods than the Marxian one, have also been suggested from time to time, and even tried in history. But most of them evade one fundamental question, namely, the question of power. How is the power to shape social destiny going to be transferred from the present ruling classes to the exploited millions ? Here, Gandhi's means of non-cooperation suggest a way which we find lacking in many of the programmes proposed by many thinkers who depend principally on the constitutional process or the slow method of educating public opinion without seriously disturbing the existing order of things. Gandhi's way is a way of revolution ; but the character of that revolution is completely non-violent. In explaining the difference between that revolution and the violent one, he has recently said :

> A non-violent revolution is not a programme of 'seizure of power'. It is a programme of transformation of relationships ending in a peaceful transfer of power.—(*H*, 17-2-46, 14.)

Non-violence and Democracy

There is however an additional reason why I prefer the revolutionary Gandhian method of conversion through non-cooperation and consequent self-suffering. And the reason is this.

Each of us has his own opinion regarding the course of human history, as well as of the role played in it by the various factors involved in the process. In a similar manner, others may entertain different views, which may be logically equally admissible : only the premises of one will be different from the premises of the other. But if each of us thinks that he has reached nearest to truth, and then arms himself with the authority to punish others for their different opinions, then there would be no end of trouble in a mad world. The proof of whether one is right or wrong will lie in one's power to inflict punishment on others ; and this, as we can all feel, is the poorest way of proving the rightness of one's own case.

Naturally, no man can live without his own opinions ; and the most decent way of convincing others of the correctness of one's own position is by converting an opponent by means of gentleness, and not by coercing him. In the propagation of truth, it would therefore be wrong to inflict punishment on others ; but it would surely be right to suffer in our own person for a course of action which we hold to be right. Self-suffering becomes a guarantee of the sincerity of one's own opinions.

This method has the additional merit of helping us to correct ourselves if we happen to be in the wrong. If suffering is limited to our own side, we do not rush to propagate half-tested truths. Such suffering, when willingly and joyfully borne, burns up within us the sources of personal error which give a wrong direction to our opinions. We have, at the same time, the additional satisfaction of feeling that we have injured no one but ourselves for what we hold to be right. This preserves a comradely feeling towards other human beings, as well as a respect for partial views of truth other than our own.

The non-violent way is thus the way of democracy. Democracy can never be spread by the infliction of punishment on others, however distasteful and injurious their ideas may appear to us to be. Self-suffering also brings the power of spreading one's own opinions by actually living it, within the reach of even the physically weakest man. In Gandhi's own words :

True democracy or the Swaraj of the masses can never come through untruthful and violent means, for the simple reason that the natural corollary to their use would be to remove all opposition through the suppression or extermination of the antagonist. That does not make for individual freedom. Individual freedom can have the fullest play under a regime of unadulterated *ahimsa*. —(*H*, 27-5-39, 143.)

While violence is directed towards the injury, including the destruction, of the aggressor, and is successful only when it is stronger than that of the opponent, non-violent action can be taken in respect of an opponent, however powerfully organised for violence. Violence *per se* of the weak has never been known to succeed against the stronger in violence. Success of non-violent action of the very weak is a daily occurrence. —(*GC*, 179.)

Indeed the weakest State can render itself immune from attack if it learns the art of non-violence. But a small State, no matter how powerfully armed it is, cannot exist in the midst of a powerful combination of well-armed States. It has to be absorbed by or be under the protection of one of the members of such a combination. —(*H*, 7-10-39, 293.)

The Gospel of Work

One thing which appeals to me very much in Gandhi's teachings is his idea that in a free society, every man should be given the fullest liberty to develop and exercise his special aptitudes and abilities, consistently with equal opportunity for others. At the same time, all men, whatever the nature of their special abilities may be, will be subject to the law of bread labour. That is to say, every able-bodied person will perform manual labour enough to produce the equivalent of what he consumes for his physical sustenance ; this labour being employed in the production of basic necessaries of life like food, dress or shelter.

When I first read Tolstoy, the fact that I was spending my days in intellectual labour of a type which could be described as being of some use to society only after the exercise of considerable mental ingenuity, made me feel restless ; and I rushed to devote myself to productive service in order to compensate for the life I was living. The work of organising a khadi centre, without any form of outside aid, relieved me immensely in a spiritual sense. But when the work was well on the way, it failed to yield the same satisfaction as I had formerly derived from it. Gradually I discovered the reason was that the institution, instead of being self-acting, depended too much upon me. I seemed to gain in personal influence; but this was a wretched compensation for organization of the masses in terms of self-rule. So I proceeded to remodel the institution in order that the local people might gradually take over the entire task of management without any help from my part. But before the new plan could be properly executed, the work was interrupted by circumstances beyond our control. I was, by chance, thrown into the company of many workers in the political field; and then I discovered for myself a new opportunity and a task, no less important than khadi organization. This was the duty of distributing the fruits of socially useful intellectual labour to my neighbours. The cause of pure scientific research became, at the same time, once more precious to me. It gained a new significance ; but its character was also changed in conformity with my newly developed social conscience.

But the question still remained to be answered : was I entitled to my daily bread. I imagined I was ; and in order to prove to myself that I had no time left beyond what was necessary for rest, I began to work harder and harder. But soon I discovered plenty of blank patches of time which could be turned to use, when I could spin and produce the cloth which I needed. Thus, although I might not find time to perform the full measure of bread labour, yet it was possible for me to perform a substantial portion of it. After long practical experience, Tolstoy had discovered a great truth, viz. that the day consists of twentyfour hours. If one spent eight hours in intellectual labour and eight more in personal needs including sleep, there still remained full eight hours for devotion to manual labour. Then I read Gandhi, once more, with care in order to find a solution for my doubts. And I learnt that he would allow me to pursue my special inclination for science provided I was prepared to satisfy not more than my natural wants, and spend the rest of my earnings for society which is its rightful owner. All our time as well as our talents is, according to Gandhi, society's own property ; and we are only servants entrusted with its rightful employment. The fruits of our labours should be at the complete disposal of the community among whom we live, and we can therefore take from the community no more than what the latter can afford to distribute to us. Thus, self-acquired pro-perty, under the present economic arrangements, is no more our own than what has been handed down to us under the existing laws of inheritance. We are trustees, on behalf of the community, of all that is necessary for the production of wealth.

With regard to wages, Gandhi had said many years ago to lawyers, accountants and engineers, that they were all worthy of their hire ; but the hire consisted of no more than their daily bread, which, of course, included all their natural wants.

. There is another aspect of the law of bread labour in Gandhi's writings which has given me an abiding interest in it. A common idea which underlies industrial civilization is that, for the sake of human growth, we have to increase the hours of leisure which a man can freely employ in work which suits his own taste and inclination. This is good so far as it goes. But there is a feeling behind both capitalistic and socialistic civilization that the work which we have unavoidably to undertake in order to sustain human life, should be reduced by mechanical appliances to the utmost possible extent. Nobody can quarrel with an attempt to avoid reducible drudgery, but the attitude towards work and leisure seems to me to have something wrong about it. The work which is essential for the life of man, should be looked upon as sacred, and made capable of developing the personality of the worker to a large extent. He will undoubtedly need some leisure to devote to work of free choice ; but the consciousness that the moral bond of bread labour unites him to the rest of mankind should uplift him and transform the labour which Nature lays upon all of us with a heavy hand, into a creative endeavour capable of unfolding the deepest petals of our being. In this will lie the victory of Man over Nature.

Self-rule

But does Gandhi's bread labour mean that every man should lead an atomistic life, that we should dissipate all that man has so far gained by the division of labour and by corporate endeavour ? Gandhi's answer is definitely, No. Organization and interdependence there must be ; and if necessary they should reach world-wide proportions. But what Gandhi insists upon is that this interdependence should on no account be based on coercion. It should be of a voluntary character, and the cooperating units should all enjoy the same measure of freedom and authority. This is not so under capitalism and violence. Both economic and military power in the modern world, are unequally distributed ; with the result that small states, as well as common people within each state, are reduced to the position of slaves within federations brought into being by the ruling classes of today.

In its place, Gandhi wishes first to rescue the individual and restore him to an adequate control over his life and destiny, before there can be interdependence and international cooperation. This is the meaning of his insistence upon decentralization, both of the productive system as well as of social authority. For the sake of adequate human development, every man should be in a position to exercise adequate authority within his own sphere of life, otherwise he might be rendered anaemic in a spiritual sense. In order to give effect to this, a very great development of democratic institutions would be necessary in all branches of social life. Old institutions have to be recast, new ones made ; and even the latter have to be remade again and again, as we learn more from their actual working.

Once such institutions function for a while and citizens get a taste of their benefit, they will naturally be eager to preserve them by means of their own strength. And all can share in the defence of un-aided democratic institutions equally, if the means of self-preservation are also democratized. As we have discussed already, this is only possible under non-violence. Violence inevitably tends to concentrate power in a few hands ; and, by that very process, the latter become external to the masses and no longer fully representative of them.

Nationalism and Internationalism

A criticism is often heard that whatever Gandhi's personal intentions may be, his endeavours will, in actual result, lead to the prosperity of the Indian bourgeoisie at the expense of the working classes. The Indian National Congress is also alleged to serve the interests of the former rather than those of the latter. In other words, both Gandhi and the Congress are supposed to be conscious or unconscious agents of Indian nationalism, in the narrow sense of that term. Such an organization can bring about a bourgeois democratic revolution only ; and the goal of socialism will remain as distant as ever. Let us examine if this is true or not.

It is quite true that Gandhi has tried to enlist the peasantry as well as the privileged classes in the cause of India's freedom, and it is also true that some capitalists have profited by their association with the national cause. But there are two points in

which he departs radically from the bourgeois form
of nationalism. The means employed by the Indian
National Congress under Gandhi's guidance, are
such that they will lead successfully to the end only
if the masses become self-acting towards the latter
part of the revolution. And the chances are that
if the masses gain success through their fully
developed conscious strength, they will also
refuse to be exploited in future by anybody who
wishes to ride upon their back. Through the non-
violent means, 'the fighters will gain no more than
the poorest Indian.'—(*H*, 12-7-42, 220.) If some
capitalists join in such a struggle, Gandhi does not
hesitate to accept their help in so far as the cause of
Swaraj for the masses gains thereby.—(*HS*, 15-7-44.)

Ever since the beginning of Gandhi's political
leadership, the Indian National Congress, on its own
part, has not espoused any interest which is exclusively the interest of the privileged classes ; nor has
it fought for any such cause by turning it into a
national issue. Its exclusive concern, whether in
peace or in war, has been the welfare of the poorest
Indian villager. The All-India Spinners' Association,
The Harijan Sevak Sangh, The Hindustani Talimi
Sangh, The Go-Seva Sangh, are all exclusively
concerned with the interests of rural humanity,
irrespective of race, caste, creed or sex. From time
to time, bodies of men, consciously or unconsciously
motivated by sectional interests, have dropped off
from the Indian National Congress. But such de-
fections have never led the Congress to make any
adjustments in their favour. The Congress under

Gandhi's guidance, has begun to feel that the more the common people of India become self-conscious and organized for non-violence, the less is there need of the help of those who may, later on, develop sectional interests. It has always kept its doors open for those members of the privileged classes who would voluntarily declass themselves and subserve the interests of labouring humanity. There is ample room for every individual here, if the above proviso is accepted.

The second difference between the Gandhian idea of nationalism and the usual one is that Gandhi does not dream of benefiting the Indian nation at the expense of any other nation. Not only so. His idea is that if India possesses anything which other countries need, but do not possess, then it is the bounden duty of India to place it voluntarily at the disposal of humanity. Exclusive possession, whether for an individual or for a nation, can never be the rule in a world based on non-violence.

Gandhi has always looked on the whole of humanity as one, and not cut up into fragments by means of hostile racial, religious, economic or political interests. It is in this respect that he departs farthest from the current cult of nationalism. If India has ever been the chosen land for him, it is because he has felt that she will be able to lead the world in the art of self-sacrifice. Obviously, such a nation will not exploit other nations, but will serve to enrich the life of humanity all over the world by its willing sacrifice. Gandhi has written :

There is no limit to extending our services to

our neighbours across State-made frontiers. God never made those frontiers.—(*YI*, 31-12-31, 427.)

We want freedom for our country, but not at the expense or exploitation of others, not so as to degrade other countries. For my own part, I do not want the freedom of India if it means the extinction of England or the disappearance of Englishmen. I want freedom of my country so that the resources of my country might be utilised for the benefit of mankind. Just as the cult of patriotism teaches us today that the individual has to die for the family, the family has to die for the village, the village for the district, the district for the province, and the province for the country, even so a country has to be free in order that it may die, if necessary, for the benefit of the world. My love of nationalism or my idea of nationalism is that my country may become free, that if need be the whole country may die, so that the human races may live. There is no room for race hatred here. Let that be our nationalism.—(*IV*, 170.)

During the last war, Gandhi expressed his sympathy for the Democratic Powers, the reason being as follows :

I believe all war to be wholly wrong. But if we scrutinise the motives of two warring parties, we may find one to be in the right and the other in the wrong. For instance, if A wishes to seize B's country, B is obviously the wronged one. Both fight with arms. I do not believe in violent warfare, but all the same B, whose cause is

just, deserves my moral help and blessings.
—(*H*, 18-8-40, 250.)

Then he proceeded to correct any possible misunderstanding by a further statement :

> Let there be no mistake on the part of English-
> men, Congressmen, or others whom my voice
> reaches, as to where my sympathy lies. . It is not
> because I love the British nation and hate the
> German. I do not think the Germans as a
> nation are any worse than the English or the
> Italians are any worse. We are all tarred with
> the same brush ; we are all members of the
> vast human family. I decline to draw any
> distinctions. I cannot claim any superiority for
> Indians. We have the same virtues and the
> same vices. Humanity is not divided into water-
> tight compartments so that we cannot go from one
> to another. They may occupy a thousand rooms,
> but they are all related to one another. I would
> not say, 'India should be all in all, let the world
> perish.' That is not my message. India should
> be all in all, consistently with the well-being of
> other nations in the world. I can keep India
> intact and its freedom also intact only if I have
> goodwill towards the whole of the human family
> and not merely for the human family which
> inhabits this little spot of earth called India.
> It is big enough compared to other smaller
> nations, but what is India in the wide world or
> in the universe ?—(*H*, 29-9-40, 304.)

SUMMARY :—The supreme lesson which Gandhi
has drawn from history is that there is a benevolent

law operating behind universal processes. Many may call it the Unknowable, but it is there all the same. Under the influence of that Law, mankind has progressed in course of time towards a deeper realization of the essential unity of life. Barriers between communities have also been gradually breaking down.

The chief purpose of human life is the realization of that Law ; and it is then the duty of every individual to set his life in accordance with the Law. He has to help in the historical process of social progress. If then we wish to break down narrownesses which cramp the growth of human life,—narrownesses which might have been inherited from the past or are the result of bringing up under institutions handed down from the past, our method of change should also be informed by a higher sense of brotherhood among men. While trying to non-cooperate with institutions, we should bear no ill-will against our opponents, but should patiently seek to convert them through self-suffering. Finally, our opponents have to be turned into willing partners with us in creating a new order of life based upon a sense of human unity.

The law of manual labour is the first moral law of life, all men have to share the common toil for the preservation of life. Such toil will deepen the feeling of fellowship among men.

A civilization based on equality is possible only if all men recognize the law of bread labour, and also place their talents, whether moral or material, whether self-acquired or inherited according to the existing laws of inheritance, at the disposal of the community for common human welfare.

Different social groups should not however lead an atomistic life ; they should voluntarily cooperate wherever cooperation is necessary. This interdependence may even reach world-wide proportions ; but the principal thing is that each unit should be free and enjoy equal rights with all.

Such a condition is possible if each community is self-contained in the matter of food and clothing, and if it also depends on its own strength for purposes of self-defence. The production of the elementary necessaries of life will have to be decentralized and the means of production placed under communal ownership. The power of successful self-defence can also be democratized and even the smallest community may gain that power if it eschews violence and depends on the non-violent method for self-defence. Under violence, there is no real safety. It leads to a race for armaments, or a helpless dependence of small communities on more powerfully armed groups. Under non-violence, it is the will to suffer which alone counts. That strength is not dependent on physical equipment, and is equally available to the weakest human being as to the smallest social group.

Freedom thus gained will help every community to cooperate on terms of equality with others, and thus lay the foundation of a truly democratic world federation.

THE NEW SYSTEM OF PRODUCTION

For a true appreciation of what Gandhi really stands for, it is necessary that his writings on any particular subject should be carefully studied in relation to the circumstances under which they were dictated. When that has been done, we shall be able to satisfy ourselves if his ideas have changed at all or not, and if so why. It will often be found that basic ideas change very little with him, but their meaning and content shows an undoubted evolution in conformity with his growing experiences as well as the natural evolution of opinions in the world round him. He learns as much from others as he learns from his own experiences.

Let us proceed in this manner to study his views on industrialism and machinery, and also his proposals for raising India from the condition into which it has been reduced by economic and political subordination.

The Charge against Industrialism

While living in South Africa, Gandhiji wrote a small book in Gujarati (1908), which was afterwards translated into English under the title *Hind Swaraj or Indian Home Rule*. This book contains a severe denunciation against 'modern civilization.' In

explaining his point, Gandhi first analysed the results
of railways and of machine-made goods on the economic life of India and then came to the conclusion
that their influence had been wholly evil.

He wrote :

Machinery has begun to desolate Europe.
Ruination is knocking at the English gates.
Machinery is the chief symbol of modern
civilization, it represents a great sin.

The workers in the mills of Bombay have
become slaves. The condition of the women
working in the mills is shocking. When there
were no mills, these women were not starving. If
the machinery craze grows in our country it will
become an unhappy land. It may be considered a
heresy, but I am bound to say that it were better
for us to send money to Manchester and use flimsy
Manchester cloth, than to multiply mills in India.
By using Manchester cloth, we would only waste
our money, but by reproducing Manchester in
India, we shall keep our money at the price of our
blood, because our moral being will be sapped,
and I call in support of my statement the very
mill-hands as witnesses. And those who have
amassed wealth out of factories are not likely to be
better than other rich men . . . I fear we will have
to admit that moneyed men support British rule ;
their interest is bound up with its stability . . .
Impoverished India can be free, but it will be hard
for an India made rich through immorality to
regain its freedom . . . It is machinery that has
impoverished India . . . I cannot recall a singel

good point in connection with machinery.
—(*IHR*, 56.)

Many years later, he said to an audience in
Europe :

Industrialism is, I am afraid, going to be a
curse for mankind. Industrialism depends entirely
on your capacity to exploit, on foreign markets
being open to you, and on the absence of competitors. It is because these factors are getting less
and less everyday for England that its number of
unemployed is mounting up daily. The Indian
boycott was a flea-bite. And if that is the state
of England, a vast country like India cannot
expect to benefit by industrialisation. In fact,
India, when it begins to exploit other nations—
as it must do if it becomes industrialised—will
be a curse for other nations, a menace to the
world. And why should I think of industrializing
India to exploit other nations ? Don't you see
the tragedy of the situation, viz. that we can find
work for three hundred millions unemployed
(through the spinning wheel and village industries
—N.K.B.), but England can find none for its three
millions and is faced with a problem that baffles
the greatest intellects of England ? The future of
industrialism is dark. England has got successful
competitors in America, Japan, France, Germany.
It has competitors in the handful of mills in
India, and as there has been an awakening in
India, even so there will be an awakening in
South Africa with its vastly richer resources
—natural, mineral and human. The mighty

Europeans look like pigmies before the mighty races of Africa. They are noble savages, after all, you will say. They are certainly noble, but no savages, and in course of a few years the Western Nations may cease to find in Africa a dumping ground for their wares. And if the future of industrialism is dark for the West, would it not be darker still for India ?—(*YI*, 12-11-31, 355.)

Indeed the West has had a surfeit of industrialism and exploitation. The fact is that this industrial civilization is a disease because it is all evil. Let us not be deceived by catchwords and phrases. I have no quarrel with steamships and telegraphs. They may stay, if they can, without the support of industrialism and all it connotes. They are not an end. We must not suffer exploitation for the sake of steamships and telegraphs. They are in no way indispensable for the permanent welfare of the human race. Now that we know the use of steam and electricity, we should be able to use them on due occasion and after we have learnt to avoid industrialism. Our concern is therefore to destroy industrialism at any cost. The present distress is insufferable. Pauperism must go. But industrialism is no remedy. The evil does not lie in the use of bullock carts. It lies in our selfishness and want of consideration for our neighbours. If we have no love for our neighbours, no change however revolutionary can do us any good.—(*YI*, 7-10-26, 348.)

It might, however, be suggested that instead of leaving production under private control, we might

subject it to full public control, and thus not only
save men from unnecessary labour but also raise the
standard of life to a height which can never be
attained by a denial of scientific advances in production. To this Gandhiji's reply is that so far as
India today is concerned, it will not be possible to
provide adequate employment for all through indus-
trialization. Even if all could be given work, it will
result in considerable disparities of wealth between the
various social groups participating in such production.
A way out might be found if we can export surplus
produce. But why should India tread the path which
England has already pursued with disastrous consequences on other nations ? It might again be
suggested that, instead of exporting to other countries,
we might gradually raise internal consumption so
that all able-bodied men might be kept fully employed. To this again, Gandhiji's reply would be that
the process of machine-production is itself of such a
nature that it tends to concentrate control over production in a few hands. Thus, even if socialization
succeeds in reducing some of the dangers of industrialism, yet it can never bring power wholly into the
hands of the common man : the latter can still be
reduced to submission by those who handle power
at the centre. This is why he wrote :

Pandit Nehru wants industrialisation because
he thinks that, if it is socialised, it would be free
from the evils of Capitalism. My own view is
that the evils are inherent in industrialism, and
no amount of socialisation can eradicate them.
—(*H*, 29-9-40, 299.)

About Machinery

Gandhiji's objection against machinery rests on the ground that it has rendered exploitation on a vast scale possible ; he, therefore, favours its regulated use. The point will be clear from the following extracts from his writings on the subject :

What I object to is the *craze* for machinery, not machinery as such. The craze is for what they call labour-saving machinery. Men go on 'saving labour' till thousands are without work and thrown on the open streets to die of starvation. I want to save time and labour not for a fraction of mankind, but for all. Today machinery merely helps a few to ride on the backs of millions. The impetus behind it all is not the philanthropy to save labour, but greed. It is against this constitution of things that I am fighting with all my might.—(*YI*, 13-11-24, 378.)

Machinery has its place, it has come to stay. But it must not be allowed to displace necessary human labour. An improved plough is a good thing. But if by some chance one man could plough up by some mechanical invention of his the whole of India and control all the agricultural produce and if the millions had no other occupation, they would starve, and being idle, they would become dunces, as many have already become. There is hourly danger of many more being reduced to that unenviable state. I would welcome every improvement in the cottage machine, but I know that it is criminal to displace hand-labour by the introduction of power-driven

3

spindles unless one is at the same time ready to give millions of farmers some other occupation in their home.—(*YI*, 5-11-25, 377.)

Q.   Are you against all machinery ?

A.   My answer is emphatically, 'No'. But I am against its indiscriminate multiplication. I refuse to be dazzled by the seeming triumph of machinery. But simple tools and instruments and such machinery as saves individual labour and lightens the burden of millions of cottages I should welcome.—(*YI*, 17-6-26, 218.)

That use of machinery is lawful which subserves the interests of all.—(*YI*, 15-4-26, 142.)

Some uninformed interviewer once asked him, 'You are against the Machine Age, I see.' To this, Gandhiji immediately replied :

To say that is to caricature my views. I am not against machinery as such, but I am totally opposed to it when it masters us.

Q.   You would not industrialise India ?

A.   I would, indeed, in my sense of the term. The village communities should be revived. Indian villages produced and supplied to Indian towns and cities all their wants. India became impoverished when our cities became foreign markets and began to drain villages dry by dumping cheap and shoddy goods from foreign lands.

Q.   You would then go back to the natural economy ?

A.   Otherwise I should go back to the city. I am quite capable of running a big enterprise, but I deliberately sacrificed the ambition, not as a sacrifice, but because my heart rebelled against it. For, I should have no share in the spoliation of the nation that is going on from day to day. But I am industrializing the villages in a different way.—(H, 27-2-37, 18.)

Gandhiji would favour
mass-production, certainly, but not based on force. After all, the message of the spinning wheel is that. It is mass-production but mass-production in people's own homes. If you multiply individual production to millions of times, would it not give you mass-production on a tremendous scale ? I would categorically state my conviction that the mania for mass-production is responsible for the world crises. Granting for the moment that machinery may supply all the needs of humanity, still, it would concentrate production in particular areas, so that you would have to go in a roundabout way to regulate distribution, whereas if there is pro-duction and distribution both in the respective areas where things are required, it is automa-tically regulated and there is less chance for fraud, none for speculation. When production and consumption thus become localised, the temptation to speed up production indefinitely and at any price disappears. All the endless difficulties and problems that our present-day economic system presents, too, would then come to an end. There would be no unnatural accumulation of hoards in the pockets of the few, and want in the midst of plenty in regard

to the rest. You see that these nations are able to exploit the so-called weaker or unorganized races of the world. Once these races gain this elementary knowledge and decide that they are no more going to be exploited, they will simply be satisfied with what they can provide themselves. Mass-production, then, at least where the vital necessities are concerned, will disappear.

Q. So you are opposed to machinery only because and when it concentrates production and distribution in the hands of the few ?

A. You are right. I hate privilege and monopoly. Whatever cannot be shared with the masses is taboo to me. That is all. —(*H*, 2-11-34, 301.)

India's Economic Problem and its Solution through Decentralization

In the *Hind-Swaraj or Indian Home Rule*, Gandhiji first suggested that common people could only regain control over their economic destiny if production was once more set to the village scale. But it was only after the Non-cooperation Movement of 1921 that he had an opportunity of experimenting on a large scale with the above idea. Suitable extracts from his writings will show how he does not favour the growth of mills in India, but would encourage village industries so that work and wealth might be made available to all, and a more equitable distribution made possible through our voluntary effort.

Multiplication of mills (he wrote) cannot

solve the problem. They will take too long to overtake the drain and they 'cannot distribute' the sixty crores (the price in rupees which India was then annually paying for the purchase of foreign cloth—N.K.B.) in our homes. They can only cause concentration of money and labour and thus make confusion worse confounded.—(*YI*, 10-12-19 *Tagore*, 487.)

Our mills cannot today spin enough for our wants, and if they did, they will not keep down the prices unless they were compelled. They are frankly money-makers and they will not therefore regulate prices according to the needs of the nation. Hand-spinning is therefore designed to put millions of rupees in the hands of poor villagers. Every agricultural country requires a supplementary industry to enable the peasants to utilise the spare hours. Such industry for India has always been spinning. —(*YI*, 16-2-21, 50.)

We want to organise our national power not by adopting the best methods of production only but by the best methods of both production and distribution.—(*YI*, 28-7-20 *Tagore*, 544.)

What India needs is not the concentration of capital in a few hands, but its distribution so as to be within easy reach of the $7\frac{1}{2}$ lakhs of villages that make this continent 1,900 miles long and 1,500 miles broad.—(*YI*, 23-3-21, 93.)

Swadeshi means a real industrial revival and consequent disappearance of grinding and growing pauperism in the land. And when

we have found ourselves able to become self-
contained without State aid regarding our cloth
supply and have solved what had appeared to
be an insoluble problem for the poverty of India,
we shall have confidence in our ability to manage
our own affairs.

Today Sir William Vincent (the then Home
Member of the Government of India) is able to
make us dance to his tune. All this will be
changed. Sir William Vincent will play a
different tune when he finds that without British
power and indeed, in spite of it, we are able to
dispense with foreign aid for the supply of our
vital needs.—(*YI*, 6-10-21, 320.)

I am more than ever convinced that, without
the spinning wheel, the problem of India's
poverty cannot be solved. Millions of India's
peasants starve for want of supplementary occupation. If they have spinning to add to their
slender resources, they can fight successfully
against pauperism and famine. Mills cannot
solve the problem. Only hand-spinning—and
nothing else—can. When India was forced to
give up hand-spinning, she had no other occupation in return. Imagine what would happen to a
man who found himself suddenly deprived of a
quarter of his bare livelihood. Over eighty-five
per cent. of her population have more than a
quarter of their time lying idle. And, therefore
even apart from the terrible drain rightly
pointed out by the G. O. M. of India, she has
steadily grown poorer because of this enforced

idleness. The problem is how to utilise these billions of hours of the nation without disturbing the rest. Restoration of the spinning wheel is the only possible answer. This has nothing to do with my special views on machinery or with the boycott of foreign goods in general. India is likely to accept the answer in full during this year. It is a madness to tinker with the problem. I am writing this in Puri in front of the murmuring waves. The picture of the crowd of men, women and children with their fleshless ribs under the very shadow of Jagannath, haunts me. If I had the power, I would suspend every other activity in schools and colleges, and everywhere else, and popularise spinning, prepare out of these lads and lasses spinning teachers, inspire every carpenter to prepare spinning wheels ; and ask the teachers to take these life-giving machines to every home, and teach them spinning. If I had the power, I would stop an ounce of cotton from being exported and would have it turned into yarn in these homes. I would dot India with depots for receiving this yarn and distributing it among weavers. Given sufficient steady and trained workers, I would undertake to drive pauperism out of India during this year. This undoubtedly requires a change in the angle of vision and in the national taste. I regard the Reforms and every-thing else in the nature of opiates to deaden our conscience. We must refuse to wait for genera-tions to furnish us with a patent solution of

a problem which is ever growing in seriousness.
Nature knows no mercy in dealing stern justice.
If we do not wake up before long, we shall be
wiped out of existence. I invite the sceptics to
visit Orissa, penetrate its villages, and find out for
themselves where India stands. They will then
believe with me that to possess or to wear, an
ounce of foreign cloth is a crime against India
and humanity.—(*YI*, 6-4-21, 108.)

Probably very few workers have noticed that
progress of hand-spinning means the greatest
voluntary co-operation the world has ever seen.
It means co-operation among millions of human
beings scattered over a very wide area and
working for their daily bread. No doubt agriculture has required much co-operative effort, but
hand-spinning requires still greater and more
honest co-operation. Wheat grows more by
nature's honesty than man's. Manufacture of
yarn in our cottages is dependent solely on
human honesty. Hand-spinning is impossible
without the willing and intelligent co-operation
of millions of human beings. We have to arrive
at a stage when the spinner like the grain-seller
is assured of a steady market for his yarn as well
as the supply of cotton sliver, if he or she
does not know the process of carding. Is it
any wonder if I claim that hand-spinning can
drive away as if by magic the growing pauperism
of the masses ? An English friend sends me a
newspaper cutting showing the progress of
machinery in China. He has evidently imagined

that in advocating hand-spinning, I am propagating my ideal about machinery. I am doing nothing of this kind. I would favour the use of the most elaborate machinery if thereby India's pauperism and resulting idleness be avoided. I have suggested hand-spinning as the only ready means of driving away penury and making famine of work and wealth impossible. The spinning wheel itself is a piece of valuable machinery, and in my own humble way I have tried to secure improvement in it in keeping with the special conditions of India. The only question that a lover of India and humanity has to address himself to is how best to devise practical means of alleviating India's wretchedness and misery. No scheme of irrigation or other agricultural improvement that human ingenuity can conceive can deal with the vastly scattered population of India or provide work for masses of mankind who are constantly thrown out of employment. Imagine a nation working only five hours per day on an average, and this, not by choice but by force of circumstances, and you have a realistic picture of India.

If the reader would visualise the picture, he must dismiss from his mind the busy fuss of the city life or the grinding fatigue of the factory life or the slavery of the plantations. These are but drops in the ocean of Indian humanity. If he would visualise the picture of the Indian skeleton, he must think of the eighty per cent of the population which is working its own fields and which has practically no occupation for at least four months in the year and which there-fore lives on the borderland of starvation. This is the normal condition. The ever recurring famines make a large addition to this enforced idleness. What is the work that these men and women can easily do in their own cottages so as to supplement their very slender resources? Does anyone still doubt that it is only hand-spinning and nothing else? And I repeat that this can be made universal in a few months' time if only the workers will. Indeed it is on a fair way to becoming universal. Experts only are needed to organise it. People are ready and what is most in favour of hand-spinning is that it is not a new and untried method, but people have up to recently been using it. Its successful re-introduction does need skilful endeavour, honesty and co-operation on the largest scale known to the world. And if India can achieve his co-operation, who shall deny that India has by that one act achieved Swaraj.

It is my claim that as soon as we have com-pleted the boycott of foreign cloth (through the production of hand-spun and hand-woven cloth—N. K. B.), we shall have evolved so far that we shall.......remodel national life in keeping with the ideal of simplicity and domesticity implanted in the bosom of the masses. We will not then be dragged into imperialism, which is built upon exploitation of the weaker races of the earth, and the acceptance of a giddy materialistic civilization protected by naval and air forces that have made peaceful living almost impossible. On the contrary, we shall then refine that imperialism into a commonwealth of nations which will combine, if they do, for the purpose of giving their best to the world and of protecting, not by brute force but by self-suffering, the weaker nations or races of the earth. Non-co-operation aims at nothing less than this revolution in the thought-world. Such a transformation can come only after the complete success of the spinning-wheel. India can become fit for delivering such a message when she has become proof against temptation and therefore attacks from outside, by becoming self-contained regarding two of her chief needs—food and clothing. —(*YI*, 29-6-21, 206.)

Toning down of
Production by Machinery

Gandhi's emphasis on the spinning wheel will not however lead to the complete extinction of the modern machine in India, and he is realist enough to recognise that.

Do I seek to destroy the mill industry, I have often been asked. If I did I should not have pressed for the abolition of the excise duty. I want the mill industry to prosper—only I do not want it to prosper at the expense of the country. On the contrary, if the interests of the country demand that the industry should go, I should

let it go without the slightest compunction.
—(*YI*, 24-2-27, 58.)

Khaddar (he wrote again) does not seek to destroy all machinery, but it does regulate its weedy growth. It uses machinery for the service of the poorest in their own cottage. The wheel is itself an exquisite piece of machinery.— (*YI*, 17-3-27, 85.)

I am personally opposed to great trusts and concentration of industries by means of elaborate machinery. But at the present moment I am concerned with destroying the huge system of exploitation which is ruining India. If India takes to khaddar and all it means, I do not lose the hope of India taking only as much of the modern machinery as may be considered necessary for the amenities of life and for labour-saving purposes.—(*YI*, 24-7-24, 246.)

The Non-cooperation Movement itself was described as :

An attempt to introduce, if it is at all possible, a human or humane spirit among the men behind the machinery. Organisation of machinery for the purpose of concentrating wealth and power in the hands of the few for the exploitation of many, I hold to be altogether wrong. Much of the organisation of the machinery of the present age is of that type. The movement of the spinning wheel is an organised attempt to displace machinery from that state of exclusiveness and exploitation and to place it in its proper state. Under my scheme, therefore, men in charge of machinery will think not of themselves or even of the nation to which they belong but of the whole human race. Thus Lancashire will cease to use machinery for exploiting India and other countries, but on the contrary will devise means for enabling India to convert in her own villages her cotton into cloth. Nor will Americans under my scheme seek to enrich themselves by exploiting the other races of the earth through their inventive skill.— (*YI*, 17-9-25, 321.)

Gandhiji's Re-affirmation of Village-centred Civilization

Commenting on the economic resuscitation of the village, Gandhiji said :

The revival of the village is possible only when it is no more exploited. Industrialisation on a mass scale will necessarily lead to passive or active exploitation of the villages as the problems of competition and marketing come in. Therefore we have to concentrate on the village being self-contained, manufacturing mainly for use. Provided this character of the village industry is maintained, there would be no objection to villages using even the modern machines and tools that they can make and can afford to use. Only they should not be used as a means of exploitation of others.—(*H*, 29-8-36, 226.)

When the war began in 1939, Gandhiji repeatedly advised his countrymen to go back to the economy of village-sufficiency in order to tide over the difficult times which were lying ahead. In one of these articles, he went forward to say :

Remember that your non-violence cannot operate effectively unless you have faith in the spinning wheel. I would ask you to read *Hind Swaraj* with my eyes and see therein the chapter on how to make India non-violent. You cannot build non-violence on factory civilization, but it can be built on self-contained villages. Even if Hitler was so minded, he could not devastate seven hundred thousand non-violent villages. He would himself become non-violent in the process. Rural economy as I have conceived it eschews exploitation altogether, and exploitation is the essence of violence. You have therefore to be rural-minded before you can be non-violent, and to be rural-minded you have to have faith in the spinning wheel.— (*H*, 4-11-39, 331.)

But will the cities of India be no longer there, need they be destroyed ? Gandhiji explained his conception of the future relation between the city and the village in the following way :

Under my scheme, nothing will be allowed to be produced by the cities which can be equally well produced by the villages. The proper function of cities is to serve as clearing houses for village product.—(*H*, 28-1-39, 438.)

If I can convert the country to my point of view, the social order of the future will be based predominantly on the charkha and all it implies.

It will include everything that promotes the well-being of the villagers. It will not exclude the industries mentioned by my correspondent so long as they do not smother the villages and village life. I do visualise electricity, ship-building, iron-works, machine-making and the like existing side by side with village handi-crafts. But the order of dependence will be reversed. Hitherto the industrialisation has been so planned as to destroy the villages and village crafts. In the State of the future it will subserve the villages and their crafts. I do not share the socialist belief that centralisation of the necessaries of life will conduce to the common welfare when the centralised indus-tries are planned and owned by the State.— (*H*, 27-1-40, 428.)

We thus see how Gandhiji is not in favour of centralization of the means of producing the vital necessaries of life, viz. food and clothing. At the same time, he is also in favour of production only for use and not for profit. Naturally this can be assured only if the machinery of production is not left at the capricious disposal of private persons. Gandhiji clearly favours collective ownership, and we shall try to illustrate his views by means of relevant extracts from his writings.

Below is given Mahadev Desai's report of a con-versation which Gandhiji had with a socialist in 1935:

A socialist holding a brief for machinery asked Gandhiji if the village industries movement was not meant to oust all machinery.

'Is not this wheel a machine?' was the counter-question that Gandhiji, who was just then spinning, gave in reply.

'I do not mean this machine, but I mean bigger machinery'.

'Do you mean Singer's sewing machine? That too is protected by the village industries movement, and for that matter any machinery which does not deprive masses of men of the opportunity to labour, but which helps the individual and adds to his efficiency, and which a man can handle at will without being its slave'.

'But what about the great inventions? You would have nothing to do with electricity?'

'Who said so? If we could have electricity in every village home, I should not mind villagers plying their implements and tools with the help of electricity. But then the village communities or the State would own power houses, just as they have their grazing pastures. But where there is no electricity and no machinery, what are idle hands to do? Will you give them work, or would you have their owners cut them down for want of work?

'I would prize every invention of science made for the benefit of all. There is a difference between invention and invention. I should not care for the asphyxiating gases capable of killing masses of men at a time. The heavy machinery for work of public utility which cannot be undertaken by human labour has its inevitable place, but all that would be owned by the State and used entirely for the benefit of the people. I can have no consideration for machinery which is meant either to enrich the few at the expense of the many, or without cause to displace the useful labour of many.

'But even you as socialist would not be in favour of an indiscriminate use of machinery. Take printing presses. They will go on. Take surgical instruments. How can one make them with one's hands ? Heavy machinery would be needed for them. But there is no machinery for the cure of idleness, but this', said Gandhiji pointing to his spinning wheel. 'I can work it whilst I am carrying on this conversation with you, and am adding a little to the wealth of the country. This machine no one can oust'. —(H, 22-6-35, 146.)

Q. Then you are fighting not against machinery as such, but against its abuses which are so much in evidence today ?

A. I would unhesitatingly say, yes ; but I would add that scientific truths and discoveries should first of all cease to be mere instruments of greed. Then labourers will not be overworked and machinery, instead of becoming a hindrance will be a help. I am aiming not at eradication of all machinery, but its limitation.

Q. When logically argued that would seem to imply that all complicated power-driven machinery should go ?

A. It might have to go, but I must make one thing clear. The supreme consideration is man. The machine should not tend to make atrophied the limbs of man. For instance, I would make intelligent exceptions. Take the case of the Singer sewing machine. It is one of the few useful things ever invented, and there is a romance about the device itself. Singer saw his wife labouring over the tedious process of sewing and seaming with her own hands, and simply out of his love for her devised the sewing machine in order to save her from unnecessary labour. He, however, saved not only her labour but also the labour of everyone who could purchase a sewing machine.

Q. But in that case there would have to be a factory for making these Singer sewing machines, and it would have to contain power-driven machinery of ordinary type ?

A. Yes, but I am socialist enough to say that such factories should be nationalised, or State controlled. They ought only to be working under the most attractive and ideal conditions, not for profit, but for the benefit of humanity, love taking the place of greed as the motive. It is an alteration in the conditions of labour that I want. This mad rush for wealth must cease, and the labourer must be assured, not only of a living wage but a daily task that is not a mere drudgery. The machine will, under these conditions, be as much a help to the man working it as to the State, or the man who owns it. The present mad rush will cease, and the labourer will work (as I have said) under attractive and ideal conditions.

This is but one of the exceptions I have in mind. The sewing machine had love at its back. The individual is the one supreme consideration. The saving of labour of the individual should be the object, and honest humanitarian consideration, and not greed, the motive. Replace greed by love and everything will come right.—(*YI*, 13-11-24, 378.)

Similarly in answer to a question regarding his ideal of India's economic constitution, he said :

According to me the economic constitution of India and for the matter of that the world should be such that no one under it should suffer from want of food and clothing. In other words, everybody should be able to get sufficient work to enable him to make the two ends meet. And this ideal can be universally realised only if the means of production of elementary necessaries of life remain in the control of the masses. These should be freely available to all as God's air and water are or ought to be ; they should not be made a vehicle of traffic for the exploitation of others.

Their monopolization by any country, nation or group of persons would be unjust. The neglect of this simple principle is the cause of the destitution that we witness today not only in this unhappy land but other parts of the world too.—(*YI*, 15-11-28, 381.)

Towards Collective Ownership

The ideal of collectivism seems to have grown deeper and more urgent with Gandhiji in recent years. When the Go-Seva Sangh Conference was held in 1942, the most important question for consideration, according to him, was 'whether cow farming should be in the hands of individuals or done collectively.' His personal opinion was expressed unequivocally : 'I myself had no hesitation in saying that she could never be saved by individual farming.' The article which he wrote on this subject entitled 'Individual or Collective ?' in the *Harijan* is of so much importance that we do not make any apology for reproducing a long extract from it.

The world today (he wrote) is moving towards the ideal of collective or co-operative effort in every department of life. Much in this line has been and is being accomplished. It has come into our country also, but in such a distorted form that our poor have not been able to reap its benefits. *Pari passu* with the increase in our population land-holdings of the average farmer are daily decreasing. Moreover what the individual possesses is often fragmentary. For such farmers to keep cattle in their homes is a suicidal policy ; and yet this is their condition today .... [Then he recommends certain practical measures for collective cow-farming, after which he says] I firmly believe too that we shall not derive the full benefits of agriculture until we take to co-operative farming. Does it not stand to reason that it is far better for a hundred families in a village to cultivate their lands collectively and divide the income therefrom than to divide the land anyhow into a hundred portions ? And what applies to land applies equally to cattle.

It is quite another matter that it may be difficult to convert people to adopt this way of life straightway. The straight and narrow road is always hard to traverse, every step in the programme of cow service is strewn with thorny problems, but only by surmounting difficulties can we hope to make the path easier. My purpose for the time being is to show the great superiority of collective cattle farming over the individual effort. I hold further that the latter is wrong and the former only is right. In reality the individual can only safeguard his independence through co-operation, in cattle farming the individual effort has led to selfishness and inhumanity, whereas the collective effort can abate both the evils, if it does not remove them altogether.—(*H*, 15-2-42, 39.)

Criticisms Answered

After having thus given in outline the high points of Gandhiji's proposed system of production, we shall now proceed to deal with a few criticisms which are usually levelled against it. Admitting that Gandhiji wants to root out all exploitation, why should he propose to go back to an age of agriculture and handicrafts, which we have already left far behind ?

Now, the resemblance between what Gandhiji

wishes to create and what actually existed in the past is not more than in appearance. Gandhiji knows very well that the past was tarnished by social inequalities, and it is from there that the sin of untouchability has descended upon our shoulders. If we go back to what seems to be crude handicrafts, it is in order to rescue the individual from submergence under centralized control against his will. Once the individual gains his freedom, i. e., a control over his economic destiny, it will be time for him to enter into voluntary co-operation with others for further raising the standard of life. This is true as much of the individual as of the basic economic or political units which he builds up freely in association with his neighbours. While thus maintaining his democratic freedom, he can naturally proceed to further interdependence in order to save unnecessary labour through the use of machinery held in common, and run for that particular purpose and not for profit.

The entire moral code, as well as the property relations being based on new principles, Gandhiji's village-centred society and civilization will be entirely different from the one which we had in India in the past. Gandhiji is himself perfectly aware of this, and consequently wrote :

Mediaeval times may have been bad, but I am not prepared to condemn things simply because they are mediaeval. The spinning wheel is undoubtedly mediaeval, but seems to have come to stay. Though the article is the same, it has become a symbol of freedom and unity as at one

time, after the advent of the East India
Company, it had become a symbol of slavery.
Modern India has found in it a deeper and
truer meaning than our fathers dreamt of.
—(*H*, 16-10-37, 300.)

Admitting that decentralization may have
certain merits, by way of providing work and
wealth to all members of society, the question
remains : Will a society which restricts heavy
industries and eschews centralized control, be able
to defend itself against either internal disruption or
foreign aggression ? In other words, is social preservation possible by means of non-violence ? The
question of defence is indeed vital ; and if Gandhiji's
productive system breaks down on this point, its
future is naturally doomed.

Now, let us consider how a nation defends itself
today by means of armed power. The technical
progress of science has been so great in modern times,
that it is no longer possible for any single nation,
however great, to defend her national integrity
merely by means of her own armed strength.
Nations have to band together against other nations
who have united for offensive purposes. But even
then, either of these groups may anyday lose its
position of vantage due to some new advance in
the science of destruction.

Their war industries may suddenly become obso-
lete, while new materials needed for war purposes,
may be found lacking within their own borders.
The security of nations thus becomes contingent

upon circumstances over which men have hardly any control. They can hope to survive in freedom or power only if luck favours them in diplomatic manoeuvres, or if nature has already endowed them with suitable raw materials, or a geographical position helpful in relation to the prevailing form of attack.

Gandhiji is consequently of opinion that this can never be the true way of saving democracy. Democracy can never be preserved unless the means of defence and self-preservation are also democratized, i.e., brought within reach of the smallest community on earth. This is possible only under non-violence. That community alone has a right to live which knows how to die in defence of its own life without inflicting death upon the aggressor. Such example converts the aggressive community, or a large and vital part of the individuals comprising it, and thus makes possible the establishment of a real war-free world through the conversion of those who are today enjoying power at the cost of others who are inefficient in a military sense. If Gandhiji's experiment succeeds in India, it is bound to save democracy in the world ; there seems to be no other way.

> Science of war (he wrote) leads one to dictatorship pure and simple. Science of non-violence can alone lead one to pure democracy.—(*H*, 15-10-38, 290.)

Setting forth the ultimate aim of social organization and his objection against totalitarianism, Gandhiji wrote :

> The end to be sought is human happiness

combined with full mental and moral development.
This end can be achieved under decentralisation.
Centralisation as a system, is inconsistent with
nonviolent structure of society.—(H, 18-1-42, 5.)

Describing his idea of village republics, he
wrote a few months later :

My idea of village Swaraj is that it is a
complete republic, independent of its neighbours
for its vital wants, and yet inter-dependent for
many things in which dependence is a necessity.
Thus every village's first concern will be to grow
its own food crops and cotton for its cloth.
It should have a reserve for its cattle, recreation
and playground for adults and children. Then,
if there is more land available, it will grow *useful*
money crops, thus excluding ganja, tobacco,
opium and the like.

The village will maintain a village theatre,
school and public hall. It will have its own
water-works ensuring clean water supply. This
can be done through controlled wells and tanks.
Education will be compulsory up to the final
basic course. As far as possible every activity
will be conducted on a co-operative basis. There
will be no castes such as we have today with
their graded untouchability. Non-violence with
its technique of Satyagraha and non-co-operation
will be the sanction of the village community.
There will be a compulsory service of village
guards who will be selected by rotation from a
register maintained by the village. The Government of the village will be conducted by the

Punchayat of five persons annually elected by the adult villagers, male and female, possessing minimum prescribed qualifications. These will have all the authority and jurisdiction required. Since there will be no system of punishments in the accepted sense this Punchayat will be the legislature, judiciary and executive combined to operate for its year of office.

Any village can become such a republic today without much interference, even from the present Government whose sole effective connection with the villages is the exaction of village revenue. I have not examined here the question of relations with the neighbouring villages and the centre, if any. My purpose is to present an outline of village government. Here there is perfect democracy based upon individual freedom. The individual is the architect of his own government. The law of non-violence rules him and his government. He and his village are able to defy the might of a world. For the law governing every villager is that he will suffer death in the defence of his and his village's honour. —(H, 26-7-42, 238.)

I am enunciating no new ideas here. They are to be found in *Indian Home Rule* (*Hind Swaraj*) which was written in 1908 when the technique of Satyagraha was still in process of formation. The Charkha had become part of this programme of love. As I was picturing life based on non-violence, I saw that it must be reduced to the simplest terms consistent with high thinking. Food and raiment will always remain the prime necessities of life. Life itself becomes impossible if these two are not assured. For non-violent defence, therefore, society has to be so constructed that its members may be able as far as possible to look after themselves in the face of an invasion from without or disturbances within.

Just as a domestic kitchen is the easiest thing in such circumstances, the takli or at most the spinning wheel and the loom are the simplest possessions for the manufacture of cloth. Society based on non-violence can only consist of groups settled in villages in which voluntary co-opera-tion is the condition of dignified and peaceful existence. A society which anticipates and provides for meeting violence with violence will either lead a precarious life or create big cities and magazines for defence purposes. It is not unreasonable to presume from the state of Europe that its cities, its monster factories and huge armaments are so intimately inter-related that the one cannot exist without the other. The nearest approach to civilisation based upon non-violence is the erstwhile village republic of India. I admit that it was very crude. I know that there was in it no non-violence of my definition and concep-tion. But the germ was there. —(*H*, 13-1-40, 410.)

In the same article, Gandhiji said :

I must continue to argue till I convert opponents or own defeat. For my mission is to convert every Indian whether he is a Hindu,

Muslim or any other, even Englishmen and finally the world, to non-violence for regulating mutual relations whether political, economic, social or religious. If I am accused of being too ambitious, I should plead guilty. If I am told that my dream can never materialise, I would answer "that is possible" and go my way. I am a seasoned soldier of non-violence, and I have evidence enough to sustain my faith. Whether, therefore, I have one comrade or more or none, I must continue the experiment.

Gandhiji's economic activities are thus a part and parcel of his organization of non-violence. Without a corresponding productive system based on non-exploitation and in which power ultimately resides with the individual, Satyagraha, in his opinion, can never become fully successful.

We thus realize how closely non-violent non-co-operation is interrelated to the rural civilization of Gandhiji's conception. The two are in fact, the integral parts of a creative revolution through which the common man can reach the goal of Swaraj or self-rule, i.e., the freedom which alone can bring within his reach the conditions necessary for the full development of his personality.

SWARAJ AND THE STATE

The Fundamentals

It was in his book *Hind-Swaraj or Indian Home Rule* that Gandhi first clearly enunciated his idea of Swaraj or self-rule. While drawing a comparison between Italy and India, he wrote :

If you believe that because Italians rule Italy the Italian nation is happy, you are groping in darkness. Mazzini has shown conclusively that Italy did not become free. Victor Emanuel gave one meaning to the expression ; Mazzini gave another. According to Emanuel, Cavour and even Garibaldi, Italy meant the King of Italy and his henchmen. According to Mazzini, it meant the whole of the Italian people, that is, its agriculturists. Emanuel was only its servant. The Italy of Mazzini still remains in a state of slavery. At the time of the so-called national war, it was a game of chess between two rival kings with the people of Italy as pawns. The working classes in that land are still unhappy. They, therefore, indulge in assassination, rise in revolt, and rebellion on their part is always expected. What substantial gain did Italy obtain after the withdrawal of the Austrian troops ? The gain was nominal. The reforms for the sake of which the war was supposed

to have been undertaken have not yet been
granted. The condition of the people in general
still remains the same. I am sure you do not wish
to reproduce such a condition in India. I believe
that you want the millions of India to be happy,
not that you want the reins of Government in
your hands. If that be so, we have to consider
only one thing ; how can the millions obtain self-
rule ? You will admit that people under several
Indian princes are being ground down. The latter
mercilessly crush them. Their tyranny is greater
than that of the English, and if you want such
tyranny in India, then we shall never agree. My
patriotism does not teach me that I am to allow
people to be crushed under the heel of Indian
princes if only the English retire. If I have the
power, I should resist the tyranny of Indian
princes just as much as that of the English. By
patriotism I mean the welfare of the whole people,
and if I could secure it at the hands of the English,
I should bow down my head to them. If any
Englishman dedicated his life to securing the
freedom of India, resisting tyranny and serving
the land, I should welcome that Englishman as
an Indian.—(*IHR*, 36.)

Long afterwards, he similarly wrote :

I, however, feel that fundamentally the disease
is the same in Europe as it is in India, in spite of
the fact that in the former country the people enjoy
political self-government. No mere transference
of political power in India will satisfy my ambition, even though I hold such transference to be a

vital necessity of Indian national life. The people of Europe have no doubt political power but no Swaraj. Asian and African races are exploited for their partial benefit, and they, on their part, are being exploited by the ruling class or caste under the sacred name of democracy. At the root, therefore, the disease appears to be the same as in India. The same remedy is, therefore, likely to be applicable. Shorn of all the camouflage, the exploitation of the masses of Europe is sustained by violence.

Violence on the part of the masses will never remove the disease. Anyway up to now experience shows that success of violence has been short-lived. It has led to greater violence. What has been tried hitherto has been a variety of violence and artificial checks, mainly dependent upon the will of the violent. At the crucial moment these checks have naturally broken down. It seems to me, therefore, that sooner or later, the European masses will have to take to non-violence if they are to find their deliverance. That there is no hope of their taking to it in a body and at once does not baffle me. A few thousand years are but a speck in the vast time-circle. Someone has to make a beginning with a faith that will not flinch. I doubt not that the masses, even of Europe, will respond, but what is more emergent in point of time is not so much a large experiment in non-violence as a precise grasp of the meaning of deliverance.

From what will the masses be delivered ?
It will not do to have a vague generalisation and
to answer 'from exploitation and degradation.'
Is not the answer this that they want to occupy
the status that Capital does today ? If so, it can
be attained only by violence. But if they want
to shun the evils of Capital, in other words, if
they would revise the view-point of Capital, they
would strive to attain a juster distribution of the
products of labour. This immediately takes us
to contentment and simplicity, voluntarily
adopted. Under the new outlook multiplicity of
material wants will not be the aim of life, the
aim will be rather their restriction consistently
with comfort. We shall cease to think of getting
what we can but we shall decline to receive what
all cannot get. It occurs to me that it ought not
to be difficult to make a successful appeal to the
masses of Europe in terms of economics and a
fairly successful working of such an experiment
must lead to immense and unconscious spiritual
results. I do not believe that the spiritual law
works in a field of its own. On the contrary, it
expresses itself only through the ordinary activities of life. It thus affects the economic, the
social and the political fields. If the masses of
Europe can be persuaded to adopt the view I have
suggested, it will be found that violence will be
wholly unnecessary to attain the aim and they
can easily come to their own by following the
obvious corollaries of non-violence. It may even
be that what seems to me to be so natural and

feasible in India, may take longer to permeate the inert Indian masses than the active European masses. But I must reiterate my confession that all my argument is based on suppositions and assumptions and must, therefore, be taken for what it is worth.—(*YI*, 3-9-25, 304.)

We make no apology for reproducing the above long passage, for the whole argument in favour of non-violence in relation to self-rule of the masses is briefly and clearly laid down in it. Gandhi has never wearied of emphasizing this argument whenever he has found an occasion to do so. (See for instance, *CP*, 3 ; *YI*, 1-12-20 in *Tagore*, 330 and *YI*, 21-5-25, 178.)

Real Swaraj

Let us now turn to the more concrete question of political power and its organization. Discussing this question, Gandhi wrote in 1925 :

By Swaraj I mean the Government of India by the consent of the people, ascertained by the vote of the largest number of the adult population, male or female, native born or domiciled who have contributed by manual labour to the service of the State and who have taken the trouble of having their names registered as voters. I hope also (to demonstrate) that real Swaraj will come not by the acquisition of authority by a few but by the acquisition of the capacity by all to resist authority when abused. In other words, Swaraj is to be attained by educating the masses into a

5

sense of their capacity to regulate and control authority.—(*YI*, 29-1-25, 40.)

Similarly he said in 1941 :

We have been. long accustomed to think that power comes only through Legislative Assemblies. I have regarded this belief as a grave error brought about by inertia or hypnotism. A superficial study of British history has made us think that all power percolates to the people from parliaments. The truth is that power resides in the people and it is entrusted for the time being to those whom they may choose as their representatives. Parliaments have no power or even existence independently of the people. It has been my effort for the last twenty-one years to convince the people of this simple truth. Civil Disobedience is the storehouse of power. Imagine a whole people unwilling to conform to the laws of the legislature and prepared to suffer the consequences of non-compliance ! They will bring the whole legislative and executive machinery to a standstill. The police and the military are of use to coerce minorities, however powerful they may be. But no police or military coercion can bend the resolute will of a people out for suffering to the uttermost.—(*CP*, 8.)

On Political Power

Closely related to Gandhi's idea that the common people should be able to control the rulers at the centre by means of non-violent non-co-operation, lies also his other opinion that men should have as little to do as possible with the State in regulating social life ; for the latter is ultimately based on violence. This leaning towards Anarchism is discernible in his writings, now and then, in spite of the fact that in actual life, he has been fighting for the establishment of a democratic State for India.

Thus in 1931, he wrote :

To me political power is not an end but one of the means of enabling people to better their condition in every department of life. Political power means capacity to regulate national life through national representatives. If national life becomes so perfect as to become self-regulated, no representation is necessary. There is then a state of enlightened anarchy. In such a State, every one is his own ruler. He rules himself in such a manner that he is never a hindrance to his neighbour. In the ideal State, therefore, there is no political power because there is no State. But the ideal is never fully realised in life. Hence the classical statement of Thoreau that that Government is best which governs the least.— (*YI*, 2-7-31, 162.)

Similarly, in course of an interview in 1934, he stated :

I look upon an increase in the power of the State with the greatest fear, because, although while apparently doing good by minimising exploitation, it does the greatest harm to mankind by destroying individuality, which lies at the root of all progress. The State represents violence in a concentrated and organised form. The individual has a soul but as the State is a soulless machine, it can never be weaned from violence to which it owes its very existence.

It is my firm conviction that if the State suppressed Capitalism, it will be caught in the coils of violence itself and fail to develop non-violence at any time. What I would personally prefer would be not a centralisation of power in the hands of the State, but an extension of the sense of trusteeship; as, in my opinion, the violence of private ownership is less injurious than the violence of the State. However, if it is unavoidable, I would support a minimum of State ownership. What I disapprove of is an organisation based on force which a State is. Voluntary organisation there must be.

Mahadev Desai reported a conversation on the same subject in the *Harijan* of 1940:

But are we not being driven to philosophical anarchism? Is that not an impossible ideal? These questions were asked by a philosophical friend some months ago and Gandhiji gave him replies which I think will be useful today.

'Does any one know true non-violence?' he asked.

Gandhiji immediately replied: 'Nobody knows it, for nobody can practise perfect non-violence.'

'Then how can it be used in politics?'

SWARAJ AND THE STATE 69

'It can be used in politics precisely as it can be used in the domestic sphere. We may not be perfect in our use of it, but we definitely discard the use of violence, and grow from failure to success.'

'You would govern non-violently. But all legislation is violence.'

'No, not all legislation. Legislation imposed by people upon themselves is non-violence to the extent it is possible in society. A society organised and run on the basis of complete non-violence would be the purest anarchy.'

'Do you think it is a realisable ideal?'

'Yes. It is realisable to the extent non-violence is realisable. That State is perfect and non-violent where the people are governed the least. The nearest approach to purest anarchy would be a democracy based on non-violence. The European democracies are to my mind a negation of democracy.'

'Do you think that non-violence or democracy that you visualise was ever realised in the olden times?'

'I do not know. But if it was not, it only means that we had never made the attempt to realise the highest in us. I have no doubt in my mind that at some stage we were wiser and that we have to grow wiser than we are today in order to find what beauties are hidden in human nature. Perfect non-violence is impossible so long as we exist physically, for we would want some space at least to occupy. Perfect non-violence whilst you

are inhabiting the body is only a theory like
Euclid's point or straight line, but we have
to| endeavour every moment of our lives'.
—(*H*, 27-7-40, 211.)

The theoretical position held by Gandhi is thus
entirely different from that of Marxian Socialism.
According to the latter, the first step needful is to
capture the State by means of violence and place it
under the dictatorship of the proletariat. The State
machinery will then be employed to root out all
forms of exploitation, and also educate men into a
new frame of mind. When this has been done, the
people's voluntary organizations will gradually take
up the functions of the State, which will then wither
away. But during the transition period, the State
should be made all-powerful for defending the life and
interests of the people. Gandhi, on the other hand,
believes that true defence is only possible under non-
violence, in which the heart of the exploiter is
changed be non-co-operation. The chief function
of the State is thus transferred from the army
to the people directly, under organised non-
violence. The people also begin to regulate their
economic as well as political life, as far as possible,
by means of voluntary associations i.e., democratic
organizations, from the present moment. In other
words, the chief difference between Marxian Socialism
and Gandhi's anarchistic ideal lies in the fact that,
in the latter, the withering away of the State
begins from the immediate present, instead of being
left over for a period when all possible opposition
has already been liquidated by means of intense

centralization of social authority, brought about through violence.

Gandhi's Practical Idealism

But in spite of his insistence upon Anarchism, Gandhi is not indifferent, like some other Anarchists, to the machinery of the State so long as it is there. His practical nature leads him towards a full democratic control of the State ; under no circumstances is he prepared to put up with totalitarianism, i.e., suppression of opposition by means of violence, even if it be in the immediate interest of the masses. Replying to an address presented to him by the citizens of Bombay just before he left for England to attend the Round Table Conference, he said :

I claim to live for the semi-starved paupers of India and Swaraj means the emancipation of these millions of skeletons. *Purna* Swaraj denotes a condition of things when the dumb and the lame millions will speak and walk. That Swaraj cannot be achieved by force, but by organisation and unity.— (*YI*, 23-4-31, 81.)

Speaking before the Federation of the Indian Chambers of Commerce, he similarly said :

It has been said that Indian Swaraj will be the rule of the majority community ; i. e., the Hindus. There could not be a greater mistake than that. If it were to be true, I for one would refuse to call it Swaraj and would fight it with all the strength at my command, for to me Hind Swaraj is the rule of all the people, is the rule of justice. Whether under that rule the ministers were Hindus or Musalmans or Sikhs, and whether the legislatures were exclusively filled by the Hindus or Musalmans or any other community, they would have to do even-handed justice. And just as no community in India need have any fear of Swaraj being monopolised by any other, even so the English should have no fear. The question of safeguards should not arise at all. Swaraj would be real Swaraj only when there would be no occasion for safeguarding any such rights I may tell you that the Congress does not belong to any particular group of men ; it belongs to all, but the protection of the poor peasantry, which forms the bulk of the population, must be its primary interest. The Congress must, therefore, truly represent the poor. But that does not mean that all other classes—the middle classes, the capitalist or zamindar—must go under. All that it aims at is that all other classes must subserve the interest of the poor.   —(*YI*, 16-4-31, 78.)

In an article written in the *Young India*, he repeated the same idea in the following terms :

I will therefore state the purpose. It is complete freedom from the alien yoke in every sense of the term, and this for the sake of the dumb millions. Every interest therefore, that is hostile to their interest, must be revised, or must subside if it is not capable of revision. —(*YI*, 17-9-31, 263.)

At the Round Table Conference in 1931, speaking as the sole representative of the Indian National Congress, he gave a picture of how things were to shape themselves if a national government

was to come into being in India. With regard to the
question of racial discrimination, he said :

I am afraid that for years to come India
would be engaged in passing legislation in order
to raise the downtrodden, the fallen, from the mire
into which they have been sunk by the capitalists,
by the landlords, by the so-called higher classes,
and then, subsequently and scientifically, by the
British rulers. If we are to lift these people from
the mire, then it would be the bounden duty of
the National Government of India, in order to set
its house in order, continually to give preference
to these people and even free them from the
burdens under which they are being crushed.
And, if the landlords, zamindars, monied men and
those who are today enjoying privileges—I do
not care whether they are Europeans or Indians—
if they find that they are discriminated against, I
shall sympathise with them, but I will not be
able to help them, even if I could possibly do so,
because I would seek their assistance in that
process, and without their assistance it would not
be possible to raise these people out of the mire.

Look at the condition, if you will, of the
untouchables, if the law comes to their assistance
and sets apart miles of territory. At the present
moment they hold no land ; they are absolutely
living at the mercy of the so-called higher castes,
and also, let me say, at the mercy of the State.
They can be removed from one quarter to another
without complaint and without being able to
seek the assistance of law. Well, the first act of

the Legislature will then be to see that in order
somewhat to equalise conditions, these people
are given grants freely.

From whose pockets are these grants to
come ? Not from the pockets of Heaven. Heaven
is not going to drop money for the sake of the
State. They will naturally come from the monied
classes, including the Europeans. Will they say
that this is discrimination ? They will be able to
see that this is no discrimination against them
because they are Europeans ; it will be discrimination against them because they have got money
and the others have got no money. It will be,
therefore, a battle between the haves and the
have-nots ; and if that is what is feared, I am
afraid the National Government will not be able
to come into being if all these classes hold the
pistol at the heads of these dumb millions and
say : You shall not have a Government of your
own unless you guarantee our possessions and our
rights.

I think I have given a sufficient indication
of what the Congress stands for and of the implications of this formula that I have suggested. On
no account will they find that there has been discrimination against them because they are English
or because they are European or Japanese or
belong to any other race. The grounds that will
be applicable to them for discrimination will be
also the grounds for discrimination against
Indian-born citizens.

I have got another formula also hurriedly

drafted because I drafted it here as I was listening to Lord Reading and to Sir Tej Bahadur Sapru. It is in connection with existing rights :

"No existing interest legitimately acquired, and not being in conflict with the best interests of the nation in general, shall be interfered with except in accordance with the law applicable to such interests."

I certainly have in mind what you find in the Congress resolution in connection with the taking over by the incoming Government of obligations that are being today discharged by the British Government. Just as we claim that these obligations must be examined by an impartial tribunal before they are taken over by us, so should existing interests be subject to judicial scrutiny when necessary. There is no question, therefore, of repudiation but merely of taking over under examination, under audit. We have here some of us who have made a study of the privileges and the monopolies enjoyed by Europeans, but let it not be merely Europeans : there are Indians—I have undoubtedly several Indians in mind—who are today in possession of land which has been practically given away to them not for any service rendered to the nation but for some service rendered, I cannot even say to the Government, because I do not think that the Government has benefited, but to some official ; and if you tell me that those concessions and those privileges are not to be examined by the State I again tell you that it will be impossible to run the machinery of Government on behalf of the have-nots, on behalf of the dispossessed. Hence, you will see here that there is nothing stated in connection with the Europeans. The second formula also is applicable to Indians, as it is applicable say, to Sir Puru- shottamdas Thakurdas and Sir Phiroze Sethna. If they have obtained concessions which have been obtained because they did some service to the officials of the day and got some miles of land, well, if I had the possession of the Government I would quickly dispossess them. I would not consider them because they are Indians, and I would just as readily dispossess Sir Hubert Carr or Mr. Benthall, however admirable they are and however friendly they are to me. The law will be no respector of persons whatsoever. I give you that assurance. After having received that assurance I am unable to go any further. So that is really what is implied by 'legitimately acquired'—that every interest must have been taintless, it must be above suspicion, like Caesar's wife, and therefore, we shall expect to examine all these things when they come under the notice of that Government.

Then you have "not being in conflict with the best interests of the nation." I have in mind certain monopolies, legitimately acquired, undoub- tedly, but which have been brought into being in conflict with the best interests of the nation. Let me give you an illustration which will amuse you somewhat, but which is on natural ground. Take this white elephant which is called New Delhi. Crores have been spent upon it. Suppose that the future Government comes to the conclusion that seeing that we have this white elephant it ought to be turned to some use. Imagine that in Old Delhi there is a plague or cholera going on, and we want hospitals for the poor people. What are we to do? Do you suppose the National Government will be able to build hospitals, and so on? Nothing of the kind. We will take charge of those buildings and put these plague-stricken people in them and use them as hospitals, because I contend that those buildings are in conflict with the best interests of the nation. They do not represent the millions of India. They may be representative of the monied men who are sitting at the table; they may be representative of His Highness the Nawab Sahib of Bhopal, or of Sir Purushottamdas Thakurdas, or of Sir Phiroze Sethna, or of Sir Tej Bahadur Sapru, but they are not representative of those who lack even a place to sleep and have not even a crust of bread to eat. If the National Government comes to the conclusion that that place is unnecessary, no matter what interests are concerned, they will be dispossessed, and they will be dispossessed, I may tell you, without any compensation, because, if you want this Government to pay compensation it will have to rob Peter to pay Paul, and that would be impossible.

It is a bitter pill which has got to be swallowed if a Government, as Congress conceives it, comes into being. In order to take away something from here, I have no desire to deceive you into the belief that everything will be quite all right. I want, on behalf of the Congress, to lay all the cards on the table. I want no mental reservation of any description whatsoever ; and then, if the Congress position is acceptable, nothing will please me better, but, if that position is not acceptable, if today I feel I cannot possibly touch your hearts and cannot carry you with me, then the Congress must continue to wander and must continue the process of proselytisation until you are all converted and allow the millions of India to feel that at last they have got a National Government.—(*NV*, 71.)

An important interview took place between Prof. N. G. Ranga and Mahatma Gandhi towards the end of 1944. A part of that interview, as reported by Shri Pyarelal in the Press, is given below :

Prof. Ranga : You say that the earth rightly belongs or should belong to the peasant. By this, do you mean only that the peasant ought to gain control over the land he cultivates or that he should also gain effective voice or power in the society and over the State in which he is obliged to live ? If the Kisans are to have only land and not effective political power, their position will be just as bad as in Soviet Russia where political power has been monopolised by the proletariat dictatorship, while peasants were first allowed to gain some holdings and later were deprived of those holdings in the name of collectivisation of land.

Gandhiji : I do not know what has happened in Soviet Russia. But I have no doubt that if we have democratic Swaraj, as it must be if the freedom is won through non-violence, the Kisans must hold power in all its phases, including political power.

Prof. Ranga : Am I right in interpreting your statement that 'land should not belong to the absentee landlord or zamindar' and that ultimately the zamindary system has to be abolished, of course through non-violent means ?

Gandhiji : Yes. But you should remember that I should visualize a system of trusteeship 'regulated by the State.' In other words, I do not want to antagonize the zamindars (and for that matter any class) without cause.

Prof. Ranga : When you say that a peasant has 'so to work as to make it impossible for the landlord to exploit him', does it include, apart from the Satyagrahic campaigns, the legislative administrative reforms that peasants may oblige the State through the exercise of their franchise and political influence to improve their individual and collective conditions and minimise the powers of the landlords?

Gandhiji : Civil disobedience and non-co-operation are designed for use when people, i. e., the tillers of the soil, have no political power. But immediately they have political power, naturally their grievances, whatever their character, will be ameliorated through legislative channels.

'But he might not have all that political power', you will perhaps say. My reply is that if Swaraj is attained by the effort of the whole people, as it must be under non-violence, the Kisans must come into their own and have the uppermost voice. But if it is not so and there is a sort of a workable compromise between the people and the Government on the basis of a limited franchise, the interests of the tiller of the soil will need close watching. If the legislature proves itself to be incapable of safeguarding the Kisan's interests they will of course always have the sovereign remedy of civil disobedience and non-co-operation. But as I said, as early as 1922 in connection with Chirala Perala, ultimately, it is not paper legislation, nor brave words or fiery speeches, but the power of non-violent organisation, discipline and sacrifice that constitute the real bulwark of the people against injustice and oppression.—(HS, 15-1-45.)

THE THEORY OF TRUSTEESHIP

**Criticism of the
Present Arrangements**

During the opening ceremony of the Benares Hindu University on the 4th of February 1916, Gandhiji delivered a speech in course of which he said :

I now introduce you to another scene. His Highness the Maharaja, who presided over our deliberations, spoke about the poverty of India. Other speakers laid great stress upon it. But what did we witness in the great pandal in which the foundation ceremony was performed by the Viceroy ? Certainly a most gorgeous show, an exhibition of jewellery which made a feast for the eyes of the greatest jeweller who chose to come from Paris. I compare with the richly bedecked noblemen the millions of the poor. And I feel like saying to those noblemen : 'There is no salvation for India unless you strip yourselves of the jewellery and hold it in trust for your countrymen in India'. Sir, whenever I hear of a great palace rising in any great city in British India or be it in the India which is ruled by our great chiefs, I become jealous at once and I say : 'Oh, it is the money that has come from the agriculturists'. Over 75% of the

6

population are agriculturists and Mr. Higginbotham told us last night in his own felicitous language that they are the men who grow two blades of grass in the place of one. But there cannot be much spirit of self-govern- ment about us if we take away or allow others to take away from them almost the whole of the results of their labour. Our salvation can only come through the farmer. Neither the lawyers, nor doctors, nor the rich landlords are going to secure it.—(*Natesan*, 322.)

While addressing a body of students in Benares once more in 1927, Gandhiji said :

Panditji has collected and has been collecting lakhs of rupees for you from Rajas and Maharajas. The money apparently comes from the wealthy princes, but in reality it comes from the millions of our poor. The education that you receive today is thus paid for by the starving villagers who will never have the chance of such education. It is your duty to refuse to have an education that is not within the reach of the poor ; but I do not ask that of you today. I ask you to render a slight return to the poor by doing a little *yajna* for them. For he who eats without doing his *yajna* steals his food, says the Gita. The *yajna* of our age and for us is the spinning wheel. Day in and day out I have been talking about it, writing about it. —(*YI*, 20-1-27, 22.)

Gandhiji's charges against present arrangements in society are based on the fact that they are built upon the exploitation of the toiling millions. The latter are not only degraded by their poverty, but society loses in a different way also. In 1937, when the Congress decided to accept office, Gandhiji wrote by way of advice :

Riches have not yet been sufficiently taxed. In this of all countries in the world, possession of inordinate wealth by individuals should be held as a crime against Indian humanity. Therefore the maximum limit of taxation of riches beyond a certain margin can never be reached. In England, I understand, they have already gone as far as 70% of the earnings beyond a prescribed figure. There is no reason why India should not go to a much higher figure. Why should there not be death duties ? Those sons of millionaires who are of age and yet inherit their parents' wealth are losers for the very inheritance. The nation thus becomes a double loser. For the inheritance should rightly belong to the nation. And the nation loses in that the full faculties of the heirs are not drawn out, being crushed under the load of riches. —(H, 31-7-37, 197.)

In a similar vein he wrote on the eve of the Salt Satyagraha in 1930 :

The greatest obstacle in the path of non-violence is the presence in our midst of the indigenous interests that have sprung up from British rule, the interests of monied men, speculators, scrip-holders, landholders, factory owners and the like. All these do not always realise that they are living on the blood of the masses, and when they do, they become as callous as the British principals whose tools and agents they are. If, like the Japanese Samurai, they could but realise that they must give up their blood-stained gains, the battle is won for non-violence. It must not be difficult for them to see that the holding of millions is a crime when millions of their own kith and kin are starving and therefore they must give up their agency. No principal has yet been found able to work without faithful agents.

But non-violence has to be patient with these as with the British principal. The aim of the non-violent worker must ever be to convert. —(*YI*, 6-2-30, 44.)

The callousness of the upper classes has often pained Gandhiji deeply, yet he has been sparing in his references to them. But there have been occasions when he has flared up and given expression to his feelings. For instance, during the celebrated trial of 1922, he said :

Little do the town-dwellers know how the semi-starved masses of India are slowly sinking to lifelessness. Little do they know that their miserable comfort represents the brokerage they get for the work they do for the foreign exploiter, that the profits and brokerage are sucked from the masses. Little do they realise that the Government established by law in British India is carried on for this exploitation of the masses. No sophistry, no jugglery in figures can explain away the evidence that the skeletons in many

villages present to the naked eye. I have no
doubt whatsoever that both England and the
town-dwellers of India will have to answer,
if there is God above, for this crime against
humanity which is perhaps unequalled in history.
—(*YI*, 23-3-22, 167.)

Similarly in answer to a correspondent he once
wrote :

What does the correspondent mean when he
refers to the 'lower orders who know no responsibility and can anyway make both ends meet' ?
Is he sure that the 'lower orders know no responsibility' ? Have they no feelings, are they not
injured by an angry word ? In what sense are
they lower except in their poverty for which
we the middle class are responsible ? And may I
inform my correspondent that the 'lower orders'
not only do not 'make the two ends meet' but
the majority of them are living in a state of semi-
starvation ? If the middle class people voluntarily suffer losses for the sake of the 'lower
classes' it would be but a tardy reparation for
their participation in their exploitation. It is
this arrogation of superiority and consequent
callousness to the sufferings of the so-called lower
classes that keeps us from Swaraj and that retards
the progress of the life-giving charkha. I invite
the correspondent to think in terms of the
masses and by taking to the charkha identify
himself with his less fortunate countrymen.
—(*YI*, 17-7-24, 240.)

Ideal Distribution

The question however is : What should be the
nature of an ideal society ? What should be its
property relations and what about the income of
people ?

In the year 1904, Gandhiji imbibed from
Ruskin the idea that

A lawyer's work has the same value as a
barber's, inasmuch as all have the same right of
earning their livelihood from their work.
—(*Auto*, 365.)

Ever since that time he has held that wages
derived from all forms of productive labour ought to
be equal. (*H*, 6-7-35, 164.) But realizing the practical
difficulties, he wrote :

My ideal is equal distribution, but so far as
I can see it is not to be realised. I therefore work
for equitable distribution.—(*YI*, 17-3-27, 86.)

Recently Gandhiji said in course of his
speeches in Noakhali that

He certainly did not consider money got
through speculation as rightly gained. Nor did
he consider it impossible for a man to shed bad or
evil habits at any time. If everybody lived by the
sweat of his brow the earth would become a
paradise.

The question of special talents hardly needed
separate consideration. If everyone laboured
physically for his bread, it followed that poets,
doctors, lawyers etc. would regard it their duty to
use those talents gratis for the service of humanity. Their output will be all the better and

richer for their selfless devotion to duty.
—(*H*, 2-3-47, 47.)

Q. Why should we insist on a Rabindranath
or Raman earning his bread by manual labour?
Is it not sheer wastage? Why should not brain
workers be on a par with manual workers? Both
perform useful social work.

A. Intellectual work is important and has
an undoubted place in the scheme of life. But
what I insist is the necessity of physical labour
for all. No man ought to be free from that
obligation. It would serve to improve even the
quality of his intellectual output. *Brahmins*
worked with their body as with their mind. But
even if they did not, body labour is a proved
necessity at the present time.

In this connection I would refer to the life of
Tolstoy and how he made famous the theory of
Bread Labour first propounded in his country by
the Russian peasant Bondaref.—(*H*, 23-2-47, 36.)

Again,

Q. You wrote about economic equality in
1941. Do you hold that all persons who perform
useful and necessary services in society, whether
farmer or bhangi, engineer or accountant, doctor
or teacher, have a moral right only to equal
wages with the rest? Of course, it is understood,
educational or other expenses shall be charge of
the State. Our question is, should not all persons
get the same wages for their personal needs? Do
you not think that if we work for this equality, it

will cut sooner under the root of untouchability than any other process ?

A. As to this he had no doubt that if India was to live an exemplary life of independence which would be the envy of the world, all the bhangis, doctors, lawyers, teachers, merchants and others would get the same wages for an honest day's work. Indian society may never reach the goal but it was the duty of every Indian to set his sail towards that goal and no other if India was to be a happy land. —(*H*, 16-3-47, 67.)

Before we proceed any further, it may be interesting to discuss one point first of all, *viz.*, what is then the difference between socialism and Gandhism ?

Gandhism versus Socialism

In Gandhi's own opinion the difference amounts to this :

My fundamental difference with Socialists is well known. I believe in the conversion of human nature and in striving for it. They do not believe in this. But let me tell you that we are coming nearer one another. —(*H*, 27-5-39, 137.)

Similarly in reply to a socialist's question, Gandhiji wrote in 1940 :

If I can convert the country to my point of view, the social order of the future will be based predominantly on the charkha and all it implies. It will include everything that promotes the well-being of the villagers. It will not exclude the industries mentioned by my correspondent

so long as they do not smother the villages and village life. I do visualise electricity, ship-building, ironworks, machine-making and the like existing side by side with village handicrafts. But the order of dependence will be reversed. Hitherto the industrialisation has been so planned as to destroy the villages and village crafts. In the State of the future it will subserve the villages and their crafts. I do not share the socialist belief that centralisation of the necessaries of life will conduce to the common welfare, when the centralised industries are planned and owned by the State. The socialistic conception of the West was born in an environment reeking with violence. The motive lying behind the Western type and the Eastern is the same—the greatest welfare of the whole society and the abolition of the hideous inequalities resulting in the existence of millions of have-nots and a handful of haves. I believe that this end can be achieved only when non-violence is accepted by the best mind of the world as the basis on which a just social order is to be constructed. I hold that the coming into power of the proletariat through violence is bound to fail in the end. What is gained by violence must be lost before superior violence.
—(*H*, 27-1-40, 428.)

Commenting further on the difference, he said :

I have claimed that I was a socialist long before those I know in India had avowed their creed. But my socialism was natural to me and not adopted from any books. It came out of my unshakable belief in non-violence. No man could be actively non-violent and not rise against social injustice, no matter where it occurred. Unfortunately Western socialists have, so far as I know, believed in the necessity of violence for enforcing socialistic doctrines.

I have always held that social justice, even unto the least and the lowliest, is impossible of attainment by force. I have further believed that it is possible by proper training of the lowliest by non-violent means to secure redress of the wrongs suffered by them. That means is non-violent non-co-operation. At times non-co-operation becomes as much a duty as co-operation. No one is bound to co-operate in one's own undoing or slavery. Freedom received through the effort of others, however benevolent, cannot be retained when such effort is withdrawn. In other words, such freedom is not real freedom. But the lowliest can feel its glow as soon as they learn the art of attaining it through non-violent non-co-operation. I am quite sure that non-violent non-co-operation can secure what violence never can, and this by ultimate conversion of the wrong-doers. We in India have never given non-violence the trial it has deserved. The marvel is that we have attained so much even with our mixed non-violence. —(*H*, 20-4-40, 97.)

In 1928 he had similarly stated that although the

ultimate ideal was common between him and the
Bolshevik Party, yet the difference lay principally in
the means ; and the difference was great inasmuch
as it was the same as the difference between violence
and non-violence.

Q. What is your opinion about the social
economics of Bolshevism and how far do you
think they are fit to be copied by our country ?

A. I must confess that I have not yet been
able fully to understand the meaning of
Bolshevism. All that I know is that it aims at
the abolition of the institution of private
property. This is only an application of the
ethical ideal of non-possession in the realm
of economics and if people adopted this ideal
of their own accord or could be made to accept
it by means of peaceful persuasion there would
be nothing like it. But from what I know of
Bolshevism it not only does not preclude the
use of force but freely sanctions it for the
expropriation of private property and maintaining
the collective state ownership of the same. And
if that is so I have no hesitation in saying
that the Bolshevik regime in its present form
cannot last for long. For it is my firm conviction
that nothing enduring can be built on violence.
But be that as it may, there is no questioning the
fact that the Bolshevik ideal has behind it the
purest sacrifice of countless men and women who
have given up their all for its sake, and an ideal
that is sanctified by the sacrifices of such master
spirits as Lenin cannot go in vain : the noble

example of their renunciation will be emblazoned for ever, and quicken and purify the ideal as time passes.—(*YI*, 15-11-28, 381.)

Violence is no monopoly of any one party. I know Congressmen who are neither socialists nor communists, but who are frankly devotees of the cult of violence. Contrariwise, I know socialists and communists who will not hurt a fly but who believe in the universal ownership of instruments of production. I rank myself as one among them.—(*H*, 10-12-38, 366.)

Some young communists questioned him in London as to how he actually proposed to bring the new order into being if he abjured the use of violence. Was it to be by persuasion ? In answer he said :

Not merely by verbal persuasion. I will concentrate on my means. Some have called me the greatest revolutionary of my time. It may be false, but I believe myself to be a revolutionary— a non-violent revolutionary. My means are non-co-operation. No person can amass wealth without the co-operation, willing or forced, of the people concerned.—(*YI*, 26-11-31, 369.)

In course of the same interview, he said :

The masses do not see in landlords and other profiteers their enemy. But the consciousness of the wrong done to them by these classes has to be created in them. I do not teach the masses to regard the capitalists as their enemies, but I teach them that they are their own enemies. The system must be destroyed and not the individual.

But what does this mean ? Why should we not,
like the socialists, look upon all exploiters as the
enemies of mankind ? Gandhiji's answer is as
follows, and the careful reader will notice how his
attitude ultimately springs from the creed of non-
violence. As President of the Kathiawad Political
Conference in 1924, he had said :

The popular saying, as is the king, so are the
people, is only a half-truth. That is to say it is
not more true than its converse, as are the people,
so is the prince. Where the subjects are watchful
a prince is entirely dependent upon them for his
status. Where the subjects are overtaken by
sleepy indifference, there is every possibility that
the prince will cease to function as a protector,
and become an oppressor instead. Those who
are not wide awake, have no right to blame their
prince. The prince as well as the people are
mostly creatures of circumstances. Enterprising
princes and peoples mould circumstances for their
own benefit. Manliness consists in making
circumstances subservient to ourselves. Those
who will not heed themselves perish. To understand this principle is not to be impatient, not
to reproach Fate, not to blame others. He
who understands the doctrine of self-help
blames himself for failure. It is on this ground
that I object to violence. If we blame others
where we should blame ourselves and wish
for or bring about their destruction, that does
not remove the root cause of the disease which

on the contrary sinks all the deeper for the ignorance thereof. —(*YI*, 8-1-25, 13.)

This was explained more fully later on :

It is because the rulers, if they are bad, are so, not necessarily or wholly by birth, but largely because of their environment, that I have hopes of their altering their course. It is perfectly true that the rulers cannot alter their course themselves. If they are dominated by their environment, they do not surely deserve to be killed, but should be changed by a change of environment. But the environment are we—the people who make the rulers what they are. They are thus an exaggerated edition of what we are in the aggregate. If my argument is sound, any violence done to the rulers would be violence done to ourselves. It would be suicide. And since I do not want to commit suicide, nor encourage my neighbours to do so, I become non-violent myself and invite my neighbours to do likewise.

Moreover, violence may destroy one or more bad rulers, but, like Ravana's heads, others will pop up in their places, for, the root lies elsewhere. It lies in us. If we reform ourselves, the rulers will automatically do so.—(*H*, 21-9-34, 250.)

The correspondent seems to imagine that a non-violent person has no feelings and that he is a silent witness to the 'slow sucking of blood going on every day in the world.' Non-violence is not a passive force nor so helpless as the correspondent will make it out to be. Barring truth, if truth is to be considered apart from non-violence, the latter is the activest force in the world. It never fails. Violence only seemingly succeeds, and nobody has ever claimed uniform success for violence. Non-violence never promises immediate and tangible results. It is not a mango trick. Its failures are, therefore, all seeming. A believer in violence will kill the murderer and boast of his act. But he never killed murder. By murdering the murderer, he added to it and probably invited more. The law of retaliation is the law of multiplying evil. —( )

Those, who seek to destroy men rather than manners, adopt the latter and become worse than those whom they destroy under the mistaken belief that the manners will die with the men. They do not know the root of the evil.

—(*YI*, 17-3-27, 85.)

Implications of Economic Equality

The essential difference between socialism and Gandhism, or as Gandhi himself has put it, socialism of the Western and Eastern types, lies therefore in the means adopted for achieving the end. All other differences are traceable to the original difference between violence and non-violence. The means being thus opposite to one another, a dissimilarity has also crept into the nature of the ideal. It has already been stated that non-violent organization can flourish only under decentralization. Besides this, there is another important point of difference between socialism and Gandhism. Let us examine where this distinction lies.

Unlike many socialists, but like some of them, such as Bernard Shaw, Gandhi holds equality of income to be the corner-stone of an ideal social order. He referred to economic equality in the pamphlet on the Constructive Programme as 'the master-key to non-violent independence.' Explaining its implications in the *Harijan* of 25-8-40, he wrote :

The real implication of equal distribution is that each man shall have the wherewithal to supply all his natural wants and no more. For example, if one man has a weak digestion and requires only a quarter of a pound of flour for his bread and another needs a pound, both should be in a position to satisfy their wants. To bring this ideal into being the entire social order has got to be reconstructed. A society based on non-violence cannot nurture any other ideal. We may not perhaps be able to realise the goal, but we must bear it in mind and work unceasingly to near it. To the same extent as we progress towards our goal we shall find contentment and happiness, and to that extent too shall we have contributed towards the bringing into being of a non-violent society.

It is perfectly possible for an individual to adopt this way of life without having to wait for others to do so. And if an individual can observe a certain rule of conduct, it follows that a group of individuals can do likewise. It is necessary for me to emphasise the fact that no one need wait for anyone else in order to adopt a right course. Men generally hesitate to make a beginning if they feel that the objective cannot be had in its entirety. Such an attitude of mind is in reality a bar to progress.

Now let us consider how equal distribution can be brought about through non-violence. The first step towards it for him who has made this ideal part of his being is to bring about the necessary changes in his personal life. He would reduce his wants to a minimum, bearing in mind the poverty of India. His earnings would be free of dishonesty. The desire for speculation would be renounced. His habitation would be in keeping with his new mode of life. There would be self-restraint exercised in every sphere of life. When he has done all that is possible in his own life, then only will he be in a position to preach this ideal among his associates and neighbours.

Indeed at the root of this doctrine of equal distribution must lie that of the trusteeship of the wealthy for the superfluous wealth possessed by them. For according to the doctrine they may not possess a rupee more than their neighbours. How is this to be brought about? Non-violently? Or should the wealthy be dispossessed of their possessions? To do this we would naturally have to resort to violence. This violent action cannot benefit society. Society will be the poorer, for it will lose the gifts of a man who knows how to accumulate wealth. Therefore the non-violent way is evidently superior. The rich man will be left in possession of his wealth, of which he will use what he reasonably requires for his personal needs and will act as a trustee for the remainder to be used for the society. In this argument, honesty on the part of the trustee is assumed.

If, however, in spite of the utmost effort, the rich do not become guardians of the poor in the true sense of the term and the latter are more and more crushed and die of hunger, what is to be done? In trying to find out the solution of this riddle I have lighted on non-violent non-co-operation and civil disobedience as the right and infallible means. The rich cannot accumulate wealth without the co-operation of the poor in society. If this knowledge were to penetrate to and spread amongst the poor, they would become strong and would learn how to free themselves by means of non-violence from the crushing inequalities which have brought them to the verge of starvation.—(*H*, 25-8-40, 260.)

A few months earlier, he had written :

A nationalist zamindar will try to live like a non-zamindar. He will regard his tenants as his co-proprietors ; in other words, he will hold his zamindari in trust for his tenants taking a moderate commission for the use of his labours and capital.—(*H*, 27-4-40, 108.)

Similarly in answer to a question he had once replied :

Q. But what about the zamindar ? Would you eliminate him ? Would you destroy him ?

A. I do not want to destroy the zamindar, neither do I feel the zamindar is inevitable.

Q. Your actual economic policy would differ from Mr. Nehru's ? He, so far as I understand him, would wipe out the zamindar.

A. Yes, we seem to differ in our ideas of village uplift and reconstruction. The difference is of emphasis. He does not mind the village uplift movement. He believes in industrialisation ; I have grave doubt about its usefulness for India. He believes in the ultimate inevitability of class conflict though he would avoid it if he could. I expect to convert the zamindars and other capitalists by the non-violent method, and therefore there is for me nothing like an inevitability of class conflict. For it is an essential part of non-violence to go along the line of least resistance. The moment the cultivators of the soil realize their power, the zamindari evil will be sterilized. What can the poor zamindar do when they say that they will simply not work the land unless they are paid enough to feed and clothe and educate themselves and their children in a decent manner ? In reality the toiler is the owner of what he produces. If the toilers intelligently combine, they will become an irresistible power. That is how I do not see the necessity of class conflict. If I thought it inevitable I should not hesitate to preach it and teach it.

—(*H*, 5-12-36, 338.)

Exploitation of the poor can be extinguished

not by effecting the destruction of a few millionaires, but by removing the ignorance of the poor
and teaching them to non-co-operate with their
exploiters. This will convert the exploiters also.
I have even suggested that ultimately it will lead
to both being equal partners. Capital as such is
not evil ; it is the wrong use that is evil. Capital
in some form or other will always be needed.
—(*H*, 28-7-40, 219.)

Is it Class Collaboration ?

Now this raises a very important and knotty
question. Does Gandhi stand by existing property
relations ? Does he aim at class collaboration ?
His earlier writings do lend some colour to such an
opinion. In 1931, for instance, he had said :

Q. If you will benefit the workers, the
peasant and the factory hand, can you avoid
class war ?

A. I can most decidedly, if only the people
will follow the non-violent method. By the
non-violent method, we seek not to destroy the
capitalist, we seek to destroy capitalism. We
invite the capitalist to regard himself as a trustee
for those on whom he depends for the making,
the retention and the increase of his capital.
Nor need the worker wait for his conversion.
If capital is power, so is work. Either power
can be used destructively or creatively. Either
is dependent on the other. Immediately the
worker realises his strength, he is in a position
to become a co-sharer with the capitalist instead

of remaining his slave. —(*YI*, 26-3-31, 49.)
Similarly he wrote in 1937 :

> A labourer's skill is his capital.   Just as the
> capitalist cannot make his capital fructify without
> the co-operation of labour even so the working
> man cannot make his labour fructify without the
> co-operation of capital.   And if both labour and
> capital have the gift of intelligence equally deve-
> loped in them and have confidence in their
> capacity to secure a fair deal, each at the hands
> of the other, they would get to respect and
> appreciate each other as equal partners in a
> common enterprise. —(*H*, 3-7-37, 161.)

In spite of thus aiming at 'equal' or 'just'
relations between capital and labour, for the time
being, we can find out what lies at the back of
Gandhi's mind, for that makes itself felt in his
writings every now and then.   Thus in 1924, he
wrote :

> The village work frightens us.   We who
> are town-bred find it trying to take to village life.
> Our bodies in many cases do not respond to the
> hard life.   But it is a difficulty which we have to
> face boldly, even heroically, if our desire is to
> establish Swaraj for the people, not to substitute
> one class rule by another which may be even
> worse.   Hitherto the villagers have died in their
> thousands so that we might live.   Now we
> might have to die so that they may live.   The
> difference will be fundamental.   The former have
> died unknowingly and involuntarily.   Their

enforced sacrifice has degraded us. If now we die knowingly, our sacrifice will ennoble us and the whole nation. Let us not flinch from the necessary sacrifice, if we will live as an independent self-respecting nation.—(*YI*, 17-4-24, 130.)

Referring to zamindars and talukdars, he wrote in 1929 :

They must regard themselves, even as the Japanese nobles did, as trustees holding their wealth for the good of their wards the ryots. Then they would take no more than a reasonable amount as commission for their labours. At present there is no proportion between the wholly unnecessary pomp and extravagance of the moneyed classes and the squalid surroundings and the grinding pauperism of the ryots in whose midst the former are living. A model zamindar would therefore at once reduce much of the burden the ryot is now bearing, he would come in intimate touch with the ryots, and know their wants and inject hope into them in place of the despair which is killing the very life out of them. He will not be satisfied with the ryot's ignorance of the laws of sanitation and hygiene. He would reduce himself to poverty in order that the ryot may have the necessaries of life. He will study the economic condition of the ryots under his care, establish schools in which he will educate his own children side by side with those of the ryots. He will purify the village well and the village tank. He will teach the ryot to sweep his roads and clean his latrines by himself doing this necessary labour. He will throw open without reserve his own gardens for the unrestricted use of the ryot. He will use as hospital, school, or the like most of the unnecessary buildings which he keeps for his pleasure. If only the capitalist class will read the sign of the times, revise their notions of God-given right to all they possess, in an incredibly short space of time the seven hundred thousand dung-heaps, which today pass muster as villages, can be turned into abodes of peace, health and comfort. I am convinced that the capitalist, if he follows the Samurai of Japan, has nothing really to lose and everything to gain. There is no other choice than between voluntary surrender on the part of the capitalist of super-fluities and consequent acquisition of the real happiness of all on the one hand, and on the other the impending chaos into which if the capitalist does not wake up betimes, awakened but ignorant famishing millions will plunge the country and which not even the armed force that a powerful Government can bring into play can avert. —(Y*I*, 5-12-29, 396.)

In 1942 he wrote :

The rich should ponder well as to what is their duty today. The monied classes have got to learn how to fight either with arms or the weapon of non-violence. For those who wish to follow the latter way the best and most effective *mantram* is तेन त्यक्तेन भुञ्जीथाः (Enjoy thy wealth by renouncing it). Expanded it means : 'Earn your crores by all means. But understand that your wealth is not yours ; it belongs to the people. Take what you require for your legitimate needs and use the remainder for society.' This truth has hitherto not been acted upon ; but, if the monied classes do not even act on it in these times of stress, they will remain the slaves of their riches and passions and consequently of those who over-power them.

But I have visions that the end of this war will mean also the end of the rule of capital. I see coming the day of the rule of the poor, whether that rule be through force of arms or of non-violence. —(*H*, 1-2-42, 20.)

A New Implication of Trusteeship

Shortly after the article quoted above was written, Shankerrao Deo questioned Gandhiji :

Q. Why first earn crores and then use them for society ? As society today is constituted the means of earning crores are bound to be impure ; and one who earns crores by impure means cannot be expected to follow the *mantram* तेन त्यक्तेन भुञ्जीथाः because in the very process of earning crores by impure means the man's character is bound to be tainted or vitiated. I request you to emphasise as much, if not more, the purity of means of earning money as on spending. If purity of means is strictly observed, then, according to me, crores could not be accumulated at all and the difficulty of spending for society will assume a very minor prospect.

Gandhiji proceeded in course of the following weeks to develop the implications of non-violence and trusteeship in fuller measure. He first said in answer to Shri Shankerrao :

In the application of the method of non-violence one must believe in the possibility of every person, however depraved, being reformed under humane and skilled treatment.

—(*H*, 22-2-42, 49.)

He also said :

But I accept the proposition that it is better not to desire wealth than to acquire it and become a trustee. I gave up my own long ago, which should be proof enough of what I would like others to do. But what am I to advise those who are already wealthy or who would not shed the desire for wealth ? I can only say to them that they should use their wealth for service.

Personally I do not believe in inherited riches. The well-to-do should educate and bring up their children so that they may learn how to be independent. The tragedy is that they do not do so. Their children get some education, they even recite verses in praise of poverty, but they have no compunction about helping themselves to parental wealth. That being so I exercise my common sense and advise what is practicable.
—(*H*, 8-3-42, 67.)

Someone asked him the following question next month :

Q. From your writings one gathers the notion that your 'trustee' is not anything more than a very benevolent philanthropist and donor, such as the first Parsi Baronet, the Tatas, the Wadias, the Birlas, Shri Bajaj and the like. Is that so? Will you please explain whom you regard as the primary or rightful beneficiaries of the possessions of a rich man? Is there to be a limit to the amount or part of the income and capital which he can spend upon himself, his kith and kin and for non-public purposes? Can one who exceeds such limit be prevented from doing so? If he is incompetent or otherwise fails to discharge his obligations as a trustee, can he be removed and called upon to render accounts by a beneficiary or the State? Do the same principle apply to princes and zamindars, or is their trusteeship of a different nature?

A. If the trusteeship idea catches, philanthropy, as we know it, will disappear. Of those you have named only Jamnalalji came near, but only near, it. A trustee has no heir but the public. In a State built on the basis of non-violence, the commission of trustees will be regulated. Princes and zamindars will be on a par with other men of wealth. —(*H*, 12-4-42, 116.)

Similarly in 1934 he had said :

Q. Suppose an artist leaves certain pictures to a son who does not appreciate their value for the nation and sells them or wastes them so that the nation stands to lose something precious through one man's folly. If you are assured that the son would never be a trustee in the sense in which you would like to have him, do you not think the State would be justified in taking away those articles from him with the minimum use of violence ?

A. Yes, the State will, as a matter of fact, take away those things and I believe it will be justified if it uses the minimum of violence. But the fear is always there that the State may use too much violence against those who differ from it. I would be very happy indeed if the people concerned behaved as trustees, but if they fail, I believe we shall have to deprive them of their possessions through the State with the minimum exercise of violence. That is why I said at the Round Table Conference that every vested interest must be subject to scrutiny and confiscation ordered where necessary—with or without compensation as the case demanded.

What I would personally prefer would be not a centralization of power in the hands of the State, but an extension of the sense of trusteeship, as in my opinion the violence of private ownership is less injurious than the violence of the State.

It is my firm conviction that if the State suppressed capitalism by violence, it will be caught in the coils of violence itself and fail to develop non-violence at any time. The State represents violence in a concentrated and organized form. The individual has a soul, but as the State is a soulless machine, it can never be weaned from the violence to which it owes its very existence. Hence I prefer the doctrine of trusteeship.

Gandhiji would allow talented people to earn more than others, if otherwise their talents are likely to be stifled.

But the bulk of his greater earnings must be used for the good of the State, just as the income of all earning sons of the father goes to the common family fund. —(*YI*, 26-11-31, 368.)

We must appeal to the good in human beings and expect response. Is it not conducive to the well-being of society that every member uses all his talents, only not for personal aggrandisement but for the good of all ? We do not want to produce a dead equality where every person becomes or is rendered incapable of using his ability to the utmost possible extent. Such a society must ultimately perish. I therefore suggest that my advice that monied men may earn crores (honestly only, of course) but so as to dedicate them to the service of all is perfectly sound. तेन त्यक्तेन भुञ्जीथाः is a *mantra* based on uncommon knowledge. It is the surest method to evolve a new order of life of universal benefit in the place of the present one where each one lives for himself without regard to what happens to his neighbour.—(*H*, 22-2-42, 49.)

We have also seen how private ownership will be without its present support in the form of the law of inheritance. That one step would, in fact, knock the base completely out of capitalism.

THE THEORY OF TRUSTEESHIP

Gandhiji thus wishes to bring about as equal a distribution as possible through the developed consciousness and non-violent strength of the toilers in the fields and factories rather than through the arm of the State. The latter comes in its time only if the former strength is there behind it.

The present inequalities are surely due to the people's ignorance. With a growing knowledge of their natural strength, inequalities must disappear. If the revolution is brought about by violence the position will be reversed, but not altered for the better. With non-violence, i.e. conversion, the new era which people hope for must be born. My approach and appeal are in terms of non-violence pure and undefiled. The French have a noble motto in Liberty, Equality, Fraternity. It is a heritage not for the French only but for all mankind.

What the French never realised, it is open to us to do. Will the princes and the princely landholders and merchants take the lead ? It is for them to take the lead, not for the 'have-nots' who have nothing to share with anybody except their pauperism and abjectness. I am addressing weekly appeals to the British Power. They are made in the same friendly spirit as this is. The British may not respond. If the 'haves', who are in fact the pillars on which the mighty British Power rests, can realise their obvious duty, the British Power must yield. It was because I had despaired of response from the

pillars, that I have thought of moving the masses
on whom the pillars rest. I may not leave a
single stone unturned to avoid what is
undoubtedly a great risk. Hence this appeal.
—(*H*, 2-8-42, 249.)

Rebutting the charge that he was a friend of
capitalists, Gandhiji said :

I am not ashamed to own that many capitalists are friendly towards me and do not fear me.
They know that I desire to end capitalism, almost,
if not quite, as much as the most advanced
socialist or even communist. But our methods
differ, our languages differ. My theory of
'trusteeship' is no makeshift, certainly no
camouflage. I am confident that it will survive
all other theories. It has the sanction of philosophy and religion behind it. No other theory is
compatible with non-violence.—(*H*, 16-12-39, 376.)

The country as well as the Government
should know me exactly as I am. I have never
concealed the fact that I am a friend of everybody,
Moderates, moneyed men, Englishmen, Americans
or any other, irrespective of caste, colour or
persuasion. My belief and practice are directly
derived from my non-violence. My non-co-operation is non-co-operation with evil, not with the
evil-doer. Underneath my non-co-operation is
my earnest desire to wean the evil-doer from the
evil or harm he is doing so that I can give him my
hearty co-operation.

Again, if I associate with so-called Moderates
or with moneyed men, I do so to seek their

co-operation in the cause I am handling. But I approach them with an open mind so that I correct myself where I find myself in the wrong. I have known no cause that I have espoused that has suffered because of such association. —(*HS*, 15-7-44.)

A Question

The reader may legitimately ask, if under the theory of trusteeship, there is provision that the State may intervene and deprive the rich man of his possessions if he does not behave properly, does not the theory become superfluous when the peoples' State comes into being and takes over all management in the interest of the masses ?

But Gandhi, as we have seen, does not admit that his theory is a makeshift. Through what arrangement then does he propose to give the rich man the satisfaction of feeling that he has not become completely subservient to the State ? That provision will be clear when we examine the following authorised report of an interview with workers in Bengal during the month of January, 1946.

In many parts of Bengal, the cultivators are Muslims and the proprietors are Hindus. Recently in some places the Muslim tillers have refused to till the land under Hindu owners. What should the Hindu owners do under the circumstances ? He was asked next.

Gandhiji replying said that the views he was going to express were strictly his own. As they all knew he was not even a four-anna Congress member and therefore he could not speak as a Congressman. He spoke only in his personal capacity as a Satyagrahi.

Although the question had been posed in a communal setting, the real cleavage as he saw it was not communal but economic. In Bengal the cultivators might be Muslim and proprietors Hindu. But in Andhra both the cultivators and proprietors were Hindus and yet the same conflict was in evidence in some parts.

His views, continued Gandhiji, on the ownership of land were well-known. The only rightful owner of the land was he who tilled it. The present proprietors were morally entitled to hold land only if they became trustees for it.

If the cultivators of the fields of a proprietor, who had become a trustee, refused to till the land for him, he would not sue them or seek otherwise to coerce them. He would leave them alone and try to earn his livelihood independently by his honest industry. If he has been discharging his function as a trustee honestly, they would come back to him before long in contrition and seek his guidance and help.

For, he would use his privilege not to fill his pockets by the exploitation of the labourers but teach the latter co-operation and organization so as to increase their produce and generally ameliorate their condition. This would mean that the proprietor must himself become a cultivator 'par excellence'.

A proprietor who regarded his property merely as a means for satisfying his lusts was not its owner but its slave. The proprietor of land in Bengal had, therefore, only to adopt his ideal of trusteeship and their troubles would end.

Q. Would the trustee's property be passed on to his children by inheritance ?

A. A proprietor who holds his property as a trust will not pass it on to his children by inheritance unless the latter in their turn become trustees and make good their claim as such. If they are not prepared for it, he should create a trust of his property.

It is demoralising for an able-bodied young man to live like a parasite on unearned income. A father should inculcate in his children the appreciation of the dignity of labour and teach them to earn their bread by their honest industry. As regards the moneyed people, all I can say from my close personal association with a large number of them, is that if a general atmosphere in favour of trusteeship, devoid of ill-will and class hatred, is created in the country they will fall in line with it.   —(*HS*, 12-1-46.)

In other words, although personally Gandhiji is not in favour of inheritance of wealth and in favour of turning every man into a willing body-labourer, yet he would not force such a condition in society by means of violence. He would wish people of wealth to turn themselves, either of their own accord or by conversion under the influence of non-violent non-co-operation undertaken by the actual producers, into a trustee. The utmost freedom that Gandhi is prepared to leave the present possessor of wealth is that he will have the right of disposal of the trust property in his keeping, which he will be allowed to pass on to his children if they prove by their acts that they have thoroughly imbibed the ideal of trusteeship like their father. In case of failure, the father is to convert the property into a trust under law. But that, as we have seen earlier, will be under the scrutiny and permission of the State, i. e. of the public.

Quite recently Gandhi has made his position very clear with respect to the theory of trusteeship. It will also be noticed from the two quotations given below that there has been some change in his ideas about the State from what was evident from his earlier writings. From the position of an uncompromising anarchist, as in theory at least he was, he has come round to the view that there can also be a State based on non-violence. Personally, I believe this is comparable to the revisions that are also taking place in communistic theory after the experiences of Russia.

Q. You have asked rich men to be trustees. Is it implied that they should give up private ownership in their property and create out of it a trust valid in the eyes of law and managed democratically? How will the successor of the present incumbent be determined on his demise?

A. In answer Gandhiji said that he adhered to the position taken by him years ago that every-

thing belonged to God and was from God. Therefore it was for His people as a whole, not for a
particular individual. When an individual had
more than his proportionate portion he became
a trustee of that portion for God's people.

God who was all-powerful had no need to
store. He created from day to day; hence men
also should in theory live from day to day and
not stock things. If this truth was imbibed by
the people generally, it would become legalized
and trusteeship would become a legalized institution. He wished it became a gift from India to
the world. Then there would be no exploitation
and no reserves as in Australia and other countries
for White men and their posterity. In these dis-
tinctions lay the seed of a war more virulent
than the last two. As to the successor, the
trustee in office would have the right to
nominate his successor subject to legal sanction.
—(*H*, 23-2-47, 39.)

Q. Is it possible to defend by means of non-
violence anything which can only be gained
through violence?

A. What was gained by violence could not
only not be defended by non-violence but the
latter required the abandonment of ill-gotten
gains.

Q. Is the accumulation of capital possible
except through violence whether open or tacit?

A. Such accumulation by private persons
was impossible except through violent means but

accumulation by the State in a non-violent society was not only possible, it was desirable and inevitable.

Q. Whether a man accumulates material or moral wealth he does so only through the help or co-operation of other members of society. Has he then the moral right to use any of it mainly for personal advantage ?

A. No, he has no moral right.

Q. How would the successor of a trustee be determined ? Will he only have the right of proposing a name, the right of finalization being vested in the State ?

A. Choice should be given to the original owner who became the first trustee, but the choice must be finalized by the State. Such arrangement puts a check on the State as well as the individual.

Q. When the replacement of private by public property thus takes place through the operation of the theory of trusteeship, will the ownership vest in the State, which is an instrument of violence or in associations of a voluntary character like village communes and municipalities which may of course derive their final authority from State-made laws ?

A. That question involved some confusion of thought. Legal ownership in the transformed condition vested in the trustee, not in the State. It was to avoid confiscation that the doctrine of trusteeship came into play retaining for the society the ability of the owner in his own right.

Nor did he, the speaker, hold that the State must always be based on violence. It might be so in theory but the practice of the theory demanded a State which would for the most part be based on non-violence.   —(*H*, 16-2-47, 25.)

Of the Future

But supposing all property now vested in private is gradually converted into trust property, and equality of income is established, as far as practicable, will that mean an end of the theory of trusteeship ? Gandhiji does not think so.   Talents will still be there ; and Gandhiji then wishes all talented persons to hold their talents in trust for society, just as he wishes their inherited or personally acquired riches to be held in trust today. That is why he said that in the future society of his conception, no

person, whether prince or princely zamindar or merchant, can be the sole owner or disposer of possessions, hereditary or self-acquired. Every individual must have the fullest liberty to use his talents consistently with equal use by neighbours, but no one is entitled to the arbitrary use of the gains from the talents. He is part of the nation or say the social structure surrounding him. Therefore he can use his talents not for self only but for the social structure of which he is but a part and on whose sufferance he lives. —(*H*, 2-8-42, 249.)

In other words, talents should be socialized just as the means of production of the elementary necessaries of life ought to be ; and this socialization should be brought about by the conversion of talented persons through organised non-violence. As such, the theory of trusteeship has a permanent value in human society.

To sum up, we may therefore say, that apart from its wider spiritual application as stated above, even within the sphere of economic life, the Gandhian theory of trusteeship thus does not make for class collaboration, but for class liquidation, as a friend of mine once very happily put it. This liquidation, which will result in all men turning into labourers and placing their mental and material resources at the service of humanity taken as a whole, will be effected not by the forceful regimentation of the exploiters by the exploited, but by a change of heart brought about among the exploiters by the non-violent non-co-operation of those on whom the former depend for the making, the retention and the employment of their wealth. In course of that struggle, the exploited will also become free from the weaknesses which have given rise to the present social inequalities. Under the new constitution of things brought about by the joint endeavour of today's hostile classes, all men will live as servants of the community, willingly and joyfully, through a complete reorientation of life's values in a new direction. Through economic equality, society will also, in its turn, secure for every man full opportunity for the development of his physical, mental and moral powers without allowing him to restrict similar opportunity in others. And the product of those talents will be shared by all in common.

SATYAGRAHA : ITS MEANING AND METHOD

I have no set theory to go by. I have not worked out the science of Satyagraha in its entirety. You can join me in my quest if it appeals to you and you feel the call. —(*H*, 27-5-39, 136.)

War and Non-violence

William James was not only a great psychologist but also a great man. He loved mankind and hated war. But he also knew that war had certain merits ; it developed the sense of responsibility and co-ordinated endeavour, comradeship, courage and enthusiasm as hardly anything else could. But he also knew that the advantages of war were more than offset by the suffering and degradation which came inevitably in its train. So he tried to find some 'moral equivalent of war' which would produce the same beneficial effect on human character, but for which we would not have to pay as dearly as in conflicts where violence, hatred and cruelty are the prime movers. The phrase quoted above was probably coined by William James himself, and in an essay written many years ago, he suggested that instead of making war itself taboo, we should change its direction or lift up its character to a higher plane. Instead of allowing men to waste their lives in fighting against one another, he proposed that we should battle against the forces of nature so that human life may be made richer and happier in the end.

But few people seem to have paid adequate attention to the great psychologist. And one of the chief reasons for the neglect seems to have been that the proposed equivalent did not help to solve the quarrels and antagonisms of mankind where they actually existed. If all men already possessed the sense of human brotherhood, if they realized from the beginning that the welfare of the part lay in the welfare of the whole, then they might turn their energy to a better purpose instead of wasting it in war. But when such a sense was itself lacking, how were the believers in unity to convert the rest into a similar belief so that a new order could be brought into being on earth ?

It is just here that the method of Satyagraha steps in as a possible and effective substitute for war. It does not propose to do away with human conflicts ; but it raises the quality of those very conflicts by bringing into operation a spirit of love and a sense of human brotherhood. Satyagraha is not a substitute for war, it is war itself shorn of many of its ugly features and guided by a purpose nobler than we associate with destruction. It is an intensely heroic and chivalrous form of war.

Many have mistaken non-violence for pacifism and in order to clear the misunderstanding, Gandhi once said in course of a speech :

I shall take up the Abyssinian question first, I can answer it only in terms of active resistant non-violence. Now non-violence is the activest force on earth, and it is my conviction that it never fails. But if the Abyssinians had adopted the attitude of non-violence of the strong, i.e. the non-violence which breaks to pieces but never bends, Mussolini would have had no interest in Abyssinia. Thus if they had simply said : 'You are welcome to reduce us to dust or ashes but you will not find one Abyssinian ready to co-operate with you, what could Mussolini have done ? He did not want a desert. Mussolini wanted submission and not defiance, and if he had met with the quiet, dignified and non-violent defiance that I have described, he would certainly have been obliged to retire. Of course it is open to anyone to say that human nature has not been known to rise to such height. But if we have made unexpected progress in physical sciences, why may we do less in the science of the soul ?

Now about the English pacifists. I know there are some great and sincere men amongst them, but they are thinking in terms of pacifism as distinguished from unadulterated non-violence. I am essentially a non-violent man, and I believe in war bereft of every trace of violence. An essentially non-violent man does not calculate the consequences. The English pacifists you are talking of calculate, and when they speak of pacifism they do so with the mental reservation that when pacifism fails, arms might be used. With them not non-violence but arms are the ultimate sanction, as was the case with Woodrow Wilson's Fourteen Points. No, someone has to arise in

England with the living faith to say that England, whatever happens, shall not use arms. They are a nation fully armed, and if they having the power deliberately refuse to use arms, theirs will be the first example of Christianity in active practice on a mass scale. That will be a real miracle.

—(*H*, 14-5-38, 111.)

During the Khilafat Movement, someone twitted Gandhi with his support of the Khilafat, which in itself was based on the rule of arms. In reply, he wrote :

A believer in non-violence is pledged not to resort to violence or physical force either directly or indirectly in defence of anything, but is not precluded from helping men or institutions that are themselves not based on non-violence. If the reverse were the case, I would, for instance, be precluded from helping India to attain Swaraj because the future Parliament of India under Swaraj, I know for certain, will be having some military and police forces, or to take a domestic illustration, I may not help a son to secure justice, because forsooth he is not a believer in non-violence.

Mr. Zacharia's proposition will reduce all commerce by a believer in non-violence to an impossibility. And there are not wanting men, who do believe that complete non-violence means complete cessation of all activity.

Not such, however, is my doctrine of non-violence. My business is to refrain from doing any violence myself, and to induce by persuasion and service as many of God's creatures as I can, to join me in the belief and practice. But I would be untrue to my faith, if I refused to assist in a just cause any men or measures that did not entirely coincide with the principle of non-violence. I would be promoting violence, if finding the Mussalmans to be in the right, I did not assist them by means strictly non-violent against those who had treacherously plotted the destruction of the dignity of Islam. Even when both parties believe in violence, there is often such a thing as justice on one side or the other. A robbed man has justice on his side, even though he may be preparing to regain the lost property by force. And it would be accounted as a triumph of non-violence, if the injured party could be persuaded to regain his property by methods of Satyagraha, i.e. love or soul-force rather than free fight.

—(*YI*, 1-6-21, 173.)

The difference between war and Satyagraha amounts to this : while the former aims at coercion, the latter aims at conversion. In war one inflicts punishment upon the adversary, in Satyagraha one draws the maximum suffering on oneself, without a trace of bitterness against the opponent as a human being.

Those who believe in war are of opinion that there can be no change of heart in a person so long as he is in possession of power. It is only when that power is broken through superior force that the time comes for a change of heart. Satyagrahis, on the

other hand, believe that it is not impossible to persuade those in enjoyment of power to part with it
willingly under the compelling influence of love as
expressed through non-violent non-co-operation. A
person can accumulate power and use it for exploitation only if the exploited co-operate with him in the
process either through fear or love of gain. If the
exploited withdraw their co-operation and refuse to
bend even under the heaviest punishment, the heart
of the exploiter, or that of a section of the group
against whom the non-co-operation is directed, is
touched, and a way opened for human reconciliation
on a higher plane. If however this method of
conversion is to succeed, it must not be mixed up
with violence at any stage. If coercive methods
are at the beck and call of those who profess to
convert, there can be no real conversion. Conversion under duress evokes the same kind of antagonism
as open violence does.

How deep Gandhi's faith in the possibility of
changing human conduct is, can be realised from the
following extract from his writings :

> When I was a little child, there used to be
> two blind master performers in Rajkot. One of
> them was a musician. When he played on his
> instrument, his fingers swept the strings with an
> unerring instinct and everybody listened spell-
> bound to his playing. Similarly there are chords
> in every human heart. If we only know how to
> strike the right chord, we bring out the music.
> —(*H*, 27-5-39, 136.)

A Progressive Educational Method

One may naturally ask the question : Should Satyagrahis then first be perfect men before they can hope to convert others or remedy social wrongs ? Gandhi does not think so ; for Satyagraha is itself an educational process. A correct experiment in non-violence enriches our experience and makes our Satyagraha increasingly effective.

Let no one understand that a non-violent army is open only to those who strictly enforce in their lives all the implications of non-violence. It is open to all those who accept the implications and make an ever-increasing endeavour to observe them. There never will be an army of perfectly non-violent people. It will be formed of those who will honestly endeavour to observe non-violence.   —(*H*, 21-7-40, 214.)

I admit at once that there is 'a doubtful proportion of full believers' in my 'theory of non-violence'. But it should not be forgotten that I have also said that for my movement I do not at all need believers in the theory of non-violence, full or imperfect. It is enough if people carry out the rules of non-violent action.

—(*GC*, 169.)

He has also written :

I adhere to the opinion that I did well to present to the Congressmen non-violence as an expedient. I could not have done otherwise, if I was to introduce it into politics. In South Africa too I introduced it as an expedient. It was successful there because resisters were a small number in a compact area and therefore easily controlled. Here we had numberless men scattered over a huge country. The result was that they could not be easily controlled or trained. And yet it is a marvel the way they have responded. They might have responded much better and shown far better results. But I have no sense of disappointment in me over the results obtained. If I had started with men who accepted non-violence as a creed, I might have ended with myself. Imperfect as I am, I started with imperfect men and women and sailed on an uncharted ocean. Thank God that though the boat has not reached its haven, it has proved fairly storm-proof. —(H, 12-4-42, 116.)

The science and art of Satyagraha is new in the sense that its large-scale application for the solution of economic, social or political wrongs is a new event in human history. Every Satyagrahi should therefore develop a truly scientific spirit, watching the results at every step, devising new experiments, modifying his opinions as well as steps with growing experience. He should hold no opinion dogmatically, but should be prepared to test every opinion even if he finds himself alone. All that men like Gandhi can do for us is to help with their richer and more varied experience ; the journey has to be undertaken by each man for himself. Constant and intelligent practice not only improves our power of action but also improves the quality of our mind.

Truth and non-violence are not for the dense. Pursuit of them is bound to result in all-round growth of the body, mind and heart. If this does not follow, either truth and non-violence are untrue, and since the former is impossible the latter will be the only conclusion.

—(*H*, 8-5-37, 98.)

You must know that a true practice of *ahimsa* means also in one who practises it, the keenest intelligence and wide-awake conscience.
—(*H*, 8-9-40, 274.)

Choice of Civil Resisters and Some Points about their Training

Those who suffer from a particular wrong should alone offer Satyagraha in order to remedy it. Others should watch the movement with sympathy or offer helpful criticism ; but should not generally join in the struggle.

It is the essence of Satyagraha that those who are suffering should alone offer it. Cases can be conceived when what may be termed sympathetic Satyagraha may be legitimately applied. The idea underlying Satyagraha is to convert the wrong-doer, to awaken the sense of justice in him, to show him also that without the co-operation, direct or indirect, of the wronged the wrong-doer cannot do the wrong intended by him. If the people in either case are not ready to suffer for their causes, no outside help in the shape of Satyagraha can bring true deliverance.

—(*H*, 10-12-38, 369.)

It was in connection with the movement for constitutional reforms in Rajkot that Gandhi said :

I think the initial mistake was made when all Kathiawadis were permitted to join Rajkot Satyagraha. That step introduced an element of weakness in the fight. Thereby we put our reliance on numbers, whereas a Satyagrahi relies solely upon God who is the help of the helpless. 'He in whose name Satyagraha was launched, will also see it through.' If the people of Rajkot had thought in these terms, there would have been no temptation to organise big processions or mass demonstrations and probably there would have been no atrocities such as Rajkot has had to experience. A genuine Satyagrahi proceeds by setting the opponent at his ease. His action never creates panic in the breast of the 'enemy'. Supposing as a result of rigid enforcement of the rules of Satyagrahis Rajkot Satyagraha had been confined to a few hundred or even a few score true Satyagrahis and they had carried on their Satyagraha in the right spirit till their last breath, theirs would have served as a heroic example. —(*H*, 20-5-39, 134.)

During the fast in May 1933, Gandhi issued a statement in course of which he said :

The movement of Civil Disobedience does not depend so much upon the quantity as on the quality of the men and women taking part in it, and if I was leading the movement, I should sacrifice quantity and insist on quality. If this could be done, it would immediately raise the level of the movement. Mass instruction on any other terms is an impossibility.—(*HC*, I, 559.)

Only those who are in the habit of obeying laws and maintaining discipline in normal times, should have the right of offering civil disobedience.

He to whom Satyagraha means nothing more than Civil Disobedience has never understood Satyagraha. No doubt the rigid interpretation of Satyagraha does include within its meaning Civil Disobedience. But only he who has mastered the art of obedience to law knows the art of disobedience to law. Only he who thoroughly knows how to construct may destroy. —(*YI*, 5-11-19, *Tagore*, 45.)

A born democrat is a born disciplinarian. Democracy comes naturally to him who is habituated normally to yield willing obedience to all laws, human or divine. I claim to be a democrat both by instinct and training. Let those who are ambitious to serve democracy qualify themselves by satisfying first this acid test of democracy. Moreover, a democrat must be utterly selfless. He must think and dream not in terms of self or party but only of democracy. Only then does he acquire the right of civil disobedience. —(*H*, 27-5-39, 136.)

Satyagrahis should develop initiative and adaptability. Decentralisation of leadership is an essential part of Satyagraha.

9

Discipline has a place in non-violent
strategy, but much more is required. In a
Satyagraha army everybody is a soldier and a
servant. But at a pinch every Satyagrahi soldier
has also to be his own general and leader. Mere
discipline cannot make for leadership. The latter
calls for faith and vision.

To create a truly non-violent atmosphere in
the country spinning with faith is necessary.
Spinning for discipline, whatever else it might be
capable of achieving, will not give that faith ;
it cannot help us to win the Satyagraha fight
which requires the non-violence of the strong.

—(*H*, 28-7-40, 227.)

There should be division of work in a Satyagraha
camp, and each Satyagrahi should devote himself
wholly to his portion of work. To resist the temptation of proving one's efficiency in every field requires
a certain amount of self-control. This is necessary
in the interest of co-ordinated and effective work.
During the Satyagraha for the establishment of the
right to use public roads by 'Untouchables' at
Vaikom, Gandhi said :

Those who remain at the Ashram are taking
as much part in the struggle as those who go and
offer Satyagraha at the barricades. Every piece
of work in connection with the struggle is just as
important as any other piece, and therefore the
work of sanitation in the Ashram is just as
important as spinning away at the barricades.
And if in this place the work of cleaning the

closets and compound is more distasteful than
spinning it should be considered far more important and profitable. Not a single minute should
be wasted in idle conversation, but we must be
absorbed in the work before us and if every one
of us works in that spirit you will see that there
is pleasure in work itself. Every bit of property,
any thing in the Ashram should be regarded by
you as your own property and not property that
can be wasted at pleasure. You may not waste
a grain of rice or a scrap of paper, and similarly
a minute of your time. It is not ours. It
belongs to the nation and we are trustees for the
use of it. —(H, 19-3-25, 95.)

Satyagrahis should not function as a party
separate from the masses, either in constructive work
or in civil resistance. They should work through
the local democratic organizations. Their relation
to the common people should be like that of sugar in
milk which enriches its taste but has no separate
existence. The common man's belief in non-violence
may not be intelligent ; but that of the Satyagrahi
should be of a different kind. The latter should
try to live up to all the implications of such
belief intelligently. Only then can an effective
bond be established between the Satyagrahi and the
masses, a relation which will help to preserve order
and non-violence even in the midst of strain or in the
face of a crisis. —(H, 14-5-38,111 ; H, 4-11-39, 331-2.)

With regard to the training of a Satyagrahi, it
should be pointed out, in the end, that although the

latter appears to be long and painful, yet we should never give it up, as the fruits of non-violence are also of inestimable value. We hope to attain results by it which have so far never been realized by means of violence.

It takes a fairly strenuous course of training to attain to a mental state of non-violence. In daily life it has to be a course of discipline though one may not like it, like for instance the life of a soldier. But I agree that unless there is hearty co-operation of the mind, the mere outward observance will be simply a mask harmful both to the man himself and others. The perfect state is reached only when mind and body and speech are in proper co-ordination. But it is always a case of intense mental struggle,

—(*YI*, 1-10-31, 287.)

If the method of violence takes plenty of training, the method of non-violence takes even more training, and that training is much more difficult than the training for violence.

—(*H*, 14-5-38, 110.)

Of course, the critics can reasonably argue that the non-violence pictured by me is not possible for masses of mankind, it is possible only for the very few highly developed persons. I have combated that view and suggested that, given proper training and proper generalship, non-violence can be practised by masses of mankind. —(*H*, 17-12-38, 384.)

One should not depend on money-aid in a

Satyagraha compaign ; it should play a minor role, if any at all. One should rely more on voluntary contributions in the shape of labour or materials, rather than on money, which is only a convenient means of buying the labour of others, even when it is not of a voluntary nature. Quality being more important, quantity may have to be sacrificed ; in time quality will multiply itself in a natural way.

What a Satyagrahi can fight for

It should be clear from the outset that a Satya-grahi must fight with clean hands and in a clean cause. The civilization envisaged by Gandhi 'eschews exploitation altogether, and exploitation is the essence of violence'. (*H*, 4-11-39, 331.) Therefore the non-violent method is useless in the defence of any object which can only be gained by means of violence.

Non-violence in the very nature of things is of no assistance in the defence of ill-gotten gains and immoral acts. —(*H*, 5-9-36, 236.)

There can be no *Satyagrah* in an unjust cause. —(*YI*, 27-4-21, 129.)

In non-violent Swaraj, there can be no encroachment upon just rights ; contrariwise, no one can possess unjust rights. —(*H*, 25-3-39, 65.)

Only property, right or privilege which can exist on the sufferance of the rest of society, can therefore be preserved by means of non-violence. The Satyagrahi should remember in this connection that 'love and exclusive possession can never go together', i.e. we can own a thing under non-violence only if everyone else who is in need of it is also not in want of it.

Q. Is it possible to defend by means of non-violence anything which can only be gained through violence ?

A. What was gained by violence could not only not be defended by non-violence but the latter required the abandonment of ill-gotten gains. —(*H*, 16-2-47, 25.)

The Demand

Gandhi's specific instructions with regard to the demand in civil disobedience are given below :

Civil disobedience can never be in general terms such as for Independence. The issue must be definite and capable of being clearly understood and within the power of the opponent to yield. —(*CP*, 28.)

Bring your demand down to its lowest proportions without sacrificing truth and justice. In other words, distinguish carefully between what is essential and what is not in the demand. Submit your demand constantly to public examination and criticism. All that is found not absolutely essential, should not be made a cause for Satyagraha.

An example can be given from the Travancore Satyagraha of 1938. Gandhi wrote :

I have been against mixing up the struggle for responsible government with the charges against the Dewan. —(*H*, 14-1-39, 424.)

I told them (the deputation from Travancore) that their cause would be damaged by persistence in the charges against the Dewan, and that the question was not one of truth or otherwise of the charges. It was one of political insight. Allegations were made that the struggle was personal. The demand for responsible government made it impersonal and raised it to a higher level. I could not be party to the conduct of a struggle which must engage and exhaust time and energy in pursuit of a personal matter to the exclusion of the most important one of Swaraj. If they concentrated on the allegations, responsible government was bound to recede into the background. —(*H*, 17-12-38, 382.)

Whereas if they got responsible government, which they were bound to, if they were united and strong in their faith in non-violence and truth, they would have control over all the Dewans, present or future. —(*H*, 14-1-39, 424.)

In choosing a demand and the immediate step for implementing it, one should also take into consideration one's capacity to suffer. The need may even arise of owning one's error, and revising a demand which has been wrongly set too high from the beginning. In 1939, while commenting on Satyagraha movements in Jaipur and Rajkot, Gandhi wrote :

What I have done by correcting myself in Rajkot is to show the true way to the Satyagrahis. In following it, they may find it necessary to lower their immediate demands but only so as to really hasten their progress to their goal. Therefore there can be no lowering out of weakening. Every lowering must be out of a due appreciation of the local situation and the capacity of the workers to cope with it. Here there is no room for demoralisation and a rout. In cases like Jaipur of course there can be no question of lowering. The demand itself is in the lowest pitch. There is no room in it for lowering anything. In essence it is one for civil liberty. Civil liberty consistent with the observance of non-violence is the first step towards Swaraj. It is the breath of political and social life. It is the foundation of freedom. There is no room there for dilution or compromise. It is the water of life. I have never heard of water being diluted.

—(H, 24-6-39, 169.)

Having thus fixed one's minimum demand, the Satyagrahi may find it necessary to put forth his maximum strength, by way of self-suffering, in order to implement it. So Gandhi wrote :

Let them not forget their limitations and above all the conditions of success, viz. strictest observance of truth and non-violence. They must be ready to face bullets without flinching but also without lifting their little finger in so-called self-defence. A Satyagrahi abjures the right of self-defence. Let it also be remembered that a Satyagrahi's minimum is also his maximum.

—(H, 9-7-38, 173.)

And its Progression

The general rule is :

In a pure fight, the fighters would never go beyond the objective when the fight began, even if they have received an accession to their strength in course of the fighting and, on the other hand, they could not give up their objective if they found their strength dwindling away. —(*SA*, 412.)

But Satyagraha has to be progressive in character, which he explained thus :

My experience has taught me that a law of progression applies to every righteous struggle. But in the case of Satyagraha the law amounts to an axiom. As the Ganges advances, other streams flow into it, and hence at the mouth it grows so wide that neither bank is to be seen and a person sailing upon the river cannot make out where the river ends and the sea begins. So also as a Satyagraha struggle progresses onward, many another element helps to swell its current, and there is a constant growth in the results to which it leads. This is really inevitable, and is bound up with the first principles of Satyagraha. For in Satyagraha the minimum is also the maximum, and as it is the irreducible minimum, there is no question of retreat, and the only movement possible is an advance. In other struggles, even when they are righteous, the demand is first pitched a little higher so as to admit of future reduction, and hence the law of progression does not apply to all of them without exception. But

I must explain how the law of progression comes
into play when the minimum is also the maximum
as in Satyagraha. The Ganges does not leave its
course in search of tributaries. Even so does the
Satyagrahi not leave his path which is sharp as the
sword's edge. But as the tributaries spontaneously
join the Ganges as it advances, so it is with
the river that is Satyagraha. Seeing that the
Immigration Act (in South Africa) was included
in the Satyagraha, some Indians ignorant of the
principles of Satyagraha insisted upon the whole
mass of the anti-Indian legislation in the
Transvaal being similarly treated. Others again
suggested a mobilisation of Indians all over South
Africa and the offering of Satyagraha against all
anti-Indian legislation in Natal, the Cape Colony,
the Orange Free State etc., while the Transvaal
struggle was on. Both the suggestions involved
a breach of principle. I distinctly said, that it
would be dishonest now, having seen the opportunity, to take up a position which was not in
view when Satyagraha was started. No matter
how strong we were, the present struggle must
close when the demands for which it was
commenced were accepted. I am confident, that
if we had not adhered to this principle, instead of
winning, we would not only have lost all along
the line, but also forfeited the sympathy which
had been enlisted in our favour. On the other
hand if the adversary himself creates new difficulties for us while the struggle is in progress,
they become automatically included in it. A

Satyagrahi, without being false to his faith, cannot disregard new difficulties which confront him while he is pursuing his own course. The adversary is not a Satyagrahi,—Satyagraha against Satyagraha is impossible,—and is not bound by any limit of maximum or minimum. He can therefore try if he wishes to frighten the Satyagrahi by raising novel issues. But the Satyagrahi has renounced all fear, tackles by Satyagraha the later difficulties as well as the former and trusts that it will help him to hold his own against all odds. Therefore as a Satyagraha struggle is prolonged, that is to say by the adversary, it is the adversary who stands to lose from his own standpoint, and it is the Satyagrahi who stands to gain. —(*SA*, 319.)

Timing a Demand

In Satyagraha, one should never try to take advantage of the opponent's weak moments. That may be a good rule when coercion is the aim ; but when conversion is the object, the idea of embarrassing the opponent, or the thought of punishing him should be taboo.

The First Step and the
Question of Publicity

A Satyagrahi must first mobilise public opinion against the evil which he is out to eradicate, by means of a wide and intensive agitation. When public opinion is sufficiently roused against a social abuse even the tallest will not dare to practise or openly to lend support to it. An

awakened and intelligent public opinion is the
most potent weapon of a Satyagrahi.

—(*YI*, 8-8-29, 263.)

Educative propaganda through newspapers may
thus form an integral part of a Satyagraha campaign. In the history of *Satyagraha in South Africa*,
Gandhi has stated :

I believe that a struggle which chiefly relies
upon internal strength cannot be wholly carried
on without a newspaper, and it is also my
experience that we could not perhaps have
educated the local Indian community, nor kept
Indians all over the world in touch with the
course of events in South Africa in any other way,
with the same ease and success as through *Indian
Opinion*, which therefore was certainly a most
useful and potent weapon in our struggle.

As the community was transformed in
course of and as a result of the struggle, so was
Indian Opinion. —(*SA*, 221.)

Newspapers and propaganda literature specially
devoted to a cause, should be self-supporting. They
should never depend on advertisements to pay their
way. Self-sufficiency should be a test and a measure
of public sympathy and support. (See *YI*, 8-10-19,
Tagore, 3.)

If this is found impracticable, Satyagrahis must
seek other means in order to give publicity to their
cause.

If the luxury of wires be denied to us,
we must manage with the post. If the postal

communication be also stopped we must use messengers. Friends travelling to and fro will oblige us. When the use of the railways is denied, we must use other methods of conveyance. No amount of slowness imposed from without can checkmate us, if we are sure within.

—(*YI*, 15-12-21, 408.)

So long as all have pen and paper or even slate and pencil, we need not despair of transmitting our thoughts in writing, if we have enough volunteers. Given a sufficient number of volunteer writers, we can multiply copies indefinitely. I can foresee many advantages in non-co-operationists being confined to their pens only. —(*YI*, 9-3-21, 73.)

Let everyone become his own walking newspaper and carry the good news from mouth to mouth. This does not mean what boys used to do in the past, viz. trumpeting about of bits of news. The idea here is of telling my neighbour what I have authentically heard. This no Government can overtake or suppress. It is the cheapest newspaper yet devised, and it defies the wit of Government, however clever it may be. Let these walking newspapers be sure of the news they give. They should not indulge in idle gossip. They should make sure of the source of information, and they will find that the public gets all the information that they need without opening their morning newspaper which, they should know, will contain garbled, one-sided information and therefore not worth the trouble of reading. —(*H*, 10-11-40, 334.)

Other Preliminary Steps

Put your adversary in the wrong, which means that you yourself should always be in the right. Sufficiently long negotiations should be carried on with the adversary directly in order, first of all, to convince him of the justice of the demand.

As a Satyagrahi, I must always allow my cards to be examined and re-examined at all times and make reparation if an error is discovered. —(*H*, 11-3-39, 44.)

The opponent should be given every opportunity to do the right.

Anyone who objects to the right thing, puts himself in the wrong. —(*H*, 13-1-40, 411.)

The Satyagrahi should also be always ready to submit his case before an impartial tribunal. But if such on offer fails, and civil resistance has to be resorted to, then the Satyagrahi will feel all the stronger for having done everything for a peaceful solution. But

What I have pleaded for (wrote Gandhiji) is desire and readiness for negotiation. It is not inconceivable that the stage of negotiation may never be reached. If it is not, it must not be for the fault of the Satyagrahi.

—(*H*, 24-6-39, 170.)

Since Satyagraha is one of the most powerful methods of direct action, a Satyagrahi exhausts all other means before he resorts to Satyagraha. He will therefore constantly and continually approach the constituted authority, he will appeal to public opinion, educate public opinion, state his case calmly and coolly before everybody who wants to listen to him, and only after he has exhausted all these avenues will he resort to Satyagraha.   —(*YI*, 20-10-27, 353.)

It will be contrary to every canon of Satyagraha to launch upon the extreme step till every other is exhausted. Such haste will itself constitute violence.   —(*H*, 24-6-39, 172.)

The aim of the non-violent worker must ever be to convert. He may not however wait endlessly. When therefore the limit is reached, he takes risks and conceives plans of active Satyagraha which may mean civil disobedience and the like. His patience is never exhausted to the point of giving up his creed.   —(*YI*, 6-2-30, 44.)

But when he has found the impelling call of the inner voice within him and launches out upon Satyagraha he has burnt his boats and there is no receding.   —(*YI*, 20-10-27, 353.)

The Campaign of Civil Disobedience

(i)   Caution

The first indispensable condition precedent to any civil resistance is that there should be surety against any outbreak of violence whether on the part of those who are identified with civil resistance or on the part of the general public.

It would be no answer in the case of an outbreak of violence that it was instigated by the State or other agencies hostile to civil resisters. It should be obvious that civil resistance cannot flourish in an atmosphere of violence. That does not mean that the resources of a Satyagrahi have come to an end. Ways other than civil disobedience should be found out. —(*H*, 18-3-39, 53.)

The greatest care is necessary when violence, not non-violence, seems to pervade the air. Indeed it may be reasonably argued that in an atmosphere surcharged with violence there is no scope for non-violence. This argument may be carried too far, so far that non-violence may be made wholly ineffective ; whereas it is claimed to be the only effective force for counteracting violence no matter how terrible. But when violence pervades the air the expression of non-violence may not be through civil disobedience. And if it is to be civil disobedience, it must be hedged in by adequate restrictions. In Satyagraha, it is never the numbers that count ; it is always the quality, more so when the forces of violence are uppermost. —(*H*, 25-3-39, 64.)

(ii) The Place of Secrecy

When Gandhiji was released from prison after civil disobedience, he said in course of a Press statement in May 1933 :

I cannot help saying that the secrecy that has attended the movement is fatal to its success. If, therefore, the movement must be continued

I would urge those who are guiding the movement in different parts of the country to discard all secrecy. I do not care if thereby it becomes difficult to secure a single civil resister.

There can be no doubt that fear has seized the common mass. The Ordinances have cowed them down and I am inclined to think that the secret methods are largely responsible for the demoralisation. —(*HC*, I, 559.)

Similarly, in 1944, he wrote :

The question most discussed with me by visitors is whether I approve of underground activities. These include sabotage, the publication of unauthorised sheets etc. It has been suggested to me that without some workers going underground, they could have done nothing. Some have contended that destruction of property, including dislocation of communications provided that safety of human life could be insured, should surely be counted as non-violence.

Examples of other nations, as having not hesitated to do all these things and much worse, have been cited. My reply is that no nation has, so far as I know, deliberately used truth and non-violence as exclusive means for the attainment of freedom. Judged by that standard, I say unhesitatingly that underground activities, even though utterly innocent in themselves, should have no place in the technique of non-violence.

Sabotage, and all it means, including destruction of property, is in itself violence.

10

Though these activities may be shown to have touched the imagination and enthusiasm, I have no doubt that they have harmed the movement as a whole. —(*HS*, 29-7-44.)

Gandhiji had already said in his Hindustani speech before the All-India Congress Committee on the 8th of August, 1942 :

Nothing should be done secretly. This is an open rebellion. In this struggle secrecy is a sin. A free man would not engage in a secret movement. It is likely that when you gain freedom you will have a C. I. D. of your own, in spite of my advice to the contrary. But in the present struggle we have to work openly and to receive bullets in our chests, without running away. In a struggle of this character all secrecy is sin and must be punctiliously avoided. —(*GC*, 147.)

When the means are violent, a well-knit party must be there to guide operations. They have to be on the look out for weak points in the enemy's armour and also make the most economical use of their own strength. Under such a scheme, the party plays the major directive role and the masses can never take the initiative in their own hands in accordance with some previously explained plan. Under violence, again, the whole body of the common people cannot make themselves equally effective; and it is only that portion of it which makes the most effective use of violence which comes to the forefront. This part may consist of the industrial proletariat or the army and police. When the revolution is over, power gravitates unequally to the several forces engaged in the revolution. It tends to collect most in the party which led the revolution, and less and less in those sections of the common people which played increasingly feebler roles in action. By this very act, the active sections who gain more power than the rest, become isolated from the masses.

In the technique of non-violence, on the other hand, the theoretical position is just the opposite. As soon as the movement is on, the front-rankers are expected to lead by the bravest and openest acts which are called forth. They may find themselves in jail, or some may lose their lives while facing severer repression. In any case, they are out of the picture at the first shot, only to leave their example to work as leaven in raising the masses. If, then, the masses respond and take up the initiative and follow in the footsteps of the leaders in the act of civil resistance, then only can Satyagraha reach a successful termination.

Even if a few members of the directive organisation remain over by chance, they do not conduct operations as a party of violence has to do. They are supposed to act only through the people's own democratic organizations, helping the people to adapt the movement to new circumstances in accordance with the principle of non-violence ; and, above all, to take every step openly without hesitation. If the movement succeeds under these conditions, it can succeed only if the people have become, more or less, self-acting. The very movement of Satyagraha puts them on their own legs. And when power comes with the revolution, it spreads evenly among the masses ; for, under non-violence, any unarmed man, woman or child can be effective, provided the heart is stout. Under violence, this cannot be so ; those who make the most effective use of violence gain the upper hand. This is why complete openness goes with non-violence, while secrecy must accompany methods of violent organization.

It has been the experience of Congress workers that secrecy becomes necessary in civil disobedience in the same proportion as previous organizational work has been lacking. And soon one also realizes practically that the more secrecy creeps in, the farther do the masses recede into the background. It can therefore be taken as a general rule that the more the masses are organized in the non-violent way, the less is there any need of secrecy.

(iii) Picking up a Law for Disobedience

In 1919, Gandhi stated in general terms :

It is open to (the Satyagrahi) to withdraw his co-operation from the State by disobeying such other laws whose breach does not involve moral turpitude.—(*YI*, Nov. 1919, *Tagore*, 7.)

Similarly, the instruction in 1939 was :

Disobedience should not be destructive, that is harmful to the country. The laws to be picked up, therefore, should be those which are harmful to the people or laws whose breach will not harm the people but are likely merely to make more work for the authorities.—(*H*, 18-3-39, 53.)

More detailed instructions were also issued in 1922 when there were proposals for a nation-wide movement of civil disobedience :

Aggressive, assertive or offensive civil disobedience is non-violent, wilful disobedience of laws of the State whose breach does not involve moral turpitude and which is undertaken as a symbol of revolt against the State. Thus disregard of laws relating to revenue or regulation of personal conduct for the convenience of the State, although such laws in themselves inflict no hardship and do not require to be altered, would be assertive, aggressive or offensive civil disobedience.

Defensive civil disobedience, on the other hand, is involuntary or reluctant non-violent disobedience of such laws as are in themselves bad and obedience to which would be inconsistent with one's self-respect or human dignity. Thus formation of volunteer corps for peaceful purposes, holding of public meetings for like purposes, publication of articles not contemplating or inciting to violence in spite of prohibitory orders, is defensive civil disobedience. And so is conducting of peaceful picketing undertaken with a view to wean people from things or institutions picketed in spite of orders to the contrary. The fulfilment of the conditions mentioned above is as necessary for defensive civil disobedience as for offensive civil disobedience.

—(*YI*, 9-2-22, 85.)

The next rule is that :

It must be a movement in which the largest number of people can take part.

—(*H*, 18-3-39, 53.)

In choosing a law for disobedience, one should not again be tempted by chances of ready popular response. Enthusiasm has its place ; but patience and cool determination count for more in the long run in Satyagraha. In 1922, Gandhi warned Congressmen against the adoption of any hasty step in the following terms :

We must not resort to non-payment (of taxes) because of the possibility of a ready response. The readiness is a fatal temptation. Such non-payment will not be civil or non-violent, but it will be criminal or fraught with the greatest possibility of violence. Not until the peasantry is trained to understand the reason and the virtue of *civil* non-payment and is prepared to look with calm resignation upon the confiscation (which can only be temporary) of their holdings and the forced sale of their cattle and other belongings, may they be advised to withhold payment of taxes.—(*YI*, 26-1-22, 57.)

Once again, while reviewing the progress of the Individual Civil Disobedience Movement towards the end of 1941, he wrote :

Enthusiasm that is froth is of no use in non-violent action. Showy demonstrations and the like have a value in the initial stages. Continuous feverish activity can only promote violence and therefore retard the steady march of non-violent action, call it battle, if that word is preferred.

—(*HS*, 31-10-41.)

(iv) Maintaining the Initiative

An able general always gives battle in his own time on the ground of his own choice. He always retains the initiative in these respects and never allows it to pass into the hands of the enemy.

In a Satyagraha campaign the mode of fight and the choice of tactics, e.g. whether to advance or retreat, offer civil resistance or organize non-violent strength through constructive work or purely selfless humanitarian service are determined according to the exigencies of the situation. A Satyagrahi must carry out whatever plan is laid out for him with a cool determination giving way to neither excitement nor depression.
—(*H*, 27-5-39, 143.)

In Satyagraha there is no such thing as disappointment or heart-burning. The struggle always goes on in some shape or other till the goal is reached. A Satyagrahi is indifferent whether it is civil disobedience or some other phase of the struggle to which he is called. Nor does he mind if in the middle of the civil disobedience march, he is called upon to halt and do something else. He must have faith that it is all for the best. My own experience hitherto has been that each suspension has found the people better equipped for the fight and for control over forces of violence. Therefore, in advising suspension, I dismiss from my mind the fear that it may lead to desertion and disbelief. If it does, I should not feel sorry, for it would be to me a sign that the deserters did not know what Satyagraha was and the movement was better without those who did not know what they were doing.

—(*H*, 1-4-39, 72.)

Just as it is necessary that the Satyagrahi should not allow the adversary to dictate or force any step upon him, in the same way, he should not allow himself to be buffetted about by every temporary event. He should have a long-range view of how the campaign should shape itself, he should maintain an intelligent appreciation of the environment, but in the matter of direction, he should form his own decision and pursue it with tact and firmness.

Those who claim to lead the masses must resolutely refuse to be led by them, if we want to avoid mob law and desire ordered progress of the country. I believe that mere protestation of one's opinion and surrender to the mass opinion is not only not enough, but in matters of vital importance, leaders must *act* contrary to the mass of opinion if it does not commend itself to their reason.—(*YI*,   )

A leader is useless when he acts against the promptings of his own conscience, surrounded as he must be by people holding all kinds of views. He will drift like an anchorless ship if he has not the inner voice to hold him firm and guide him.—(*YI*, 23-2-22, 112.)

(v) How the Campaign grows

In the course of a struggle, Satyagrahis may find themselves isolated, and the people leaving the path of non-violence in their impatience. Under such circumstances, it may be necessary to modify the programme of civil resistance and take some dramatic step which will strike the imagination of the people, and restore confidence in the possibility of full resistance through non-violence.

For this purpose, it is necessary that, at every stage, there should be a band of Satyagrahis prepared to give non-violent expression to the resistance surging in the form of violence in the mass mind ; and this should be done by facing the most intense form of repression possible. The programme for the masses should be tuned to a lower key than that of the trained Satyagrahis.

The person responsible for conducting a Satyagraha campaign should, therefore, keep a wise and watchful eye on the sufferings of the common people. Persistence in suffering, for its own sake, is wrong in any form of warfare, whether violent or non-violent. A retreat may be called upon as a preparation for an intenser endeavour in the future.

Resistance, violent or non-violent, has to be well thought out. Thoughtless resistance will be regarded as bravado in military parlance, and violence or folly in the language of non-violence. Retreat itself is often a plan of resistance and may be a precursor of greater bravery and sacrifice. Every retreat is not cowardice which implies fear to die. Of course a brave man would more often die in violently or non-violently resisting the aggressor in the latter's attempt to oust him. But he will be no less brave if wisdom dictates present retreat. —(H, 12-4-42, 109.)

A wise general does not wait till he is actually routed ; he withdraws in time in an orderly manner from a position which he knows he would not be able to hold. —(H, 22-10-38, 304.)

This is so far as the mass movement is concerned. For the Satyagrahi himself, however, there is no retreat ; only he must adapt his steps to the changed circumstances in the midst of the campaign. Gandhi's instruction in this respect has been that

There is no time limit for a Satyagrahi nor is there a limit to his capacity for suffering. —(YI, 19-2-25, 61.)

They must develop infinite faith in the capacity of ahimsa to neutralise every person of himsa. True ahimsa lay in running into the mouth of himsa. They must shed their fear and disbelief in the power of ahimsa to achieve the seemingly impossible.—(H, 29-4-39, 104.)

Consequently there may come a time in the latter reaches of Satyagraha when life has to be staked in a brave all-out endeavour. Under such circumstances :

We must tell the people what they should do. They will act according to capacity. If we begin to judge their capacity and give directions accordingly, our directions will be halting and even compromising which we should never do. —(GC, 310.)

For the Satyagrahi, the road is clear.

Just as one must learn the art of killing in the training for violence, so one must learn the art of dying in the training for non-violence. —(H, 1-9-40, 268.)

But even then, Gandhi has issued a note of warning :

Let us all be brave enough to die the death of a martyr, but let no one lust for martyrdom.

—(H, 13-1-27, 10.)

Fasting in Satyagraha

Satyagraha is undertaken in order to remedy a wrong. The ideal condition is that in which the Satyagrahi, after withdrawing his co-operation from the present system, is able to employ the whole of his energy in building up the new social order without wasting any time in combating the old. But such a condition is only an ideal ; in actual life, the Satyagrahi has to employ the method of civil resistance in order to counteract the existing forces. It may however be possible that due to inadequate preparation, or the presence of an atmosphere of violence, his civil resistance has every likelihood of being diverted into fruitless channels. What should the Satyagrahi do under the circumstances to canalize the forces of violence and restore the non-violent form of resistance among the masses ?

Placed under such a contingency, Gandhiji has, on several occasions in the past, resorted to the method of fasting, if need be, to death. Sometimes the fast has been undertaken in order to find an opportunity of reasoning with his own self in an intensity of solitude, or as he has put it, 'to come face to face with God by crucifying the flesh'. But in spite of its claim as being an exclusively private affair, such fasts have actually exercised tremendous influence on public opinion because of the position Gandhiji enjoys, and have thus been effective in bringing about desirable changes in the public mind.

There is also another kind of fasting which is more directly in tune with the method of Satyagraha in which the object is to appeal to the good sense of the person against whom Satyagraha is directed. While undertaking such a fast, the Satyagrahi should not, on any account, be actuated by any sort of ill-will against his adversary, for it is his purpose to convert and not to coerce, even by the indirect pressure of public opinion roused by means of the fast.

I have been driven (wrote Gandhi) to the conclusion that fasting unto death is an integral part of Satyagraha programme, and it is the greatest and most effective weapon in its armoury under given circumstances.

Non-violence in its positive aspect as benevolence (I do not use the word love as it has fallen into disrepute.) is the greatest force because of the limitless scope it affords for self-suffering without causing or intending any physical or material injury to the wrong-doer. The object always is to evoke the best in him. Self-suffering is an appeal to his better nature, as retaliation is to his baser. Fasting under proper circumstances is such an appeal *par excellence*. If the politician does not perceive its propriety in political matters, it is because it is a novel use of this very fine weapon. —(*H*, 26-7-42, 248.)

Fasting is a fiery weapon. It has its own science. No one, as far as I am aware, has a perfect knowledge of it. Unscientific experimentation with it is bound to be harmful to the one who fasts, and it may even harm the cause espoused. No one who has not earned the right to do so should, therefore, use this weapon. A fast may only be undertaken by him who is associated with the person against whom he fasts. The latter must be directly connected with the purpose for which the fast is being undertaken. —(*H*, 13-10-40, 322.)

When Gandhi finished his twentyone-day's fast in 1943 while in prison, the Home Member of the Government of India said in course of a speech before the Legislative Council, 'I must confess that speaking for myself it is certainly repugnant to Western ideas of decency to exploit against an opponent his feelings of humanity, chivalry and mercy or to trifle with such a sacred trust as one's own life in order to play on the feelings of the public for the sake of some purely mundane object'. To this Gandhiji replied as follows :

I must tread with extreme caution upon the ground with which you are infinitely more familiar than I can be. Let me however remind you of the heroic fast of the late Mac Swiney. I know that the British Government let him die in imprisonment. But he has been acclaimed by the Irish people as a hero and a martyr. Edward Thompson in his *You have lived through all this* says that the late Mr. Asquith called the British Government's action as a 'political blunder of the first magnitude.' The author adds : 'He was allowed to die by inches, while the world watched with a passion of admiration and sympathy and innumerable British men and women begged their Government not to be such a damned fool'. And is it repugnant to Western ideas of decency to exploit (if the expression must be retained) against an opponent his feelings of humanity, chivalry or mercy ? Which is better, to take the opponent's life, secretly or openly, or to credit him with finer feelings and evoke them by fasting and the like ? Again, which is better, to trifle with one's own life by fasting or some other way of self-immolation, or to trifle with it by engaging in an attempt to compass the destruction of the opponent and his dependents ?   —(GC, 79.)

Now and again, Gandhi has issued instructions as to how fasts are actually to be undertaken. Once he wrote :

Judged by my standard, the majority of fasts do not at all come under the category of Satyagraha fasts and are, as they are popularly called, hunger strikes undertaken without previous preparation and adequate thought.

—(*H*, 18-3-39, 56.)

I know that fasting like Satyagraha is very much abused nowadays. One finds people fasting on the slightest pretext. Often there is violence behind such fasting. If for no other reason than for this practical reason of preventing thoughtless imitation, I was most reluctant to undertake this (Rajkot) fast. But an inner urge brooks no denial. I can only therefore warn the people, who may wish hereafter to fast for redress of grievances, real or imaginary, against imitating me. Fasting like some potent medicines can only be taken on rare occasions and under expert guidance. It is wrong, it is sinful for everybody to consider himself an expert. —(*H*, 11-3-39, 46.)

During the Rajkot Fast, an objection was raised that the fast had turned the whole movement from being a public into a private affair. It was thus harmful to the spirit of democracy, for too much apparently depended on one person's activities. Gandhi defended himself by writing :

The fast is a most efficacious weapon in the armoury of non-violence. That it can be used only by the fewest possible persons is no objection to its use. It would be foolish for me not to use the talents given to me by God on the ground that others or all do not possess some of them.

I have never heard it said that use of special
talents placed at the service of democracy can
retard its even growth. I hold that such use
stimulates it as the Rajkot fast undoubtedly has.
And why is the Rajkot fast to be condemned,
if the nation benefited by the previous fasts ? It
is open to the critics to say that the previous
ones were also criticized. So they were. But
my point is that the nation gained by every one
of them. What does arrest the growth of the
democratic spirit is the outbreak of violence. I
must ask the public to believe me when I say
that if my fast did nothing else, it prevented
much violence. —(*H*, 15-4-39, 88.)

The Object of a Campaign

The object of war is to inflict punishment on the
opponent so as to reduce him by fear to obey the
will of the conqueror. The aim of Satyagraha, on
the other hand, is to convert the wrong-doer and
then enlist his support in building up a new social
order without the injustices of the present.

The steps by which the Satyagrahi proposes to
do so are the following. He first withdraws his
co-operation from a system which has been proved
wrong. At the same time, he tries to build up a
new way of life through suitable constructive work.
But the rulers of the old order do not permit him
to proceed in peace. They are interested in the
maintenance of the status quo, and, in order to
retain old privileges, they inflict punishment on the
Satyagrahi for his withdrawal of co-operation.

The violence of the rulers, which was formerly implicit or camouflaged, now becomes explicit. Gandhi has, therefore, compared Satyagraha to the aseptic form of treatment.

Satyagraha or the way of non-resistance to evil is the aseptic method in which the physician allows the poison to work itself out by setting in motion all the natural forces and letting them have full play.—(*H*, 9-7-38, 173.)

Early in 1921, he had written :

We must not retort. Inaction on our part will kill Government madness. For violence flourishes on response, either by submission to the will of the violator, or by counter-violence. My strong advice to every worker is to segregate this evil Government by strict non-co-operation, not even to talk or speak about it, but having recognised the evil, to cease to pay homage to it by co-operation.—(*YI*, 30-3-21, 98.)

The Satyagrahi bravely endures the repression which is meted out to him by the adversary, for the burden of existing iniquities is more unbearable for him than the suffering which results from his peaceful effort to do away with the evil.* Through his patience, he hopes to reach the heart of the adversary ; but he never resists the violence of the aggressor by any form of counter-violence. When this point has been reached, the way is opened for an appeal to the adversary's reason. The latter

---

* Cf. 'In fact, (the Satyagrahi) invites imprisonment and other uses of force against himself. This he does because and when he finds the bodily freedom he seemingly enjoys to be an intolerable burden.' (*YI*, 10-11-21, 361.)

begins to realize the wrong he had been inflicting on brave and just men, and he finds himself in a mood to reconsider the justice of their demands.

Gandhi has written in this context :

I have come to this fundamental conclusion that if you want something really important to be done you must not merely satisfy reason, you must move the heart also. The appeal of reason is more to the head but the penetration of the heart comes from suffering. It opens up the inner understanding of man.

—(*YI*, 5-11-31, 341.)

The Satyagrahi then goes another step forward, and seeks the co-operation of his erstwhile opponent in undoing the wrongs of the past.

My non-co-operation is non-co-operation with evil, not with the evil-doer. Underneath my non-co-operation is my earnest desire to wean the evil-doer from the evil or harm he is doing so that I can give him my hearty co-operation.

—(*HS*, 15-7-44.)

My non-co-operation though it is part of my creed is a prelude to co-operation. My non-co-operation is with methods and systems, never with men.—(*YI*, 12-9-29, 300.)

The end of non-violent 'war' is always an agreement, never dictation, much less humiliation of the opponent.—(*H*, 23-3-40, 53.)

Q. But, is not non-violent rebellion, a programme of seizure of power ?

A. Therein lies the fallacy. A non-violent revolution is not a programme of 'seizure of power'. It is a programme of transformation of relationships ending in a peaceful transfer of power.—(*H*, 17-2-46, 14.)

Negotiation

The Satyagrahi should consequently be prepared for an honourable settlement at every moment. But

it is not inconceivable that the stage of negotiation may never be reached. If it is not, it must not be for the fault of the Satyagrahis.
—(*H*, 24-6-39, 70.)

The Satyagrahi's approach should be direct, and he should take the initiative whenever an opening presents itself for negotiation with the opponent. During the Satyagraha at Travancore for constitutional reforms in 1939, Gandhiji advised Satyagrahis in the following terms :

I am convinced that direct negotiation should be opened with the authorities. Hitherto the State Congress people have talked at the authorities and the latter at them. The result has been a widening of the gulf between the two. It would not do for a Satyagrahi to argue that the approach must be mutual. That assumes the existence of the spirit of Satyagraha in the authorities, whereas Satyagraha is offered in respect of those who make no claim to be Satyagrahis. Hence the first and the last work of a Satyagrahi is ever to seek an opportunity for an honourable approach. Now this is impossible so long as the heart is steeled against a belief even in the possibility, let alone advisability, of such approach. And hitherto, the impossibility has been unquestionably assumed. I have been a tacit party to it. I now know better. If the leaders have active ahimsa in them, they must cultivate a belief in the perfect possibility and necessity of such approach. And if they have that belief, the way will surely be open to them. In my own person, I have always acted on that principle.—(*H*, 10-6-39, 153.)

The method of Satyagraha requires that the Satyagrahi should never lose hope so long as there is the slightest ground left for it. For he never despairs of being able to evoke the best in his opponent, his mission being to convert the opponent, not humiliate or defeat him. He therefore even knocks at his opponent's door if it becomes necessary, as I did often with General Smuts. It so happened that the last opening, when even I had the least hope, proved the prelude to success.

There ought to be no demoralisation among the ranks. It is up to the lieutenants to be in constant touch with them and explain to them the reason for, and the bearing on the struggle of, each step. For whether there is actual battle or merely preparation, the education of the masses continues without interruption. It is a great mistake to suppose that the revolutionary instinct will die, if the garnered energies of the people

have no outlet. This may be true of violent
revolution but it is utterly wrong of non-violent
revolution. I am quite convinced that we would
put ourselves in the wrong if in our impatience
we precipitate the battle or, which is the same
thing, bang the door on negotiations. The battle
will come at the right time when it is clear
beyond doubt that there is no escape from it.

—(*H*, 17-2-40, 2.)

With regard to the tactics of negotiation itself,
Gandhi's advice is that we should take care of the
fundamentals and the other things will then take
care of themselves.

All compromise is give and take, but there
can be no give and take on fundamentals. Any
compromise on fundamentals is a surrender. For
it is all give and no take. The time for compromise can only come when both (parties) are of
one mind on fundamentals.—(*H*, 30-3-40, 72.)

Is not Satyagraha giving an ell when an inch
is asked for by the wrong-doer, is it not giving the
cloak also when only the coat is demanded ? It
may be asked why this reversal of the ordinary
process ? The ordinary process is based on
violence. If my life were regulated by violence in
the last resort, I would refuse to give an inch lest
an ell might be asked for. I would be a fool if I
did otherwise. But if my life is regulated by non-
violence, I should be prepared to and actually
give an ell when an inch is asked for. By so
doing I produce on the usurper a strange and even

pleasurable sensation. He would also be
confounded and would not know what to do with
me. So much for the 'enemy'. I, having made up
my mind to surrender every non-essential, gain
greater strength than ever before to die for the
defence and preservation of what I hold to be
essential. Full surrender of non-essentials is a
condition precedent to accession of internal
strength to defend the essential by dying.

—(*H*, 20-10-40, 333.)

The Mental Front in Satyagraha

The central duty of the Satyagrahi is to
preserve a feeling of respect for the personality
of his opponent throughout the struggle against
him.

A genuine Satyagrahi proceeds by setting
his opponent at his ease. His action never creates
panic in the breast of the 'enemy'.

—(*H*, 20-5-39, 134.)

A non-violent action accompanied by non-
violence in thought and word should never
produce enduring violent reaction upon the
opponent. —(*H*, 24-6-39, 172.)

During the Rajkot Satyagraha, Gandhi had an
interview with a high State official, after which he
told the members of the Praja Parishad :

There was one thing in that interview that
galled me and to which I wish to draw your
particular attention. He had an unmixed contempt for the Parishad people. I had noticed this
before. But now it hurt me. Why should your

Satyagraha excite his contempt of all things ? I can understand ahimsa inspiring a kind of fear, the sort of fear that a mother feels when her child gets offended and goes to sleep hungry without taking food. But genuine Satyagraha should never excite contempt in the opponent even when it fails to command regard or respect. This is not super-refinement on my part. Satyagraha is nothing if not a ceaseless quest after perfection. A Satyagrahi, therefore, turns the searchlight inward relentlessly to weed out all the defects that may be hidden there still. Thereby he increases his capacity to serve the cause he has espoused a thousandfold.

—(*H*, 6-5-39, 113.)

If the feeling of fellowship is absent with regard to one's opponent, then civil disobedience is sure to degenerate into disobedience for the sake of coercion. If it is retained, even at the cost of much mental strain, then with every advance in Satyagraha, the tension decreases and is gradually replaced by a sense of friendliness and charity, in spite of the repression which the opponent may still be showering on the Satyagrahi. When there is this feeling of expansion, the Satyagrahi may feel confident that he is on the right track, while, if there is a feeling of contraction, it is an indication that he is on the wrong track.

This does not however mean that the Satyagrahi should refrain from following his course merely for the sake of preserving the good temper of his

opponent. For the process of evoking the best in
one's opponent, may be quite distinct from maintaining his temper unruffled.

Our aim is not merely to arouse the best in
(our opponent) but to do so whilst we are prose-
cuting our cause. If we cease to pursue our
course, we do not evoke the best in him but we
pander to the evil in him. The best must not be
confounded with good temper. When we are
dealing with any evil, we may have to ruffle the
evil-doer. We have to run the risk, if we are to
bring the best out of him. I have likened non-
violence to aseptic and violence to antiseptic
treatment. Both are intended to ward off the
evil, and therefore cause a kind of disturbance
which is often inevitable. The first never harms
the evil-doer.—(*H*, 30-3-40, 72.)

Many years ago, he had similarly written :

I accept the interpretation of Ahimsa,
namely, that it is not merely a negative state of
harmlessness but it is a positive state of love,
of doing good even to the evil-doer. But it does
not mean helping the evil-doer to continue the
wrong or tolerating it by passive acquiescence.
On the contrary, love, the active state of Ahimsa,
requires you to resist the wrong-doer by disso-
ciating yourself from him even though it may
offend him or injure him physically. Thus if my
son lives a life of shame, I may not help him to
do so by continuing to support him, my love
for him requires me to withdraw all support

from him although it may mean even his death. And the same love imposes on me the obligation of welcoming him to my bosom when he repents. But I may not by physical force compel my son to become good.

Non-co-operation is not a passive state, it is an intensely active state—more active than physical resistance. Passive resistance is a misnomer. Non-co-operation in the sense used by me must be non-violent and therefore neither punitive nor vindictive nor based on malice, ill-will or hatred. It follows therefore that it would be sin for me to serve General Dyer and co-operate with him to shoot innocent men. But it will be an exercise of forgiveness or love for me to nurse him back to life, if he was suffering from a physical malady.

—(*YI*, 25-8-20 , *Tagore*, 322.)

With the above object in view, the Satyagrahi should bear in mind the following instructions.

Do not concentrate on showing the misdeeds of the Government, for we have to convert and befriend those who run it. And after all no one is wicked by nature. And if others are wicked, are we the less so ? That attitude is inherent in Satyagraha.   —(*H*, 30-3-40, 71.)

All the songs and speeches betokening hatred must be taboo.   —(*YI*, 2-4-31, 58.)

The Satyagrahi should refrain from taking advantage of moments when the adversary is embarrassed by outside conditions. Then, it is better

to postpone mass civil disobedience and confine it
to picked individuals. The principle of non-
embarrassment should not however be turned into a
fetish. If the moral harm due to postponement of
civil resistance is likely to be more than the gain on
the other side, then civil disobedience has to be
launched in spite of the risks of misunderstanding
and antagonisation. Only, the Satyagrahi should
take double care that he is not actuated by hatred or
anger. His moral responsibility increases many
times ; and he must let his action show that the
intention is not to harm the wrong-doer but to do
him good.

One of the most illustrative examples of this
type of Satyagraha has been the Quit-India demand
of the Indian National Congress. The Congress
had been pursuing a policy of non-embarrassment,
and confined itself to symbolic Individual Civil
Disobedience alone before 1942. But the growing
menace of Japanese aggression made the Government so panicky, and it executed the Denial and
Evacuation Policy with so much thoughtlessness
and disregard of the sufferings of the uprooted
peasantry, that the mind of the average Indian was
brought to the verge of moral ruin : secretly they
longed for British defeat in Japanese hands.

If constructive work had been carried out with
faith and efficiency, and effective arrangements
made for warding off famine by the people's own
efforts, that in itself would have instilled self-
confidence among the masses. Then the movement

for Swaraj could easily have been postponed till the
end of the war. But progress in this respect was
inadequate ; and out of a sense of frustration, there
grew an undercurrent of anti-British feeling which
was likely to burst forth any moment with disastrous
consequences.

It was in order to stem that tide that Gandhi
conceived the Quit-India demand. Only by
relinquishing political power could the British effect
a moral transformation among the Indian people
which would make the cause of the United Nations
their own. In fact, the demand was not even based
on the organized strength of the Indian people,
much less on the temporary weakness of the British
power ; but it was based, as expressly stated again
and again by Gandhiji, on the moral urgency of the
step, imperative from the point of view of the self-
interest of the United Nations.

If, however, the British failed to do the right,
Gandhi proposed to take all risks and plunge the
country in a bold movement of civil resistance, the
nature of the contemplated steps being outlined in
a private circular to the members of the Working
Committee*. The British, in their short-sighted-
ness might misunderstand ; the strength of the
Indian people might be found wanting, they might
turn violent and thus invite their own defeat ; and
lastly, this might precipitate Japanese invasion of
India. But in spite of all these possibilities, the risk

*Published in *Gandhiji's Correspondence with the Government 1942-44*,
2nd Edition, Navajivan Publishing House, Ahmedabad, pp. 356-360.

had to be run if the British did not concede the morality of the Quit-India demand,

> for the risk of remaining supine in the face of the greatest world conflagration known to history was infinitely greater. If non-violence is the greatest force in the world, it must prove itself during the crisis.—(*GC*, 171.)*

Earlier, Gandhiji had written :

> Of course the people must not, on any account, lean on the Japanese to get rid of the British power. That were a remedy worse than the disease. But as I have already said, in this struggle every risk has to be run in order to cure ourselves of the biggest disease—a disease which has sapped our manhood and almost made us feel as if we must for ever be slaves. It is an insufferable thing. The cost of the cure, I know, will be heavy. No price is too heavy to pay for the deliverance.—(*H*, 31-5-42, 172.)

In spite of all the care which a Satyagrahi can bestow, his movement may take an unexpected turn. Under such an event, Gandhi has ever found refuge in a mental attitude of total self-surrender. In the introduction to *Satyagraha in South Africa*, he has written :

> That is the beauty of Satyagraha. It comes up to oneself, one has not to go out in search for it. That is a virtue inherent in the principle itself. A Dharma-yuddha, in which there are no secrets to be guarded, no scope for cunning and

*See also letter to Generalissimo Chiang Kai-shek, *GC*, 230.

no place for untruth, comes unsought ; and a man
of religion is ever ready for it. A struggle which
has to be previously planned is not a righteous
struggle. In a righteous struggle God Himself
plans campaigns and conducts battles. A
Dharma-yuddha can be waged only in the name of
God, and it is only when the Satyagrahi feels
quite helpless, is apparently on his last legs and
finds utter darkness all around him, that God
comes to the rescue. God helps when one feels
oneself humbler than the very dust under one's
feet. Only to the weak and helpless is divine
succour vouchsafed. —(*SA*, 5.)

A Last Word about Practice

The careful student who has followed the
discussion so far, will not have failed to notice that
what is really done in Satyagraha is to substitute the
principle of authority by the principle of freedom in
effecting social change. The modern world has done
so, in theory at least, in the field of education. But
it seems reluctant to believe in the substitution in
matters affecting large masses of mankind ; there,
the mind of man still clings to its old faith in
punishment and war.

Among certain communities, a curious dichotomy
seems to prevail. They would employ the principle
of freedom where members of their own group are
concerned, but retain their old belief in punishment
where others are involved. But as life and mind
cannot be divided into water-tight compart-
ments, the use of coercive methods in one sphere of

social life gradually corrupts the other spheres as well. As in Gresham's Law, a bad method drives out the good from circulation. Probably, this is the reason why, with mounting success in war, community after community is replacing the democratic method by that of authority even in the matter of bringing about internal social change.

Satyagraha, which is truly a democratic form of revolution, is designed not merely to bring about large-scale social or political changes, but its purpose is to permeate all walks of life, whether private or public. It is the considered opinion of Gandhi, as well as of social philosophers like Dewey, that unless our personal life in the family, the school or the religious community is ruled by the spirit of Democracy, the narrow, one-sided attempt to root out war by means of constitutional arrangements, has hardly any chance of success. In Gandhi's language, it might be said that unless the Satyagrahi practises Truth and Non-violence in his personal life, he can never hope to succeed in applying them successfully to the larger problems of social life.

The natural implication of this is that a Satyagrahi should ceaselessly experiment with the non-violent method wherever there are jars in life, be the occasion great or small. If he does so with unflagging perseverance and adequate intelligence, then his experiences will help him to deal with larger social problems when he is called upon to do so.

There is need for a last word of caution. Let the Satyagrahi not strain too much ; he should not, in other words, imitate forcibly the behaviour of others far in advance of him. He should find his own pace, and try to increase it according to his own ability. Let him, above all, be true to himself ; no man is expected to do more than he can.

In physical education, if someone strains himself in trying to lift a load far beyond his capacity, the remedy lies in giving his muscles rest. It is the same with Satyagraha. Indeed, the spirit of haste or impatience is itself a product of pride or anger, in the last resort. All good things take their own time to grow. There was once a fakir of the name of Lalan Shah in Bengal who said in one of his poems : 'Brother, why this hurry ? Can you help the rose to bloom by means of a sword ?'

Summary of Instructions to Civil Resisters

1.   Only those who suffer from a wrong should offer resistance against it. Do not count on outside aid, it fails in the last resort. In the final heat, one has to rely on oneself or the justice of one's cause, or on Truth and God, as some would prefer to say.

2.   Adequate propaganda is an integral part of Satyagraha.

3.   Civil resistance should be resorted to only after all other attempts at honourable settlement, including an offer of impartial arbitration, have failed.

4.   The Satyagrahi should preserve the initiative in his own hands, and not allow it to pass into the hands of his opponent.

He must also refuse to be led by the masses against the promptings of his own judgement.

5. Keep the demands low, but consistent with Truth and Justice. 'In aiming beyond our capacity we are likely to lose all.' —(H, 10-6-39, 153.)

6. Satyagraha should be progressive in character.

7. There should be no impatience, no hurry, no bluff and no attempt to cover inner weaknesses from oneself. 'Non-co-operation is not a movement of brag, bluster, or bluff. It is a test of our sincerity. It requires solid and silent self-sacrifice.'

—(YI, 12-1-21, 13.)

8. Always seek avenues of co-operation with the adversary on honourable terms. The end of non-violent 'war' is always an agreed solution in conformity with the claims of justice and true human welfare.

9. In a negotiation, do not surrender essentials, sacrifice non-essentials. Be prepared to go to the farthest length in self-suffering in defence of the essential. Before settlement, there must be agreement on fundamentals. Keep one angle of the square right, the rest will follow.

10. When in doubt, apply the following test : if there is a feeling of expansion you are on the right track, if of contraction you are likely to be wrong.

THE CONSTRUCTIVE PROGRAMME AND CIVIL DISOBEDIENCE

A labour worker's aim should be to raise the moral and intellectual height of labour and thus by sheer merit to make him or her capable not merely of bettering his or her material condition but making labour master of the means of production instead of being the slave that it is. Capital should be labour's servant, not its master. —(*HS*, 28-10-44.)

In course of a correspondence with Shapurji Saklatwala, the Communist member of the British Parliament, Gandhiji wrote many years ago :

It is a most dangerous thing to make political use of labour until labourers understand the political condition of the country and are prepared for the common good. Labour, in my opinion, must not become a pawn in the hands of the politician on the political chess-board. It must, by its sheer strength, dominate the chess-board. —(*Indian Annual Register*, 1927, Part II, pp. 118-22.)

The question to be dealt with now is this : how does the constructive programme help in preparing the masses for self-rule ? The answer was given by Gandhiji in the draft resolution sent to the Working Committee from Allahabad on April 27, 1942 :

The true building up of Swaraj consists in the millions of India wholeheartedly working the constructive programme. Without it the whole nation cannot rise from its age-long torpor. Whether the British remain or not it is our duty

always to wipe out unemployment, to bridge the
gulf between rich and poor, to banish communal
strife, to exorcize the demon of untouchability,
to reform dacoits and save the people from them.
If crores of people do not take a living interest
in this nation-building work, freedom must remain
a dream and unattainable by either non-violence
or violence.   —(*GC*, 354.)

Civil Resistance in relation to Constructive Work

Gandhi is clearly of opinion that :

Civil disobedience is but a minor part of
Satyagraha.—(*H*, 25-3-39, 61.)

The question has been, more or less, fully dealt
with in the pamphlet *Constructive Programme* : *its
meaning and place*, where we find :

Civil Disobedience is not absolutely necessary
to win freedom through purely non-violent efforts,
if the co-operation of the whole nation is secured
in the constructive programme. But such good
luck rarely favours nations or individuals. Therefore it is necessary to know the place of Civil
Disobedience in a nation-wide non-violent effort.

It has three definite functions :

1. It can be effectively offered for the
redress of a local wrong.

2. It can be offered without regard to effect,
though aimed at a particular wrong or evil, by way
of self-immolation in order to rouse local consciousness or conscience. Such was the case in
Champaran when I offered Civil Disobedience

without any regard to the effect and well knowing that even the people might remain apathetic. That it proved otherwise may be taken, according to taste, as God's grace or a stroke of good luck.

3. In the place of full response to constructive effort, it can be offered as it was in 1941. (Referring to the Individual Civil Disobedience Movement.) Though it was a contribution to and part of the battle for freedom, it was purposely centred round a particular issue, i.e. free speech. Civil Disobedience can never be directed for a general cause such as for Independence. The issue must be definite and capable of being clearly understood and within the power of the opponent to yield. This method properly applied must lead to the final goal.

I have not examined the full scope and possibilities of Civil Disobedience. I have touched enough of it to enable the reader to understand the connection between the constructive programme and Civil Disobedience. In the first two cases, no elaborate constructive programme was or could be necessary. But when Civil Disobedience is itself devised for the attainment of Independence, previous preparation is necessary, and it has to be backed by the visible and conscious effort of those who are engaged in the battle. Civil Disobedience is thus a stimulation for the fighters and a challenge to the opponent. It should be clear to the reader that Civil Disobedience in terms of Independence without the co-operation of the millions by way of constructive effort is mere bravado and worse than useless.

—(*CP*, 28.)

We can put the matter in a different way thus. If the constructive programme is worked in the right spirit, the new order of life can be built up without the intervention of civil disobedience, if Satyagrahis are diligent enough and the public sufficiently responsive. The first of the provisos may be fulfilled, but the second is often lacking ; the reason being that energy is sooner called forth in common men if we talk in terms of a struggle than when we ask them to go in for an apparently unexciting effort to replace an existing economic order by painful, day-to-day programme. Common people seem to feel that they can throw up a spurt of sudden energy but will fail if. the flood has to be chained and diverted to irrigate a dry plain.

This is, in fact, the reason why the so-called revolutionary energy of the masses comes in short, temporary, discontinous upsurges. Such energy may easily lend itself to violent expression ; but if we mean to conserve the force, it has to be canalized through non-violent resistance ; and when the moment of flood-burst is over, to utilize the energy through the constructive programme so that it does not run waste but is fully utilized to water the parched fields of social life.

The Satyagrahi must, above all, realize one thing. In non-violence, destruction of the old order is through construction. Even the purpose of civil resistance is not principally to destroy, but to evoke the best in the opponent so that we may, later on, secure his aid also in the work of construction. The constructive programme is *not*, therefore, a means of marking time between two civil disobedience movements, just as the farmer's task is not merely to canalize the flood-waters when the rains are on and the river is full. All through the year, he has to work on the soil which has been rendered fertile by the flood of last year. He can also prepare for the next ; but in the meantime, he must daily labour on the fields, otherwise there will be no crops.

The constructive programme is also not a means of establishing mass contacts, so that the masses can be properly directed and guided when a movement is on. It is infinitely more than that ; its purpose is to bring the economic and political destiny of the common people within their own control through determined co-operative effort ; and this in itself is a task extremely valuable on its own account. As long as full political power is not gained, it is quite possible that we shall not be able to make very much headway in the required direction. But even the little change which the masses can bring about in their own economic and social life, under a leadership whose purpose is to keep itself always in the background and stimulate local initiative, can bring about miraculous transformation in the morale of the people. Once they realize what they are striving for, their courage is restored and they gain something for which they can pay a heavy price either in labour or in suffering through non-violent resistance.

But all this requires that the leadership shall be good, and inspired by faith in non-violence. Such faith, of course, may not be had for the asking ; but it grows once we make the right start and persevere in a scientific spirit with regard to our social experiments.

Local and Partial Struggles

Personally, Gandhiji has been responsible for numerous struggles against local and specific wrongs. Thus he has either himself led or been connected with peasant movements in Champaran, Kaira, Bardoli ; of a movement for civic rights at Vaikom ; for constitutional reforms in Travancore, Jaipur, Mysore, Rajkot ; for establishing public control over religious institutions at Guru-ka-bagh, and so on. But he has always been chary in using partial struggles as a means of preparing the masses for Swaraj or the political independence of India. The reason has been clearly set forth in answer to the second question in the next chapter of this book entitled 'An Interview with Mahatma Gandhi.'

On 1-10-38, Gandhi warned prospective Satya-grahis in the following terms :

It is not enough that they are truthful and non-violent. It is necessary also for them to know their own capacity for suffering. Liberty is a dame exacting a heavy price from her wooers. And unless there are many who are prepared to pay the price, the few enthusiastic that are to be found everywhere would do well to conserve their energy. They will do well to undertake constructive service of the people without having an ambitious political programme. The ability to gain political ends will surely come from constructive service. Wisdom and patience will give them a power which in time will become irresistible. —(*H*, 1-10-38, 274.)

Similarly on 8-4-39, he wrote :

I am afraid I must plead guilty to being over-confident and hasty in launching previous civil disobedience campaigns. No harm seems to have accrued to the country because I had always my hand on the pulse of the country and thank God had no hesitation in retracing the step taken if I scented danger or discovered an error of judgement or calculation. This much harm must, however, be admitted. The people having become used to laxity about previous preparation now find it irksome to conform to the strictness in the observance of the unexciting rules of preparation. And yet they are much the most important part of Satyagraha training. Potent and active non-violence cannot be cultivated unless the candidate goes through the necessary stages which require a lot of plodding. If, however, I have succeeded in showing that repression, if properly understood, evokes natural and spontaneous resistance in a Satyagrahi, perhaps this knowledge will rob the constructive effort and the waiting of their seeming insipidity. Indeed the fact that these things appear insipid betrays want of appreciation of Satyagraha and the beauty and efficacy of non-violence. In other

words, the spirit of Satyagraha has not sunk
deep and violence still lurks even though unconsciously in the seeker's breast.—(*H*, 8-4-39, 80.)

Constructive Work viewed as
Discipline for Non-violence

On the eve of the Salt Satyagraha in 1930,
Gandhiji wrote :

> I know that many have refused to see any
> connection between the constructive programme
> and civil disobedience. But for one who believes
> in non-violence it does not need hard thinking to
> realise the essential connection between the
> constructive programme and civil disobedience *for
> Swaraj.* I want the reader to mark the qualifica-
> tion. Constructive programme is not essential
> for local civil disobedience for specific relief as in
> the case of Bardoli. Tangible common grie-
> vance restricted to a particular locality is enough.
> But for such an indefinable thing as Swaraj
> people must have previous training in doing things
> of all-India interest. Such work must throw
> together the people and their leaders whom they
> would trust implicitly. Trust begotten in the
> pursuit of continuous constructive work becomes
> a tremendous asset at the critical moment.
> Constructive work therefore is for a non-violent
> army what drilling etc. is for an army designed
> for bloody warfare. Individual civil disobedience
> among an unprepared people and by leaders not
> known to or trusted by them is of no avail, and
> mass civil disobedience is an impossibility. The

more therefore the progress of the constructive programme, the greater is there the chance for civil disobedience.—(*YI*, 9-3-30, 13.)

In 1940, he repeated more emphatically :

I have said and I repeat that there is no Swaraj for the masses except through khadi and other village crafts. For there is no non-violent disobedience without sustained constructive effort. A living, continuous mass contact is impossible without some constructive programme requiring almost daily contact of the workers with the masses.—(*H*, 23-3-40, 56.)

It gives Staying Power

The Ahmedabad Labour Union has of late started a great experiment which is likely to prove of great interest and importance to all labour organizations. The essence of the experiment consists in training its members to a supplementary occupation in addition to their principal occupation in the mills so that in the event of a lock-out, strike or loss of employment otherwise, they would always have something to fall back upon instead of being faced with the prospect of starvation. A mill-hand's life is ever full of vicissitudes. Thrift and economy no doubt provide a sort of remedy and it would be criminal to neglect them. But the savings thus made cannot carry one far, seeing that the vast bulk of our mill labourers are always struggling on the margin of bare subsistence. Moreover it would never do for a working man during strike or unemployment to rest idly at home. There is nothing more injurious to his morale and self-respect than enforced idleness. The working class will never feel secure or develop a sense of self-assuarance and strength unless its members are armed with an unfailing subsidiary means of subsistence to serve as a second string to their bow in a crisis.

The idea of subsidiary occupation for the mill-hands was first conceived by me during the eventful twentythree days' strike of the Ahmedabad mill-hands in the year 1918. It occurred to me then that if the strike was to be successful the mill-hands must have an occupation that would maintain them wholly or partly. They must not rely upon doles. During the strike many of them were employed on unskilled labour. It was then that I mooted my suggestion to teach mill-hands a subsidiary occupation.

An organized and systematic effort is now being made by the Labour Union in that direction. Mill-hands are being taught to select occupations which they can practise in their leisure hours at home and which would give them substantial relief in times of unemployment. These are ginning, cleaning, carding and spinning of cotton, weaving, tailoring, soap and paper making, typesetting, etc.

I hold that a working knowledge of a variety of occupations is to the working class what metal is to the capitalist. A labourer's skill is his capital. The intelligence of the working man is cramped by his soulless, mechanical occupation which leaves him little scope or chance to develop his mind. It has prevented him from realizing the power and full dignity of his status. He has been taught to believe that his wages have to be dictated by capitalists instead of his demanding his own terms. Let him only be organized along right lines and have his intelligence quickened, let him learn a variety of occupations, and he will be able to go about with his head erect and never be afraid of being without means of sustenance.

It is the grossest of superstitions for the working man to believe that he is helpless before the employers. The effort of the Labour Union in Ahmedabad is to dispel this superstition in a concrete manner. Its experiment, therefore, ought to be welcomed by all concerned. Success will depend on an inflexible determination on the part of the Labour Union to follow up the good beginning that has been made, with unflagging perseverance. It must have the right sort of instructors who can arouse among the workers an intelligent interest in their work. A handicraft plied merely mechanically can be as cramping to the mind and soul as any other pursuit taken up mechanically. An unintelligent effort is like a corpse from which the spirit has departed.

—(*H*, 3-7-37, 161.)

Constructive work with its three-fold use thus forms the best preparation for mass civil disobedience for the attainment of Swaraj. Its capacity to build up the new social and economic order even without the intervention of civil resistance was discussed previously. Its present uses are, when briefly stated, the following :

(a) The masses gain an idea of the exploitation-free social and economic order which they are going to build up through their own effort. It gives them something worth striving for.

(b) It generates the type of self-reliance and internal cohesion which prove useful also in times of non-violent resistance.

(c) It gives staying power in a long-drawn struggle ; so preserves morale.

(d) A bond of trust is created between active civil resisters and the average citizen through constructive work pursued continuously in peace time. This trust proves to be of immense help in moments of national crisis; then the Satyagrahi finds himself in a position to channel the upsurge of the masses along effective, non-violent lines.

Organizational Questions

It is now necessary to deal with certain questions of detail, viz. whether constructive work should be undertaken under the auspices of the Indian National Congress or outside it. Gandhiji has generally advised constructive workers to keep out of active politics; they should hold no elective post in the Congress so long as they are engaged in executing the constructive programme. But if a moment arrives when they feel impelled to join the political struggle, they will have to resign from the constructive organisation before throwing themselves into the struggle. With this end in view, the AISA, the AIVIA etc. have been kept outside the control of the Congress, although they owe their origin to resolutions passed by the Congress itself.

With regard to labour organization, Gandhi's opinion is clearly expressed in the report of an interview with Prof. Ranga quoted below :

Prof. Ranga :—You suggest that the existing Kisan organisations should be reformed where necessary. I quite recognise the need for Congressmen who have been working among Kisans to re-orientate the general political attitude of the Kisan class organisations so that they will recognise the need for a united political leadership for winning our national freedom. I am also convinced that the National Congress provides for us all—especially for peasants—the most effective weapon and leadership to win freedom. But is there any harm if we organise peasants into a 'Kisan Congress' which accepts the political leadership of the Congress ?

Gandhiji :—There may be gross self-deception in this presentation. When I said that the Kisan Sabhas should be reformed, I meant that up till now Kisan Sabhas have been formed not to wrest power from the Government but to capture the Congress. That applies to the student and labour organisations too.

Prof. Ranga :—You are partially right. That

was so in the past. But we have now completely abandoned that idea. Since you made your statement on the subject in 1929 the thing was completely given up. We have adopted the word Congress not in a spirit of rivalry but because we want to be identified with the Congress. We will have double membership. Every member of the Kisan Congress will also be enrolled as a member of the National Congress.

Gandhiji :—Then why not run the Congress ? Why set up an independent and parallel organisation ? Don't you see when Kisan Sabhas are 'bona fide' organisations they are the Congress ? Today only a fraction of India's population is represented on the Congress register. Congress aspires to represent the whole nation. It claims by right of service to speak even for those who are not on its register. When it becomes a fully national organisation 'de jure' as it is today by moral right, the bulk of its membership will naturally consist of the Kisans and they will be in a position to dictate its policy.

Prof. Ranga :—The trouble is that some of our Congress colleagues think we are ousting them from their legitimate position of power and privilege. They may not be prepared to welcome our existence or trust our 'bona fides'. We want to avoid conflicts within the Congress by willingly accepting the political leadership of the Congress. For executing our economic programme we want to have a separate class-conscious organisation which will derive power both for itself and the Congress from its contact with the masses. Unless we do that, others will come and confuse the Kisans.

Gandhiji :—Here you have involved yourself in a fallacy. You should work to make the Congress fully representative of the Kisans. Unless we get down to this fundamental thing and work from bottom upward there will be no Swaraj. Every Cogressman must make up his mind to make the Congress an honest organisation, and therefore a Kisan organisation. As for rights they should follow as a natural corollary from the performance of service. Otherwise there is only usurpation.

Prof. Ranga :—You have tried for the last twentyfive years to rebuild the Congress organisation and you know the result. I along with others must plead guilty for my share in the responsibility for failure. I must confess we have not got the confidence that we shall be able to so behave and act that the Con-. gress will in the end become a Kisan organisation. Our fear is that by following your line of action, in spite of ourselves we shall allow ourselves to be exploited by vested interests. The very fact that the Birlas and their like are today prepared to give you shelter and you accept it from them prevents radical reform. Therefore, though I shall feel the wrench I shall feel unable to work on your lines.

Gandhiji :—Then you admit that whilst you work under the aegis of the Congress, you will at the same time run a parallel, independent organisation. My mind runs in a straight line. I do not understand this zigzag. This can only lead to trouble when Congress becomes an effective organisation. I am thinking of the millions of our down-trodden countrymen who do not know what to hope and what not to hope. A parallel organisation will only further confuse their minds. It would be more logical to keep out of the Congress altogether.

Prof. Ranga :—We enter the Congress but we do not fight for position and power. Can you not treat us on the same footing as the Ahmedabad Labour Union ?

Gandhiji :—Well, the proof of the pudding is in the eating. It will all depend on the spirit in which it is done. I have already expressed my apprehension. It is for you to remove it. You can model your organisation after the Ahmedabad Labour Union. All the Labour Union members are on the Congress register. They are under the discipline of the Congress. Yet they are a power in the Congress and in the Municipality. You should confine yourself to Andhra alone. All Kisans should be automatically on your register. But the purpose of enrolment should be educative, to make the Kisans Congress-minded and politically conscious.

CONSTRUCTIVE PROGRAMME & CIVIL DISOBEDIENCE 193

Prof. Ranga :—I am glad you are laying special stress on adequate wages which will assure a minimum and decent standard of living for the landless peasants. Do you not also recognise the need for achieving minimum prices for agricultural produce which will assure labouring proprietors a decent and minimum standard of living ?

Gandhiji :—Of course I do.

Prof. Ranga :—The Bombay A.I.C.C. Resolution assures the masses that the power in the National Government and Swaraj India ought to belong to the toilers in the fields, in factories and elsewhere. Can we say that the spirit of the resolution means that the Congress therefore stands for the achievement of Democratic-Kisan-Mazdoor-Praja-Raj after the attainment of Swaraj ?

Gandhiji :—Not only after but before also. The Congress stands for Democratic-Kisan-Mazdoor-Praja-Raj.

Prof. Ranga :—Do not your new instructions envisage the development of Kisan organisations from village upwards, to provide for peasant leadership and co-operative action, but working in harmony with the local National Congress Committee and their leadership ? I may say that the Haripura session of the Congress has recognised the right of Kisans to have their own class organisations. But we are anxious, in the light of these four years' experience, that

13

Congressmen shall take the lead in organising Kisans into their own unions so that there can be real unity and co-operation between Kisan organisations and Congress Committees.

Gandhiji :—Kisan organisation and Congress organisation are to me convertible terms. National Congress organisations to be true have either to be a Kisan organisation or nothing else.

Prof. Ranga :—Can we organise landless agricultural labour into their separate unions wherever there are workers to undertake such responsibilities in order to win for them the barest economic and social justice ? I do not envisage such unions in rivalry with the local peasant unions but as a supplement to them.

Gandhiji :—Yes, but as part of Congress re-organisation work.—(*HS*, 15-1-45.)

Regarding Workers' Expenses

The Gandhi Seva Sangh was originally started to support whole-time constructive workers with a minimum allowance to meet their needs. In the account given by Mahadev Desai of one of its annual meetings we find :

Many of the Sangh members, it must be remembered, content themselves with a bare maintenance wage. Some are allowed stipends from the Sangh and some find their expenses from other sources. Everyone is, or at any rate is expected to be, armed with the faith that the labourer is worthy of his hire. But there are places where this hire may not be obtainable from the people who are served. The worker has, in such a case, to fall back on some means of livelihood. What may these means be ?

This was Gandhiji's reply : 'Any occupation, clean, honourable and calculated to serve as an example to the people would be good enough. I may give as examples scavenging, spinning and weaving. The occupation should, if possible, be such as touches the interest of the masses and may spur them on to use their hands and feet. One may win one's livelihood by teaching and similar other pursuits, but it all depends on one's needs, of which the maximum must always be fixed.—(*H*, 3-6-39,145.)

After mass civil disobedience was withdrawn in 1934, Gandhi's advice to erstwhile civil resisters was :

They must engage themselves in nation-building activities, the spread of khaddar through personal hand-spinning and hand-weaving, the spread of communal unity of hearts by irreproachable personal conduct towards one another in every walk of life, the banishing of untouchability in every shape or form in one's own person, the spread of total abstinence from intoxicating drinks and drugs by personal contact with individual addicts and, generally, by cultivating personal purity. These are services which provide maintenance on a poor man's scale. Those for whom the poor man's scale is not feasible should find place in small unorganised industries of national importance which give better wages.—(*HC*, I, 570.)

AN INTERVIEW WITH MAHATMA GANDHI

On the 9th and 10th of November 1934, we had a fairly long interview with Mahatma Gandhi at Wardha. The questions discussed related to fundamental social and political matters, and therefore a report of the interview will be of interest to the public. The report was submitted to Gandhiji for correction, and he sent it back in the following form for publication in the *Modern Review*, where it was published in October 1935.

Question I

While working in a village we have found that the chief obstacle to any real improvement in the condition of the villagers are two in number.

(1) They have forgotten the art of co-operation among themselves or of joining hands in order to resist any encroachment upon their rights.

(2) They live practically enslaved by those who merely own the land while doing no work, and control the money resources of the village. This slavery, which is due partly to their own character and partly to our complete neglect of their education, have left the masses absolutely devoid of any will of their own.

What should be our principal object in khadi-work or other forms of village reconstruction? Khadi-work in some portions of Bengal has degenerated into a mere method of giving a little relief to the villagers, while it has failed to restore the will which alone can bring about any lasting transformation in their condition.

Our question is, should khadi be merely that sort of humanitarian work or should we use it chiefly as an instrument of political education ? Our experience has been that unless the ultimate objective is kept clearly in mind, it degenerates easily into a work of no significance.

Answer I

The two issues of khadi and political organization should be kept absolutely separate. There must be no confusion. The aim of khadi is humanitarian, but so far as India is concerned, its effect is bound to be immensely political.

The Salvation Army wants to teach people about God. But they come with bread. For the poor bread is their God. Similarly, we should bring food to the mouths of the people through khadi. If we succeed in breaking the idleness of the people through khadi, they will begin to listen to us. Whatever the Government might do, it does leave some food for the villagers. Unless we can bring food to them, why should the people listen to us ? When we have taught them what they can do through their own efforts, they will begin to listen to us.

That trust can be best generated through khadi. While working out the khadi programme, our aim should be purely humanitarian, that is economic. We should leave out all political considerations whatsoever. But it is bound to produce important

political consequences, which nobody can prevent
and nobody need deplore.

[NOTE :—The expression 'our aim should be purely
humanitarian, that is economic' does not mean that the khadi-
worker should merely aim at providing some relief within the
present social and economic framework. He should really aim
at building up a new productive system based on the people's
own effort and under their own control. The organizer should
try to reduce unemployment to the utmost extent rather than
aim at doubling or trebling the quantity of khadi produced for
sale in distant markets.

The advice that the worker 'should teach the people what
they can do through their own efforts' implies that he should
function in such a manner that, in the end, the people can be
independent of his aid. In other words, his object should be to
leave the common people self-acting in the end.

For the sake of efficiency also, he should not mix up
constructive work with political propaganda. The growth of
initiative and self-confidence, through khadi organization, will
in its own time, bear political consequences. There need not be
any hurry for achieving quick results, in the usual sense of the
term 'political.' When the masses have gained so much in self-
development that they can see a wrong and are able to remedy
it principally by their own non-violent effort, then their resistance becomes natural and of the right type.—N.K.B.]

Question II

Could we not start small battles on local and
specific issues against capitalism in the villages and
use them as a means of strengthening the people or
bringing about a sense of co-operation among them,
in preference to the khadi method ? When we have
a choice between the two, which should we prefer ?
If we have to sacrifice all the work that we have
built up in the villages in connection with khadi

while fighting against the money-lender or the landed proprietor, for say, a reduction in the rate of interest or increase in the share of agricultural produce, then what shall we do, provided the latter is more capable of evoking self-confidence among the villagers than the khadi method of organization ?

Answer II

It is a big proviso you have added at the end of the question. I cannot say if fights on local and specific issues against capitalists are more likely to generate the kind of determination and courage needed in a non-violent campaign. But if I concede you that point, then khadi would have to be sacrificed under the circumstances you quote. As a practical man, claiming to be an expert in non-violent methods, I should advise you not to go in for that type of work in order to train the masses in self-consciousness and attainment of power.

We are fighting for Swaraj in the non-violent way. If many workers in different parts of India engage in local battles of the sort you describe, then in times of necessity, the people all over India will not be able to make a common cause in a fight for Swaraj. Before civil disobedience can be practised on a vast scale, people must learn the art of civil or voluntary obedience. Our obedience to the Government is through fear ; and the reaction against it is either violence itself or that species of it which is cowardice. But through khadi we teach the people the art of civil obedience to an institution which they have built up for themselves. Only when they have learnt that art, can they successfully disobey something which they want to destroy in the non-violent way. That is why I should advise all workers not to fritter their fighting strength in many-sided battles, but to concentrate on peaceful khadi-work in order to educate the masses into a condition necessary for a successful practice of non-violent non-co-operation. With their own exploitation, boycott of foreign cloth through picketing may easily be violent ; through the use of khadi it is most natural and absolutely non-violent.

Question III

Is love or non-violence compatible with possession or exploitation in any shape or form ? If possession and non-violence cannot go together, then do you advocate the maintenance of private ownership of land or factories as an unavoidable evil which will continue so long as individuals are not ripe or educated enough to do without it ? If it be such a step, would it not be better to own all the land through the State and place the State under the control of the masses ?

Answer III

Love and exclusive possession can never go together. Theoretically when there is perfect love there must be perfect non-possession. The body is our last possession. So a man can only exercise perfect love and be completely dispossessed if he is prepared to embrace death and renounces his body for the sake of human service. But that is true in theory only. In actual life, we can hardly exercise perfect love, for the body as a possession will always remain with us. Man will ever remain imperfect and it will always be his part to try to be perfect. So that perfection in love or non-possession will remain an unattainable ideal so long as we are alive, but towards which we must ceaselessly strive.

Those who own money now are asked to behave like trustees holding their riches on behalf of the poor. You may say that trusteeship is a legal fiction. But if people meditate over it constantly and try to act up to it, then life on earth would be governed far more by love than it is at present. Absolute trusteeship is an abstraction like Euclid's definition of a point, and is equally unattainable. But if we strive for it, we shall be able to go farther in realizing a state of equality on earth than by any other method.

Q. If you say that private possession is incompatible with non-violence, why do you put up with it?

A. That is a concession one has to make to those who earn money, but who would not voluntarily use their earnings for the benefit of mankind.

Q. Why then not have State ownership in place of private ownership and thus minimize violence?

A. It is better than private ownership. But that too is objectionable on the ground of violence. It is my firm conviction that if the State suppressed capitalism by violence, it will be caught in the coils of violence itself and fail to develop non-violence at any time. The State represents violence in a concentrated and organized form. The individual has a soul, but the State is a soulless machine, it can never be weaned from the violence to which it owes its very existence. Hence I prefer the doctrine of trusteeship.

Q. Let us come to a specific instance. Suppose an artist leaves certain pictures to a son who does not appreciate their value for the nation and sells them or wastes them, so that the nation stands to lose something precious through one man's folly. If you are assured that the son would never be a trustee in the sense in which you would like to have him, do you not think the State would be justified in taking away those things from him with the minimum use of violence ?

A. Yes, the State will, as a matter of fact, take away those things ; and I believe it will be justified if it uses the minimum of violence. But the fear is always there that the State may use too much violence against those who differ from it. I would be very happy indeed if the people concerned behaved as trustees ; but if they fail, I believe we shall have to deprive them of their possessions through the State with the minimum exercise of violence. That is why I said at the Round Table Conference that every vested interest must be subjected to scrutiny, and confiscation ordered where necessary, with or without compensation as the case demanded.

What I should personally prefer would be not a centralization of power in the hands of the State, but an extension of the sense of trusteeship as, in my opinion, the violence of private ownership is less injurious than the violence of the State. However, if it is unavoidable, I would support a minimum of State ownership.

[NOTE—In other places, Gandhiji has made it abundantly clear that what he actually desires is that every talented man should be converted into the theory of trusteeship through the non-violent non-co-operation of those on whose co-operation he depends for a full exercise of his talents. The rich people of today have thus to be converted so that they willingly place all their riches at the service of the community. What Gandhi wants is that this conversion should be effected by the people's own awakened effort rather than through the arm of the State. —N. K. B.]

Q. Then, Sir, shall we take it that the fundamental difference between you and the socialists is that you believe that men live more by self-direction or will than by habit, and they believe that men live more by habit than by will, that being the reason why you strive for self-correction, while they try to build up a system under which men will find it impossible to exercise their desire of exploiting others ?*

A. While admitting that man actually lives by habit, I hold it is better for him to live by the exercise of the will. I also believe that men are capable of developing their will to an extent that will reduce exploitation to a minimum. I look upon an increase in the power of the State with the greatest fear, because, although while apparently doing good by

* 'Habit' was here used in the sense of 'environmental pressure' or 'conditioning by environment.'—N. K. B.

minimizing exploitation, it does the greatest harm to mankind by destroying individuality, which lies at the root of all progress. We know of so many cases where men have adopted trusteeship, but none where the State has really lived for the poor.

Q. But have not those cases of trusteeship which you sometimes cite been due to your personal influence rather than to anything else ? Teachers like you come infrequently. Would it not be better, therefore, to trust to some organization to effect the necessary changes in man, rather than depend upon the casual advent of men like yourself ?

A. Leaving me aside, you must remember that the influence of all great teachers of mankind has outlived their lives. In the teachings of each prophet like Mohammed, Buddha or Jesus, there was a permanent element and there was another suited to the needs and requirements of the times. It is only because we try to keep up the permanent with the impermanent aspects of their teaching that there is so much distortion in religious practice today. But that apart you can see that the influence of these men has sustained after they have passed away.

However, what I disapprove of is an organization based on force which the State is. Voluntary organization there must be.

Question IV

What then, Sir, is your ideal social order ?

Answer IV

I believe that every man is born in the world

with certain natural tendencies. Every person is born with certain definite limitations which he cannot overcome. From a careful observation of these limitations the law of *varna* was deduced. It establishes certain spheres of action for certain people with certain tendencies. This avoided all unworthy competition. Whilst recognizing limitations the law of *varna* admitted of no distinction of high and low, on the one hand it guaranteed to each the fruits of his labours and on the other it prevented him from pressing upon his neighbour. This great law has been degraded and fallen into disrepute. But my conviction is that an ideal social order will only be evolved when the implications of this law are fully understood and given effect to.

Q.   Do you not think that in ancient India there was much difference in economic status and social privileges between the four *varnas* ?

A.   That may be historically true. But misapplication or an imperfect understanding of the law must not lead to the ignoring of the law itself. By constant striving we have to enrich the inheritance left to us. This law determines the duties of man. Rights follow from a due performance of duties. It is the fashion nowadays to ignore duties and assert or rather usurp rights.

Q.   If you are so keen upon reviving *varna-shrama* why do you not favour violence as the quickest means ?

A.   Surely the question does not arise. Definition

and performance of duties rules out violence altogether.

Q. Should we not confine our pursuit of truth to ourselves and not press it upon the world, because we know that it is ultimately limited in character ?

A. You cannot so circumscribe truth even if you try. Every expression of truth has in it the seeds of propagation, even as the sun cannot hide its light.

APPENDIX

During the Round Table Conference in 1931, Gandhiji's theoretical position with regard to the State was nearer that of a socialist than that of an uncompromising anarchist. (See p. 72.) But during 1934, when the above interview took place, the tendency towards anarchism seemed to be stronger; this was the period when he was trying to develop the All-India Village Industries Association which is a voluntary organization designed to bring economic power into the hands of the common people even in opposition to the prevailing forces of capitalism and the capitalistic State. Ever since the Congress accepted office in 1937, Gandhiji's faith in the possibility of modification of the character of the State so as to serve the economic interests of the poor has increased; this being evident from his later writings already quoted in the previous chapters. (Pp. 69, 79, 83, 106.) Quite recently, a question was asked in Noakhali as to what attitude the State should maintain towards religious instruction. The answer given by him, which is quoted below, clearly shows how he favours a completely secular State, guided not by the interest of any denominational religion, but by a purely ethical code ; and we know from other sources that the foundation of his ethics lies in the complete welfare of the individual, consistent with the welfare of the whole human race.

Q. Do you consider religion to be exclusively a personal matter ? Should religious instruction form part of the school curriculum as approved by the State ? Do you favour separate schools for children belonging to different denominations for facility of religious instruction ? Or, should religious instruction be left in the hands of private bodies ? If so, do you think it is right for the State to subsidize such bodies ?

A. As to this question he said that he did not believe in State religion even though the whole community had one religion. The State interference would probably always be unwelcome. Religion was purely a personal matter. There were in reality as many religions as minds. Each mind had a different conception of God from that of the other.

He was also opposed to State aid partly or wholly to religious bodies. For he knew that an institution or group, which did not manage to finance its own religious teaching, was a stranger to true religion. This did not mean that the State schools would not give ethical teaching. The fundamental ethics was common to all religions.—(*H*, 16-3-47, 63.)

GANDHI AND THE INDIAN NATIONAL CONGRESS

The Beginnings of Satyagraha

While living in South Africa, Gandhi was first drawn into a situation when he employed the method of Satyagraha in order to remedy a wrong from which the Indian settlers had been suffering. Answering a question put to him by the Rev. J. J. Doke in 1907, he said :

> Some years ago, when I began to take an active part in the public life of Natal, the adoption of this method occurred to me as the best course to pursue, should petitions fail, but, in the then unorganised condition of our Indian community, the attempt seemed useless. Here, however, in Johannesburg, when the Asiatic Registration Act was introduced, the Indian community was so deeply stirred, and so knit together in a common determination to resist it, that the moment seemed opportune. Some action they would take ; it seemed to be best for the Colony, and altogether right, that their action should not take a riotous form, but that of Passive Resistance. They had no vote in Parliament, no hope of obtaining redress, no one would listen to their complaints. The Christian churches were indifferent, so I proposed this pathway of suffering, and after much discussion,

it was adopted. In September, 1906, there was a large gathering of Indians in the old Empire Theatre, when the position was thoroughly faced, and, under the inspiration of deep feeling, and on the proposal of one of our leading men, they swore a solemn oath committing themselves to Passive Resistance.—(*Doke*, 89.)

Satyagraha began under these circumstances ; and the careful student who would follow the history of its development should read Gandhi's *An Autobiography or the Story of My Experiments with Truth* and *Satyagraha in South Africa* for further details. In these books, he will learn how Gandhi gradually came to the conclusion that without abundant inner discipline, which must proceed side by side with a change in outward life and action, Satyagraha is impossible. We also learn how for a collective practice of the new way of life he first founded the Phoenix Settlement in Durban in 1904, and the Tolstoy Farm in 1910. In both of these places, Satyagrahis tried to remodel their daily life in conformity with the law of human brotherhood and of equality, as well as a due recognition of the law of manual labour, which Gandhi considers to be the corner-stone of the new social order.

From South Africa, Gandhi came back to India in January 1915. For a short while, he was with Rabindranath at Santiniketan ; but when news came in February of the expiry of Gokhale, he immediately left for Bombay. One of Gokhale's last requests to Gandhi had been that he should acquaint himself first-hand with the condition of the country for one whole year before taking any active share in social or political reform. Gandhi obeyed this advice with due respect ; but, in the meanwhile, he formed his first settlement at Kochrab near Ahmedabad on the 25th of May 1915, from where the Ashram was shifted to the banks of the Sabarmati in June 1917.

The annual session of the Indian National Congress was held in 1916 at Lucknow ; and while Gandhi was attending it, a peasant from Bihar, named Rajkumar Shukla, came to him with a tale of woe resulting from the oppression of indigo-planters in the district of Champaran. Accordingly, he went to Champaran in April 1917, initiated an enquiry, had to disobey Government orders for the first time, and a great peasant movement was thus initiated in Bihar. The result was that a form of serfdom which had persisted for over a century came to an end. Bihar as well as India thereby gained its first object lesson in the method of non-violent resistance to right a proved wrong.

Early in 1918, there was a dispute between mill-owners and labourers in Ahmedabad. Shrimati Anasuya Sarabhai, who had interested herself in the welfare of labourers from 1916, sought Gandhi's advice and assistance with respect to the labourers' cause. The latter reached Ahmedabad from Champaran in March 1918, and soon after had to undertake a fast in order to influence the strikers so that they might not depart from the non-violent method. The mill-owners gave in within a short time; and then the work of organizing a labour union along non-violent lines was taken up in hand. The Ahmedabad Textile Workers' Association was formed in February 1920. Its aims and methods being of a different order, it has so far kept aloof from other labour organizations in the country. In 1926, the Association added the following clause to its aims and objects, and this was done at the instance of Gandhiji, 'in due course, to secure nationalization of the textile industry.'

Then followed a small peasant movement in the Kaira District of Gujarat in 1918, the story of which is told in the *Autobiography*, as well as in greater detail in Shankerlal Parekh's Gujarati narrative.

The Rowlatt Agitation, 1919

The Great War was then over, and the economic condition of the common people was one of dire distress; while expectations raised by promises made rather freely by the British Government during the pendency of the War, had made the people restless for some kind of political change. It was in this atmosphere that the Government of India took the country by surprise by initiating the Anarchial and Revolutionary Crimes Act, otherwise known as the Rowlatt or the Black Act.

It was in connection with this Act that Gandhi came forward with his proposal for a nation-wide Satyagraha for the first time in India. It was on the 1st of March 1919, that he

addressed a letter to the Press, and in it we find a
remarkable statement as to why he offered the
country a form of direct action against the proposed
measure. In that letter he said :

I enclose herewith the Satyagraha pledge
regarding the Rowlatt Bills. The step taken is
probably the most momentous in the history of
India. I give my assurance that it has not
been hastily taken. Personally I have passed
many a sleepless night over it. I have endeavoured duly to appreciate the Government's
position, but I have been unable to find any
justification for the extraordinary Bills. I have
read the Rowlatt Committee's Report. I have
gone through its narrative with admiration. Its
reading has driven me to a conclusion just
opposite of the Committee's. I should conclude
from the reports that secret violence is confined
to a microscopic body of the people. The existence of such men is truly a danger to the
society. But, the passing of the Bills, designed
to affect the whole of India and its people and
arming the Government with power out of all
proportion to the situation sought to be dealt
with, is a greater danger. The Committee utterly
ignores the historical fact that the millions of
India are by nature the gentlest on the earth.
Now look at the setting of the Bills. Their
introduction is accompanied by certain assurances given by the Viceroy regarding the Civil
Service and British commercial interests. Many
of us are filled with the greatest misgivings about

the Viceregal utterance. I frankly confess I do not understand its full scope and intention. If it means that the Civil Service and British commercial interests are to be held superior to those of India and its political and commercial requirements, no Indian can accept the doctrine. It can but end in a fratricidal struggle within the Empire.

The Reforms may not come, the need of the moment is the proper and just understanding upon the vital issue. No tinkering with it will produce real satisfaction. Let the great Civil Service Corporation understand that it can remain in India only as its trustee and servant, not in name but in deed and let the British commercial houses understand that they can remain in India only to supplement her requirements and not to destroy indigenous art, trade and manufacture, and you have two measures to replace the Rowlatt Bills.

They, I promise, will successfully deal with any conspiracy against the State.

Sir George Lowndes simply added fuel to the fire when he flouted public opinion. He has forgotten his Indian history or he would have known that the Government he represents has before now surrendered its own considered opinion to the force of public opinion.

It will now be easy to see why I consider the Bills to be the unmistakable symptom of the deep-seated disease in the governing body. It needs, therefore, to be drastically treated. Subterranean violence will be the remedy by the impetuous, hot-headed youths, who will have grown impatient of the spirit underlying the Bills and circumstances attending their introduction. The Bills must intensify hatred and ill-will against the State, of which deeds of violence are undoubtedly an evidence. The Indian Covenanters, by their determination to undergo every form of suffering, make an irresistible appeal to the Government, towards which they bear no ill-will, and provide to the believers in efficiency of violence as a means of securing redress of grievance with the infallible remedy and withal a remedy that blesses those that use it and also those against whom it is used. If the Covenanters know the use of this remedy, I fear no ill from it. I have no business to doubt their ability. They must ascertain whether the disease is serious enough and that the mild measures have utterly failed. The rest lies in the lap of the gods.

The Satyagraha Vow

Being conscientiously of opinion that the Bills known as the Indian Criminal Law (Amendment) Bill No. 1 of 1919 and the Criminal Law (Emergency Powers) Bill No. 2 of 1919 are unjust, subversive of the principle of liberty and justice and destructive of the elementary rights of individuals, on which the safety of the community as a whole and the State itself is based, we solemnly affirm that in the event of these Bills becoming law and until they are withdrawn, we shall refuse civilly to obey those laws and such other laws as a committee to be hereafter appointed may think fit and we further affirm that in this struggle we will faithfully follow the truth and refrain from violence to life, person or property.—(*PU*, 33.)

The Satyagraha Sabha was accordingly formed in Bombay and the statement issued by it in March 1919, said :

> The Committee contemplated by the Satyagraha Pledge has advised that for the time being laws regarding prohibited literature and registration of newspapers may be civilly disobeyed.
>
> With reference to prohibited literature the Committee has selected the following prohibited works for dissemination :
>
> "Hind Swarajya" by M. K. Gandhi.
>
> "Sarvodaya or Universal Dawn" by M. K. Gandhi (being a paraphrase of "Unto This Last.")
>
> "The Story of a Satyagrahi" by M. K. Gandhi (being a paraphrase of the "Defence and Death of Socrates" by Plato.)
>
> "The Life and Address of Mustafa Kamil Pasha" (Printed at the International Printing Press.)
>
> In making this selection, the Committee has been guided by the following considerations :
>
> (1) To cause as little disturbance as possible among the governors and the governed ;

(2)　Until Satyagrahis have become seasoned, disciplined and capable of handling delicately organized movements, to select such laws only as can be disobeyed individually ;

(3)　To select, as a first step, laws that have evoked popular disapproval and that from the Satyagraha standpoint, are the most open to attack ;

(4)　To select laws whose civil breach would constitute an education for the people, showing them a clear way out of the difficulties that lie in the path of honest men desiring to do public work ;

(5)　Regarding prohibited literature, to select such books and pamphlets as are not inconsistent with Satyagraha, and which are therefore, of a clean type and which do not, either directly or indirectly, approve of or encourage violence.

—(*PU*,47.)

The Movement was launched actually an the 6th of April 1919 ; and on that day Gandhiji, Sarojini Naidu, Jamnadas Dwarkadas, Umar Sobani and other Covenanters sold signed copies of the pamphlets in the streets of Bombay. The signature of the hawkers was attached so that the Government might have no difficulty in detecting or punishing the responsible persons. Besides these individual Satyagrahis, there was also a programme for the rest of India. The day was to begin with a fast ; and when tendering his evidence before the Hunter

Commission, Gandhi described the genesis of the Rowlatt Bill Satyagraha in the following terms :

> When the Rowlatt Bills were published, I felt that they were so restrictive of human liberty that they must be resisted to the utmost. I observed too that the opposition to them was universal among Indians. I submit that no State, however despotic, has the right to enact laws which are repugnant to the whole body of the people, much less a Government guided by constitutional usage and precedent such as the Indian Government. I felt too that the oncoming agitation needed a definite direction if it was neither to collapse nor run into violent channels.
>
> I ventured therefore to present Satyagraha to the country, emphasizing its Civil Resistance aspect. And as it is purely an inward and purifying movement, I suggested the observance of fast, prayer and suspension of all work for one day, the 6th of April. There was a magnificent response throughout the length and breadth of India, even in little villages, although there was no organization and no great previous preparation.—(*YI*, Nov. 1919, *Tagore* 7.)

The following week was marked by unprecedented enthusiasm everywhere. Here and there, acts of violence were noticeable, and the Government immediately stepped in with severe measures of repression. The Jallianwalla Bagh Massacre took place on the 13th of April 1919, this being followed by a revolting phase of military rule in the

Punjab. In response to the advice of numerous
friends, and more specially due to certain indications
of a conciliatory nature from the Government side,
Gandhi formally suspended this first all-India
Satyagraha on the 21st of July 1919.

The Khilafat Agitation, 1920

The feelings of the Indian Mussulmans were,
in the meanwhile exasperated by the terms of peace
offered to Turkey; for they went directly against
the assurances given by Premier Lloyd George
when Indian Mussulman soldiers had been drafted
to fight against their co-religionists in that country.
The Khilafat was in danger and the Indian
Mussalman began to feel that something drastic
ought to be done in order to preserve the honour of
the Khalif of Islam.

The reason why Gandhi made common cause
with the Muslims in connection with a specifically
religious question is best given in his own words.
While addressing a letter to the Viceroy in the
middle of June 1920, he said :

> The peace terms and Your Excellency's
> defence of them have given the Mussalmans of
> India a shock from which it will be difficult for
> them to recover. The terms violate Ministerial
> pledges and utterly disregard the Mussalman
> sentiment. I consider that, as a staunch Hindu
> wishing to live on terms of closest friendship
> with my Mussalman countrymen, I should be an
> unworthy son of India if I did not stand by them
> in their hour of trial.

Three courses were open to the Mahomedans in order to mark their emphatic disapproval of the utter injustice to which His Majesty's Ministers have become party if they have not actually been perpetrators of it. They are (1) resort to violence, (2) to advise emigration on a whole (sale) scale, (3) not to be party to the injustice by ceasing to co-operate with the Government. Your Excellency must be aware that there was a time when the boldest though also the most thoughtless among the Mussalmans favoured violence and that Hijrat (emigration) has not yet ceased to be the battle-cry. I venture to claim I have succeeded by patient reasoning in weaning the party of violence from its ways. I confess that I did not attempt to succeed in weaning them from violence on moral grounds but purely on utilitarian grounds. The result for the time being at any rate has however been to stop violence. The school of Hijrat has received a check if it has not stopped its activity entirely.

I hold that no repression could have prevented a violent eruption if the people had not had presented to them a form of direct action involving considerable sacrifice and ensuring success if such direct action was largely taken up by public.

Non-co-operation was the only dignified and constitutional form of such direct action. For it is a right recognised from time immemorial of the subjects to refuse to assist the ruler who misrules. At the same time I admit non-co-

operation practised by the mass of people is
attended with grave risks. But in a crisis such
as has overtaken the Mussalmans of India, no
step that is unattended with large risks can
possibly bring about the desired change. Not to
run some risks will be to court much greater risks
if not virtual destruction of law and order.

—(*IAR*, 1921, 199.)

The Reforms

Wrong after wrong was thus piled upon India in
direct opposition to the sentiments and opinions
of the whole nation ; and the measure of civil
liberty was in danger of being very seriously restricted. The Reforms hardly promised relief, and
in December 1919, a resolution was tabled by the
radical wing of the Indian National Congress under
the leadership of Tilak, to characterize the proposed
measures as 'inadequate, unsatisfactory, and disappointing.' The Resolution was actually moved by
C. R. Das ; and Gandhi who proposed an amendment,
which included deletion of the word 'disappointing',
stated in his speech :

I do believe that what we are getting falls
far short of the Congress ideals. My amendment
also means that we may not say these Reforms
are disappointing, disappointing in the sense in
which that word is used. Here I suggest to you
that if a man comes to me and disappoints me,
I do not co-operate with him. If I get a sour
loaf I reject it, and I do not take it. But if I
get a loaf which is not enough, which has not

sufficient condiments in it, I shall use it, I shall add condiments to it and shall take a bit. Therefore my amendment means nothing more and nothing less than that we should stare the situation in the face as it exists before the country today and if Tilak Maharaj tells you that we are going to make use of the Reforms Act as he must, and as he already told Mr. Montagu, as he has told the country that we are going to take the fullest advantage of the Reforms, then I say, be true to yourself, be true to the country and tell the country that you are going to do it. But if you want to say, after having gone there, you will put any obstruction, say that also. But on the question of propriety and obstruction, I say, Indian culture demands that we shall trust one who extends a hand of fellowship. The Indian culture demands trust and full trust, and if you are sufficiently manly we shall not be afraid of the future, but face the future in a manly manner and say, 'All right, Mr. Montagu, all right, all officials of the bureaucracy, we are going to trust you. We shall put you in a corner and when you resist us and when you resist the advance of the country, then we say, you do so at your peril !' That is the manly attitude that I suggest. —(*IAR*, 1920, 381.)

Gandhiji then went on to suggest that we should co-operate by accepting the Reforms, and not say one thing when we mean another. It was plainly the call of unadulterated truth in regulating political relations between the State and its subjects, a new thing which appeared on the Indian horizon, just as Satyagraha had already made its appearance in order to canalize the hatred of the nation into a line of healthy and fruitful activity.

The Non-co-operation
Movement 1921-23

The Congress had set up a commission of enquiry into the Punjab happenings; and Gandhiji was one of the members of that Committee. The recommendations of the Committee, after the guilt of the civil and military authorities had been clearly established, were of a very modest nature. But the Government of India, as well as the Government of Britain and the European community in India were all determined to flout the verdict of the nation.

Accordingly, the Indian National Congress met at a special session in Calcutta in September 1920, where, under Gandhiji's suggestion, it adopted the programme of progressive, non-violent non-co-operation for the redress of the Khilafat and Punjab wrongs, as well as for the establishment of Swarajya in place of the Reforms which the nation had ultimately decided to boycott. While moving the Resolution, Gandhiji said :

Non-co-operation, as you will see from the Resolution itself, has been conceived as a measure of discipline and self-sacrifice. Unless we are able to evolve discipline, non-co-operation is an impossibility. Non-co-operation in an angry atmosphere is an impossibility. I would yield to no one in my feelings with reference to the wrongs that have been done to this country, but I have learnt by bitter experience, through a period of close upon thirty years, the one supreme lesson, namely, to conserve my anger, to control it, and just as heat conserved is transmuted into energy, so also our anger, conserved and controlled, can result in a power that becomes irresistible throughout the world, and I want my country to control its anger at this critical period in its history.

I have been told that I am doing nothing but wrecking the Congress, and that by my mad resolution, I shall be breaking the Congress and the political life of the country. I have said already that this Congress is not a party organization, but that this Congress provides, and ought to provide, a platform for all shades of opinion, for all groups, for all parties. A minority need not leave this platform and this organization but that minority may look forward to translating itself into a majority, if its opinion commends itself to the country. All that is necessary is that no man may, under the Congress banner, place anything before the country as the Congress policy, if that particular policy has been condemned or rejected by the Congress. I venture to submit to you that if I find myself in a minority, and still if you will provide for me a platform on the Congress stage, you will not find me going away from the Congress, but leave me to convert the minority into the majority. I do not want to go into the details of the programme, for the reason that every step recommended to you is given to you in the programme itself. There are no two opinions as to the wrong that is done to the Khilafat. The Mussalmans of India cannot remain as honourable men, and followers of the faith of their Prophet, if they do not vindicate its honour at any cost. The Punjab has been cruelly and barbarously treated, and inasmuch as a single Punjabi was made to crawl on his belly, the whole of India crawled that day on her belly, and it is that humiliation which you and I, if we claim to be worthy sons and daughters of India, must be pledged to remove. And it is in order to remove these two wrongs that the country has been agitating itself and others for a number of months. But we have not been able to bend the British Government by our will. Can the country with all the passion, with all the feeling that it has shown in these two things rest satisfied with mere empty exhibition of angry feeling ? You could not have listened to a more passionate discourse upon the wrongs of the Punjab than in the pages of the address delivered by our respected President. How is the Congress to vindicate, to justify its existence and its honour, if it cannot enforce justice from un-willing hands, if it cannot enforce candid repen-tance before receiving a single gift, howsoever rich it may be, from those blood-stained hands ? Therefore it is that I have ventured to place before this country a scheme of non-co-operation and I would ask you to reject any other non-co-operation except as detailed by me, not because that programme has been framed by me, but I ask you to reject any other scheme unless you deliberately come to the conclusion that that is a better scheme of non-co-operation than the one I have presented to you. I venture to claim for this scheme of non-co-operation that if this has sufficient response in the country, I make bold to reiterate the statement that you can gain your Swaraj in one year under my conditions, not by passing this Resolution by this vast audience, but by an enforcement of this Resolution by this very audience from day to day in a progressive manner, and the progressive stages therein fixed, due regard being had to the condition of the country.

There was another way before the country, save non-co-operation, and that was drawing the sword. But India does not possess the sword, and if it had possessed the sword, I know that India would not have listened to this gospel of non-co-operation, and I want to suggest to you that even if you want to wrest justice from unwilling hands by methods of violence, two things, indispensable in this programme, discipline and self-sacrifice, will still be necessary. I have not yet known a war gained by rebels, but I have known wars gained, as you have known, by a disciplined army capable of dying every one of them, at their posts. If you want to give a pitched battle in arms to the British Government, to the English Nation or to combined powers of Europe, we shall have to train ourselves in

15

discipline and self-sacrifice. It is to that stage that
I am desirous and eager to bring my country. I
confess to you that I have become impatient. I
see that in intelligence we are not wanting, but
we have not got the spirit of national self-sacrifice
and national discipline. We have evolved discipline and self-sacrifice, as perhaps no nation has
done, in our domestic affairs. I have come to
plead before you to extend the doctrine to national
life, in other words I have come here, and I am
travelling from one end of India to the other end
in order to test whether the country has really
evolved a national spirit, whether at the altar (of)
the Nation, the country is ready to dedicate its
riches, its children, its all. And if the country is
ready to dedicate its all, without reservation, I
promise Swaraj in no time.

—(*IAR*, 1921, Part III, 109.)

The Resolution itself stated in part :

And inasmuch as a beginning should be
made by the classes who have hitherto moulded
and represented public opinion and inasmuch as
Government consolidates its power through titles
and honours bestowed on the people, through
schools controlled by it, its law-courts and Legislative Councils, and inasmuch as it is desirable
in the prosecution of the movement to take the
minimum risk and to call for the least sacrifice
compatible with the attainment of the desired
object, this Congress earnestly advises—

(*a*) surrender of titles and honorary offices

and resignation from nominated seats in local bodies ;

(*b*) refusal to attend Government Levees, Durbars, and other official and semi-official functions held by Government officials or in their honour ;

(*c*) gradual withdrawal of children from schools and colleges owned, aided or controlled by Government and in place of such schools and colleges establishment of National schools and colleges in the various Provinces ;

(*d*) gradual boycott of British courts by lawyers and litigants and establishment of private arbitration courts by their aid for the settlement of private disputes ;

(*e*) refusal on the part of the military, clerical and labouring classes to offer themselves as recruits for service in Mesopotamia ;

(*f*) withdrawal by candidates of their candidature for election to the Reformed Councils and refusal on the part of the voters to vote for any candidate who may, despite the Congress advice, offer himself for election ;

(*g*) boycott of foreign goods ;

And inasmuch as non-co-operation has been conceived as a measure of discipline and self-sacrifice without which no nation can make real progress, and inasmuch as an opportunity should be given in the very first stage of non-co-operation to every man, woman and child, for such discipline and self-sacrifice, this Congress

advises adoption of Swadeshi in piece-goods on
a vast scale, and inasmuch as the existing mills
of India with indigenous capital and control do
not manufacture sufficient yarn and sufficient
cloth for the requirements of the nation, and are
not likely to do so for a long time to come, this
Congress advises immediate stimulation of further
manufacture on a large scale by means of reviving
hand-spinning in every home and hand-weaving
on the part of the millions of weavers who have
abandoned their ancient and honourable calling
for want of encouragement.—(*IAR*, 1921, 107.)

While explaining the details of the programme,
Gandhiji wrote in the *Young India* :

I do not rely merely upon the lawyer class
or highly educated men to enable the Committee
to carry out all the stages of non-co-operation.
My hope lies more with the masses so far as the
later stages of non-co-operation are concerned.
—(*YI*, 18-8-20, *Tagore*, 370.)

In answer to the question whether the masses
would not more readily respond to a programme of
suspension of taxes rather than to the one actually
suggested, Gandhiji wrote :

So far as response is concerned, I agree with
the editor (of the *Swadeshmitran*) that the
quickest and the largest response is to be expected
in the matter of suspension of payment of taxes,
but, as I have said, so long as the masses are
not educated to appreciate the value of non-
violence even whilst their holdings are being

sold, so long must it be difficult to take up the
last stage in any appreciable extent.

—(*YI*, 18-8-20, *Tagore*, 328.)

The call was therefore to more caution, more
discipline, more organization so that the upsurge of
the nation might flow within the bounds of non-
violence. Gandhi was also trying to give a shape to
the feelings of the nation, not through action
specifically confined to the upper classes, but through
a programme in which the masses were likely to
play an increasingly important part.

The progress of the nation (Gandhiji wrote)
cannot be arrested by any person or class. The
uneducated artisans, the women, the men in the
street are taking their share in the movement.
The appeal to the educated classes paved the way
for them. The goats had to be sifted from the
sheep. The educated classes had to be put upon
their trial. The beginning had to be made by and
through them.—(*YI*, 20-4-21, 123.)

Again :

We have been trying to act on the masses
from the commencement. We regard them as
our mainstay, for it is they who have to attain
Swaraj. It is neither the sole concern of the
monied men nor that of the educated class. Both
must subserve their interest in any scheme of
Swaraj, and as soon as the masses have attained
sufficient self-control and learnt mass discipline,
we shall not hesitate if necessary to advise
them to suspend payment of taxes to a

Government that has never truly looked after
their welfare and that has exploited and terrorised
them every time they have shown the least
symptom of rising against their exploitation.

—(*YI*, 20-4-21, 124.)

There was nation-wide response when the
movement of Non-co-operation was launched. Lacs of
people took to spinning, national schools and
arbitration boards were formed in all Provinces, and
volunteers who had signed a pledge were allowed to
court arrest by disobeying Government orders. But
even this form of individual civil disobedience
resulted in the imprisonment of 30,000 people. The
tempo began to rise ; and every one looked forward
with anxious expectation to the time when mass
civil disobedience itself would be launched in the
shape of a no-tax campaign.

Gandhiji had chosen the peasants of Bardoli
Taluka in Surat District for the first experiment, where
it would be possible for him to keep the movement
completely under personal observation and control.
Accordingly, he sent a letter to the Viceroy
intimating his decision of inaugurating the no-tax
campaign. This was on the 1st of February 1922,
the decision to this effect having been taken by
the Working Committee on the 29th of January.

In the meanwhile, boycott and picketing, coupled
with processions, had given rise to sporadic cases of
violence which tended to show that the control over
the forces of violence was not yet as much as desired
by Gandhiji. On the 5th of February, a mob at Chauri

Chaura in the district of Gorakhpur set fire to the Police station, when 22 persons were killed altogether. Gandhi had been following the acts of mob-violence, as well as the Governmental measures of reprisal, with anxious care ; and when the Chauri Chaura incident took place, he suddenly decided to withhold the campaign at Bardoli, although the decision had already been communicated to the Viceroy. The Working Committee met again at Bardoli on 12-2-22, and Gandhi placed a programme of constructive activities for the whole nation, which had to be executed before the people could be allowed to think once more in terms of non-co-operation. In the Bardoli Resolution it was decided that :

> 'Mass civil disobedience contemplated at Bardoli and elsewhere be suspended, and this suspension be continued till the atmosphere is so non-violent as to ensure the non-repetition of popular atrocities such as at Gorakhpur or hooliganism such as at Bombay and Madras.'

> Moreover all activities 'specially designed to court arrest and imprisonment, all volunteer processions, public meetings, merely for the purpose of defiance of the notifications regarding such meetings' were stopped till further instructions, and a new programme of constructive work was laid down.—(*IAR*, 1923, I, 74.)

Soon after this, Gandhiji was arrested and convicted to six years' rigorous imprisonment ; but he was released before his time in February 1924 after a major surgical operation.

Some have seen in the withdrawal at Bardoli, Gandhi's fear of the masses actually coming into power. But Gandhi's reason was otherwise. After release from prison, when he once more took up the work of editing the *Young India*, he wrote :

> So long as the organizers strictly keep within the limits which they have prescribed for themselves there is no cause for calling off Satyagrah. The friend cites Chauri Chaura as an illustration. In doing so, he has betrayed confusion of thought or ignorance of facts. The Bardoli Satyagrah was suspended because Congress and Khilafat men were implicated in the Chauri Chaura outrage.
>
> —(*YI*, 19-6-24, 201.)

> Whenever I have suspended civil disobedience I have done so not by reason of any outbreak of violence, but upon the discovery of such violence as had been initiated or encouraged by Congressmen who should have known better. Any outbreak of violence would not have brought about suspension, for instance, the Moplah outbreak. But Chauri Chaura did, for the simple reason that persons connected with the Congress were involved in it.—(*YI*, 29-10-25, 368.)

What Gandhi really wanted was that the masses should come into power ; and he thought that this was only possible through non-violence. A successful violent revolution might transfer power from the present rulers to a certain section of the population which made the most effective use of violence ; but that would surely not be Swaraj in terms of the masses, for by that very act, the party of violence would become external to the masses. In 1925, he therefore wrote :

> I contend that the revolutionary method cannot succeed in India. If an open warfare were a possibility, I may concede that we may tread the path of violence that the other countries have and at least evolve the qualities that bravery on the battlefield brings forth. But the attainment of Swaraj through warfare I hold an impossibility for any time that we can foresee. Warfare may give us another rule for the English rule, but not self-rule in terms of the masses. The pilgrimage to Swaraj is a painful climb. It requires attention to details. It means vast organizing ability, it means penetration into the villages, solely for the service of the villagers. In other words, it means an awakening of national consciousness among the masses. It will not spring like the magician's mango. It will grow almost unperceived like the banian tree. A bloody revolution will never perform the trick. Haste here is most certainly waste.
>
> —(*YI*, 21-5-25, 178.)

The Period 1922-29

The Bardoli Resolution caused a lot of restlessness among Congressmen and many did not like that political action should be thus held up for an indefinite period, while they were to mark time in

slow, colourless village work.   There was accordingly
a strong desire among many Congressmen to enter
the Councils, which had been previously boycotted,
and there give fight to the bureaucracy from within.
The element of struggle involved in such an
enterprise seemed to be more satisfying ; and there
was consequently a steady growth of feeling in
favour of Council entry after the suspension of 1922.
This was clearly reflected in the presidential
address of the Gaya Congress in December 1922,
where Deshbandhu C. R. Das said :

> I confess that I am not in favour of the
> restrictions which have been put upon the practical
> adoption of any system of civil disobedience, and
> in my opinion, the Congress should abolish those
> restrictions.   I have not yet been able to under-
> stand why to enable a people to civilly disobey
> particular laws, it should be necessary that at
> least 80 per cent. of them should be clad in pure
> "Khadi".   I am not much in favour of general
> mass civil disobedience.   To my mind the idea
> is impracticable.

>   ...   .

> There is no opposition in idea between such
> civil disobedience as I have mentioned and
> the entry into the Councils for the purpose,
> and with the avowed object of either ending
> or mending them.   I am not against the boycott
> of Councils.   I am simply of opinion that the
> system of the Reformed Councils with their steel

frame of the Indian Civil Service covered over by a dyarchy of deadlocks and departments, is absolutely unsuitable to the nature and genius of the Indian nation. It is an attempt of the British Parliament to force a foreign system upon the Indian people. India has unhesitatingly refused to recognize this foreign system as a real foundation for Swaraj. These Councils must therefore be either mended or ended. Hitherto we have been boycotting the Councils from outside. We have succeeded in doing much— the prestige of the Councils is diminished, and the country knows that the people who adorn those chambers are not the true representatives of the people. But though we have succeeded in doing much, these Councils are still there. It should be the duty of the Congress to boycott the Councils more effectively from within.

—(*IAR*, 1923, I, 835.)

In the same session of the Congress, the Congress Khilafat Swaraj Party was formed with Deshbandhu Das as its leader. The Party favoured Council entry, but otherwise accepted wholeheartedly the creed of the Congress as well as the principle of non-violent non-co-operation.—(*IAR*, 1923, I, 872 *n*.)

When Gandhiji came back from prison, he marked the new development ; and, in spite of entreaties from his political supporters, did nothing to arrest the growth of the Swaraj Party. On the contrary, he issued a statement in which he paid a glowing tribute to the patriotism of the members of the Party, and advised his own supporters, hitherto called No-changers, to devote themselves to the constructive programme with redoubled enthusiasm, so that they might prove their faith by the success of their action. —(*HC*, I, 270.)

The attitude which Gandhi bore towards the Swaraj Party found a magnificent expression after Deshbandhu Das's death in the middle of 1925. Shortly after, the Working Committee meeting was held in Calcutta, as well as a meeting of the Swaraj Party Council. After attending both of them, Gandhi addressed the following letter to Pandit Motilal Nehru, the new leader of the Swaraj Party.

Calcutta, 19th July '25

Dear Panditji,

During these few days I have been taxing myself what special exclusive contribution I can make to the memory of Deshbandhu and the situation created by Lord Birkenhead's speech. And I have come to the conclusion that I should absolve the Swaraj Party from all obligations under the pact of last year. The result of this act is that the Congress need no longer be predominantly a spinning association.

I recognize that under the situation created by the speech the authority and the influence of the Swaraj Party need to be increased. I would fail in my duty if I neglected a single step within my power to increase the strength of the Party. This can be done if the Congress becomes a predominantly political body.

Under the pact the Congress activity is restricted to the constructive programme mentioned therein. I recognise that this restriction should not continue under the altered circumstance that faces the country. Not only do I, therefore, personally absolve you from the restriction, but I propose to ask the forthcoming meeting of the A. I. C. Committee to do likewise and place the whole machinery of the Congress at your disposal so as to enable you to bring before that body such political resolutions as you may consider necessary in the interest of the country. In fact, I would have you regard me at your disposal in all such matters in which I can conscientiously serve you and the Swaraj Party.—(*IAR*, 1925, II, 33.)

In spite of this sympathetic attitude, it was clear about this time that Gandhi was becoming more and more estranged from the mind of educated India. As President of the Belgaum Session of the Congress in 1924, he had proposed that membership to the Congress should be paid in yarn and not in coin. This proposal had then raised a heated controversy, with the result that yarn came to be recognized as an alternative, though not the sole, form of subscription. The reaction is reflected in the presidential address delivered at the Maharastra Provincial Conference on 11th May 1925.

It said in part :

Mr. Gandhi effected unity at Belgaum and it is owing to that fact that some scope is left in

the Congress and its subordinate institutions for
political thought.   Otherwise, our whole political
work would have begun and ended in counting the
Tilak Swarajya Fund and in measuring the
length in miles of yarn spun, in numbering how
many untouchables took their seats on the
carpets along with the touchables and in
inventing a metre for calculating the degrees to
which the Hindu Mahomedan quarrels rise or
fall. But at Belgaum, Swarajya Party was recognized as part of the Congress and therefore,
struggle with the Government, though it be on
national grounds, remained a topic for such
political gatherings ; hence was it that the
political colour of these bodies was maintained
intact. Some one might object that struggle
with Government on principles of reason cannot
be the sole politics of the country. True, but
the whole creative power of the people depends
upon ratiocination. Where there is no appeal
to intellect, there can be no activity. To be brief,
I feel that to restrict reasoning or to keep aloof
from it, is to renounce the springs of active force.

The self-determination of India depends on
the co-ordination of the Congress and the
Councils. As the electorate of the Councils is
free for all kinds of people, so must the Congress-
electorate be. He who consents in writing to
the aims and the methods of the Congress must
be a Congress-member. He should not have to
pay any kind of subscription either in yarn or
in money. Looking at the thousands of spectators

gathered at Nagpur, Mahatma Gandhi exclaimed that the Congress had really become a Congress of the masses! Can the Congress not belong to the masses if Congressmen take their seats on all representative institutions ranging from the village Panchayats to the Legislative Councils?

When the Congress adopted the yarn quali-fication, it was said that workers alone are entitled to be Congress-members. For that purpose the constitutions of Russian Bolshevik bodies were drawn upon. But it was forgotten that the Bolshevik bodies were secret societies, while the Congress was an open, political organization. The latter must include even sympathizers. How can the definition of a worker be confined to a spinner? Yarn franchise is a measure of the spread of the doctrine of Ahimsa. My humble request to Mahatmaji would be that he should now go out of the Congress. May his party be triumphant after a lapse of say ten or twenty thousand years! When Shivaji, Pratapsinha, Ranjitsinha, Shri Ram and Shri Krishna fail to follow you, oh, what can miserable men like ourselves do? —(*IAR*, 1925, I, 398.)

Perhaps it was on this account that Gandhiji wrote with a tinge of sorrow in August 1925:

I must no longer stand in the way of the Congress being developed and guided by educated Indians rather than by one like myself who has thrown in his lot entirely with the masses, and who has fundamental differences with the mind of educated India as a body. I shall want to act upon them but not by leading the Congress. The best way in which I can help that activity is by removing myself out of the way, and by concentrating myself solely upon constructive work with the help of the Congress and in its name, and that too, only so far as educated India will permit me to do.—(*HC*, I, 285.)

But in spite of the rise of the Swaraj Party, the majority of Congress members were still in favour of the continuance of Gandhiji's leadership. There was a fairly large number of devoted workers who tried to carry out the constructive programme in different parts of India. But, somehow, they felt themselves estranged from educated people, as a class ; with the result that many of them developed doctrinaire tendencies in self-defence. In isolated cases, this even gave rise to a spirit of intolerance towards the Swaraj Party itself. A quotation from the manifesto of the Congress Karmi Sangha in Bengal issued in the middle of 1926 bears testimony to this :

It is well-known how the Congress was sharply divided into two or more hostile camps for about three years after the Gaya Congress. After the Cawnpore Congress in December 1925, when the Congress practically adopted the Swarajist programme, it was felt that time had come when an attempt should be made to re-unite all Congress workers with a view to further the constructive programme which had for some years past been neglected owing to the preoccupation of the leaders with the Legislative Councils.

After Deshbandhu's death it became increasingly eminent that the Congress leaders had very little faith in village re-organization, formation of peasant and labour unions, or other items of the constructive programme. All that really interested them was wordy warfare inside the Legislature and inspite of the occasional mention of civil disobedience in their speeches and writings, the fact could no longer be concealed that what they really cared for was a histrionic display of their dialectic skill inside the Legislature. They would neither find money for reviving the moribund Congress organization in the villages nor would they undertake the organization of agricultural and industrial labour. All the work that they really wanted the Congress workers to do was to serve as their canvassing agents at the time of the elections.

—(*IAR*, 1926, I, 93.)

It was natural that in the prevailing atmosphere of party bickering, many of those who devoted themselves to the constructive programme, should miss its real significance. Instead of developing local initiative to the required extent, they drafted money from outside in order to create and even run the centres of constructive activity. In an anxiety to prove the superiority of the Gandhian programme, such workers very often concentrated on increasing the output of Khadi instead of building up the spirit of co-operation and sense of self-reliance, which alone should have been the chief aim of economic decentralization. Even the inventions

16

which were made in connection with the spinning
wheel had a wrong end in view. Arrangements
which had been found suitable in power-mills were
adapted to hand-spinning, with the result that such
attachments could not be turned out by village
craftsmen and had to be imported from the cities.
Lacs of rupees and an enormous amount of honest
labour ran to waste in this manner. In order to
systematize this work, the All-India Spinners'
Association, which was an expert organization, was
therefore founded in September 1925 out of the older
All-India Khaddar Board, which had been functioning
since the Non-co-operation days. (See draft constitution in *IAR*, 1925, II, 27.)

In the meanwhile, Gandhi repeatedly indicated
the spirit in which constructive work should be
carried out so that it might serve the purpose of
organizing the masses for Swaraj. In one issue of
the *Young India*, he wrote :

The village work frightens us. We who are
town-bred find it trying to take to village life.
Our bodies in many cases do not respond to the
hard life. But it is a difficulty which we have
to face boldly, even heroically, if our desire is to
establish Swaraj for the people, not substitute one
class-rule by another, which may even be worse.
Hitherto the villagers have died in their thousands
so that we might live. Now we might have to
die so that they may live.—(*YI*, 17-4-24, 130.)

The Congress must progressively represent
the masses. They are as yet untouched by
politics. They have no political consciousness

of the type our politicians desire. Their politics are confined to bread and salt—I dare not say butter, for millions do not know the taste of ghee or even oil. Their politics are confined to communal adjustments. It is right however to say that we the politicians do represent the masses in opposition to the Government. But if we begin to use them before they are ready, we shall cease to represent them. We must first come in living touch with them by working for them and in their midst, we must share their sorrows, understand their difficulties and anticipate their wants. With the pariahs we must be pariahs and see how we feel to clean the closets of the upper classes and have the remains of their table thrown at us. We must see how we like being in the boxes, miscalled houses, of the labourers of Bombay. We must identify ourselves with the villagers who toil under the hot sun beating on their bent backs and see how we would like to drink water from the pool in which the villagers bathe, wash their clothes and pots and in which their cattle drink and roll. Then and not till then shall we truly represent the masses and they will, as surely as I am writing this, respond to every call.

'We cannot all do this, and if we are to do this, good-bye to Swaraj for a thousand years and more', some will say. I shall sympathize with the objection. But I do claim that some of us at least will have to go through the agony and out of it only will a nation full, vigorous and free be born. —(*YI*, 11-9-24, 300.)

With reference to the aims of labour organization, he wrote in reply to a letter of Mr. Shapurji Saklatvala, the Communist member of the Parliament,

Labour, in my opinion, must not become a pawn in the hands of the politician on the political chess-board. It must, by its sheer strength, dominate the chess-board. —(*IID*, 26.)

Thus Gandhi's idea was that upper class interests should be liquidated voluntarily while labour should 'evolve its own leadership and its own self-reliant, self-existing organization.' 'The idea,' he wrote, 'is to take from capital labour's due share and no more, and this not by paralysing capital, but by reform among labourers from within and by their own self-consciousness ; not through the cleverness and manoeuvring of non-labour leaders.'—(*IID*, 26.)

I will not commit the sin of becoming their patron, but on learning that I had assisted in impoverishing them, (I must) associate myself with them in work. —(*YI*, 13-10-21, 325.)

A similar sentiment was expressed in a different context thus :

Even as a cup of milk which is full up to the brim does not overflow when sugar is gently added to it, the sugar accomodating itself in the milk and enriching its taste, in the same way,

I would like you to live...so as not to become interlopers, so as to enrich the life of the people in whose midst you may be living.

—(*Ceylon*, 116, date 1927.)

We have already said how the constructive work was not actually carried out in the spirit in which its author wanted it to be. Even among workers, who did not favour Council-entry, there were growing signs of impatience for some form of political struggle ; and this led to numerous minor Satyagraha campaigns between the years 1923 and 1929. Such were Midnapur, Mulshipet, Vaikom, Tarakeswar, Gurudwara, Chirala Perala, Patuakhali, Nagpur, Neill, Bardoli, and a host of similar campaigns undertaken for the redress of local grievances of a social, civic or economic nature. Some of them were conducted well, but a few suffered from the amateurish fashion in which the principle of non-violence was adhered to. Indeed, these move-ments afforded workers capital exercise in the conduct of non-violent campaigns on their own initiative.

The growing impatience of politically conscious workers was manifest in a different way also. After the secularization of the Turkish State by Kemal Pasha in November 1922, the Khilafat Movement, as such, lost all its meaning with the Indian Mussulmans ; but unfortunately, the group-conscious-ness centring round a religious faith which had crystallized itself during the days of the Khilafat, now recoiled upon the community, and led to its estrangement from the rest of the Indian nation.

The Congress workers also, in their days of favourable opportunity, had neglected to identify the economic interest of the masses, whether Muslim or Hindu, with their own, through the execution of the Gandhian programme. Congress was dominated more by middle class workers, who had not yet shed their own interests completely, rather than by the true representatives of the exploited millions. The result was that there came about a growing estrangement between these middle class political workers and the middle class leadership of the Muslim community. The climax was reached when riots broke out in various portions of India between the Hindus and Mussulmans, and in course of these riots, Congress workers hardly succeeded in playing the part they should have played according to their professed ideal of non-violence, or of identification with the interest of the masses.

India seemed to be passing through a period of insufficient action, and of stock-taking of ideals. But the party of violence, which had so long given left-handed support to the Congress programme, now grew more restless and planned to revive its own programme, which had been held in abeyance for a number of years. Gandhi watched the growing tendency with anxiety, and began to think of some way out of the impasse.

The opportunity presented itself when the Indian National Congress adopted the vow of Independence at its Lahore session in the winter of 1929. Some step had immediately to be taken in order to implement the Resolution ; and the Congress formally handed over leadership to Gandhi to lead the nation in an all-embracing Satyagraha struggle.

Civil Disobedience, 1930-34

Commenting on the proposed struggle, Gandhi wrote :

> The Congress cannot stay its hands after having passed the Independence Resolution. It was no bluff, no showy nothing. It was a deliberate definite change in the Congress mentality. It is then as much up to the critics as to me to devise ways and means of achieving independence.
>
> There is undoubtedly a party of violence in the country. It is growing in strength. It is as patriotic as the best among us. What is more, it has much sacrifice to its credit. In daring it is not to be surpassed by any of us. It is easy enough to fling unkind adjectives at its members, but it will not carry conviction with them. I am not now referring to the frothy eloquence that passes muster for patriotism. I have in mind that secret, silent persevering band of young men and even women who want to see their country free at any cost. But whilst I admire and adore their patriotism I have no faith whatsoever in their method. They and I are as poles asunder. India's salvation does not lie through violence. I am convinced that their methods have cost the country much more than they know or will care to admit. Let them study the Reforms which they claim were a result of their activity. Assuming that their claim is just, let them remember that

the Reforms have cost more than the country could at all pay. But they will listen to no argument however reasonable it may be, unless they are convinced that there is a programme before the country which requires at least as much sacrifice as the tallest among them is prepared to make. They will not be allured by our speeches, resolutions or even conferences. Action alone has any appeal for them. This appeal can only come from non-violent action which is no other than civil resistance. In my opinion it and it alone can save the country from impending lawlessness and secret crime. That even civil resistance may fail and may also hasten the lawlessness is no doubt a possibility. But if it fails in its purpose, it will not be civil resistance that will have failed. It will fail, if it does, for want of faith and consequent incapacity in the civil resisters. This argument may not appeal to the critic. I shall be sorry, if it does not. Even so, he will perhaps admit the purity of my motive.

We must cease to dread violence, if we will have the country free. Can we not see that we are tightly pressed in the coil of violence? The peace we seem to prize is a mere makeshift, and it is bought with the blood of the starving millions. If the critics could only realize the torture of their slow and lingering death brought about by forced starvation, they would risk anarchy and worse in order to end that agony. The agony will not end till the existing rule of spoliation has ended. I would have waited if I could have been convinced that the condition of the masses has undergone progressive amelioration under British rule. Alas, he who runs may see that it has progressively deteriorated under that rule. It is a sin, with that knowledge, to sit supine, and for fear of imaginary anarchy or worse, to stop action that may prevent anarchy, and is bound, if successful, to end the heartless spoliation of a people who have deserved a better fate. —(*YI*, 23-1-30, 28.)

Hatred and ill-will there undoubtedly are in the air. They are bound sooner or later to burst into acts of fury if they are not anticipated in time. The conviction has deepened in me that civil disobedience alone can stop the bursting of that fury. The nation wants to feel its power more even than to have independence. Possession of such power *is* independence.

That civil disobedience may resolve itself into violent disobedience is, I am sorry to have to confess, not an unlikely event. But I know that it will not be the cause of it. Violence is there already corroding the whole body politic. Civil disobedience will be but a purifying process and may bring to the surface what is burrowing under and into the whole body. And British officials, if they choose, may regulate civil disobedience so as to sterilize the forces of violence. But whether they do so, or whether as many of us fear, they will, directly or indirectly, consciously or uncon-

sciously, provoke violence, my course is clear.
With the evidence I have of the condition of the
country and with the unquenchable faith I have
in the method of civil resistance, I must not be
deterred from the course the Inward Voice seems
to be leading me to.　—(*YI*, 23-1-30, 29.)

His instruction to would-be Satyagrahis was :

The Government will spread out its red
paws in what it will call self-defence, the party
of violence may commit the mistake of seeing its
chance of coming out in the open. The non-
violent party must then prove its creed by being
ground to powder between the two millstones.
If there is such a party, all is well for India and
the world. My hope and plans are built upon
an ever-increasing faith in the existence of that
party of true non-violence.　—(*YI*, 6-2-30, 45.)

On the 2nd of March 1930, Gandhi sent a letter
to the Viceroy through a personal envoy, who happened to be an Englishman, in which he recounted
the wrongs which India had suffered from subjection,
and then intimated his resolve to launch the campaign of civil disobedience, if such remedy as lay
within the ruling power's capacity to effect, was not
forthcoming. The last portion of that classic letter
bears quotation in full :

A radical cutting down of the revenue, therefore, depends upon an equally radical reduction
in the expenses of the administration. This
means a transformation of the scheme of Government. This transformation is impossible without

independence. Hence, in my opinion, the spontaneous demonstration of 26th January, in which hundreds of thousands of villagers instinctively participated. To them Independence means deliverance from the killing weight.

Not one of the great British political Parties, it seems to me, is prepared to give up the Indian spoils to which Great Britain helps herself from day to day, often, in spite of the unanimous opposition of Indian opinion.

Nevertheless, if India is to live as a Nation, if the slow death by starvation of her people is to stop, some remedy must be found for immediate relief. The proposed conference is certainly not the remedy. It is not a matter of carrying conviction by argument. The matter resolves itself into one of matching forces. Conviction or no conviction, Great Britain would defend her Indian commerce and interests by all the forces at her command. India must consequently evolve force enough to free herself from that embrace of death.

It is common cause that, however disorganized, and, for the time being, insignificant it may be, the party of violence is gaining ground and making itself felt. Its end is the same as mine. But I am convinced that it cannot bring the desired relief to the dumb millions. And the conviction is growing deeper and deeper in me that nothing but unadulterated non-violence can check the organized violence of the British Government. My experience, limited though it undoubtedly is, shows that non-violence can be an intensely active force. It is my purpose to set in motion that force, as well against the organized violent force of the British rule as the unorganized violent force of the growing party of violence. To sit still would be to give rein to both the forces above mentioned. Having an unquestioning and immovable faith in the efficacy of non-violence, as I know it, it would be sinful on my part to wait any longer.

The non-violence will be expressed through Civil Disobedience, for the moment confined to the inmates of the Satyagraha Ashram, but ultimately designed to cover all those who choose to join the movement with its obvious limitations.

I know that in embarking on non-violence, I shall be running what might fairly be termed a mad risk. But the victories of Truth have never been won without risks, often of the bravest character. Conversion of a Nation that has consciously or unconsciously preyed upon another far more numerous, far more ancient and no less cultured than itself, is worth any amount of risk.

I have deliberately used the word 'conversion'. For my ambition is no less than to convert the British people, through non-violence, and thus make them see the wrong they have done to India. I do not seek to harm your people. I want to serve them, even as I want to serve my own. I believe that I have always served them.

I served them up to 1919 blindly. But when my eyes were opened and I conceived Non-co-operation, the object still was to serve them. I employed the same weapon that I have, in all humility, successfully used against the dearest members of my family. If I have equal love for your people with mine, it will not long remain hidden. It will be acknowledged by them, even as the members of my family acknowledged it after they had tried me for several years. If the people join me, as I expect they will, the sufferings they will undergo, unless the British Nation sooner retraces its steps, will be enough to melt the stoniest hearts.

The plan through Civil Disobedience will be to combat such evils as I have sampled out. If we want to sever the British connection, it is because of such evils. When they are removed, the path becomes easy. Then the way to friendly negotiation will be open. If the British commerce with India is purified of greed, you will have no difficulty in recognizing our Independence. I respectfully invite you then to pave the way for immediate removal of those evils, and thus open a way for a real conference between equals, interested only in promoting the common good of mankind through voluntary fellowship and in arranging terms of mutual help and commerce equally suited to both. You have unnecessarily laid stress upon the communal problems that unhappily affect this land. Important though they undoubtedly are for the consideration of any scheme of government, they have little bearing on the greater problems which are above communities and which affect them all equally. But if you cannot see your way to deal with these evils and my letter makes no appeal to your heart, on the 11th day of this month, I shall proceed, with such co-workers of the Ashram as I can take, to disregard the provisions of the Salt Laws. I regard this tax to be the most iniquitous of all from the poor man's standpoint. As the Independence movement is essentially for the poorest in the land, the beginning will be made with this evil. The wonder is that we have submitted to the cruel monopoly for so long. It is, I know, open to you to frustrate my design by arresting me. I hope that there will be tens of thousands ready, in a disciplined manner, to take up the work after me, and, in the act of disobeying the Salt Act, to lay themselves open to the penalties of a law that should never have disfigured the Statute Book.

I have no desire to cause you unnecessary embarrassment, or any at all, so far as I can help. If you think that there is any substance in my letter, and if you will care to discuss matters with me, and if to that end you would like me to postpone publication of this letter, I shall gladly refrain, on receipt of a telegram to that effect soon after this reaches you. You will, however, do me the favour not to deflect me from my course, unless you can see your way to conform to the substance of this letter.

This letter is not in any way intended as a threat but is a simple and sacred duty peremptory on a civil resister. Therefore, I am having it specially delivered by a young English friend who believes in the Indian cause and is a full believer in non-violence, and whom Providence seems to have sent to me, as it were, for the very purpose. —(HC, I, 374.)

Thus began the Salt Satyagraha of 1930. The public responded in a manner beyond all expectation. Forest laws were also defied, and in numerous localities taxes were also refused. An important feature of the Movement was the picketing of liquor and foreign cloth shops. The Government of India responded by issuing ordinance after ordinance in order to render picketing criminal, with the result that common people everywhere gained fresh opportunity of civil disobedience where taxes had not been suspended or salt could not be manufactured. In accordance with Gandhi's advice, women were largely entrusted with the task of peaceful picketing and persuasion of addicts; and a tremendous wave of enthusiasm swept over the land when women were, for the first time, called upon to share the burden of Satyagraha on a footing of equality with men. During the whole of 1930, more than a hundred thousand men were sent to jail, while Government opened fire in Peshawar, Sholapur, Midnapur and a number of other places in course of which 103 people lost their lives, according to the official estimate. —(HC, I, 410.)

The non-official estimate was however higher ; and some of the reports published by non-official bodies (e.g. regarding Midnapur) were suppressed by the Government.

After a run of about a year, a partial success was registered in the Delhi Pact of March 5, 1931, in which the Salt Regulations were partially relaxed, though no statutory changes were made in the Regulation itself. The British Government now opened negotiation with different political parties in the country ; and on the 29th of August 1931, Gandhi sailed for England to attend the Second Round Table Conference as the sole spokesman on behalf of the Indian National Congress. With the British, he pleaded for

Complete freedom from the alien yoke in every sense of the term, and this for the sake of the dumb millions. Every interest therefore, (he said) which is hostile to their interest, must be revised, or must subside if it is not capable of revision. —(*YI*, 17-9-31, 263.)

The Round Table Conference led nowhere ; and in the plenary session, Gandhi said :

I shall hope against hope, I shall strain every nerve to achieve an honourable settlement for my country, if I can do so without having to put the millions of my countrymen and country-women and even children through this ordeal of fire. It can be a matter of no joy and comfort to me to lead them again to a fight of that character, but if a further ordeal of fire has to be our lot I shall approach that with the greatest joy and with the greatest consolation that I was doing what I felt to be right, the country was doing what it felt to be right, and the country will have the additional satisfaction of knowing that it was not at least taking lives, it was giving lives : it was not making the British people directly suffer, it was suffering. Professor Gilbert Murray told me — I shall never forget that, I am paraphrasing his inimitable language—'Do you not consider for one moment that we Englishmen do not suffer when thousands of your countrymen suffer, that we are so heartless ? ' I do not think so. I do know that you will suffer ; but I want you to suffer because I want to touch your hearts ; and when your hearts have been touched then will come the psychological moment for negotiation. Negotiation there always will be ; and if this time I have travelled all these miles in order to enter upon negotiation, I thought that your countryman, Lord Irwin, had sufficiently tried us through his ordinances, that he had sufficient evidence that thousands of men and women of India and thousands of children had suffered; and that, ordinance or no ordinance, lathis or no lathis, nothing would avail to stem the tide that was onrushing and to stem the passions that were rising in the breasts of the men and women of India who were thirsting for liberty.

Whilst there is yet a little sand left in the glass, I want you to understand what this Congress stands for. My life is at your disposal.

17

The lives of all the members of the Working Committee, the All-India Congress Committee, are at your disposal. But remember that you have at your disposal the lives of all these dumb millions. I do not want to sacrifice those lives if I can possibly help it. Therefore, please remember, that I will count no sacrifice too great if, by chance, I can pull through an honourable settlement. You will find me always having the greatest spirit of compromise if I can but fire you with the spirit that is working in the Congress, namely, that India must have real liberty. Call it by any name you like ; a rose will smell as sweet by any other name, but it must be the rose of liberty that I want and not the artificial product. If your mind and the Congress mind, the mind of this Conference and the mind of the British people, means the same thing by the same word, then you will find the amplest room for compromise, and you will find the Congress itself always in a compromising spirit. But so long as there is not that one mind, that one definition, not one implication for the same word that you and I and we may be using, so long there is no compromise possible. How can there be any compromise so long as we each one of us has a different definition for the same words that we may be using. It is impossible, Prime Minister, I want to suggest to you in all humility that it is utterly impossible then to find a meeting ground, to find a ground where you can apply the spirit of compromise. And I am very grieved to have to say up to now I have not been able to discover a common definition for the terms that we have been exchanging during all those weary weeks.—(*NV*, 108.)

Gandhi reached India on the 28th of December 1931 ; but in the meanwhile events had taken place in the N. W. F. Province, the U. P. and Bengal which proved beyond doubt that the mood of the ruling class had remained unaffected, and they were determined to pursue their policy of repression without respite. Gandhi's request to interview the Viceroy was refused, and the Working Committee accordingly authorized him to renew the Satyagraha campaign. Gandhi himself was arrested on the 4th of January 1932, and within a short time, the prisons of British India were once more filled to overflowing.

During the Salt Satyagraha of 1930-31, the Government had experienced that mere imprisonment with *lathi*-charges, accompanied by a little amount of shooting, was not enough. Heavy fines were therefore imposed on convicted Congressmen and common people were also subjected to punitive taxes. These measures, specially directed against the propertied classes, seemed to have some effect. The number of Congressmen who repeatedly broke the law and offered themselves for conviction, dwindled within a short time ; and a general feeling of frustration began to pervade the atmosphere of the country.

In the meanwhile, great developments were taking place in the offing. While Gandhi was in prison, the British Government did not remain idle. They proposed constitutional reforms based on a broader franchise ; but there was a sinister effort to divide the Hindu population of India into politically exclusive sections by means of separate electorates for 'upper' and 'lower' caste Hindus. The announcement of Premier Macdonald's Communal Award was made on the 17th of August 1932. Gandhi, who was then in detention at the Yeravda prison in Poona immediately undertook 'a fast unto death' unless the whole of India was prepared to do away with the taint of untouchability, and thus indirectly render the Communal Award nugatory. The fast began on the 20th of September 1932, and threw the whole country into the throes of a social revolution. Hindu leaders rushed to Poona, where they met members of the 'untouchable' castes, and gave special undertakings to safeguard the interests of the latter, as an earnest of their desire to remove the stain of untouchability permanently from Hindu society. The Yeravda Pact was signed on the 24th of September, and the contents were cabled to the British Government who had to modify the Award in the light of these new developments. Gandhi then broke his fast in prison.

He was subsequently released in May 1933. In August 1933, civil disobedience was revived once more, and he was again sent to prison for a term of one year. In the previous period of incarceration, special facilities had been granted to him to write for the paper *Harijan*, on social, i.e. non-political matters. But as this privilege was denied in August

1933, he dicided to go on fast ; so the Government released him once more on the 23rd of the same month. Immediately on release, Gandhiji undertook an extensive tour throughout India in order to help the cause of the Harijans. The tour began in November 1933 and ended ten months later.

In the meanwhile, mass civil disobedience had given place to individual civil disobedience in July 1933 ; and this too was ultimately withdrawn in a formal way in May 1934 ; from which period, Gandhi was to remain the sole representative of civil resisters. The movement of civil resistance which had begun in March 1930, thus came to an end after a chequered career of a little over four years.

Crystallization of Ideas and Interests between 1932 & 1935

The Indian National Congress had been fighting for independence, but its main strength still lay in middle class workers. The masses had not been organized to the point when they could, more or less, dominate the political chess-board, although that was the goal set by Gandhi before Congress workers. The sacrifice and sufferings entailed by the civil disobedience movement had evidently not been enough to bring them victory ; so, it was obvious that the coming years should once more be spent in intensive constructive work. As we have seen, Gandhi himself began a drive against untouchability by his all-India tour in November 1933. In the meanwhile, the weekly *Harijan* had been started even while he was in prison ; and the Harijan Sevak

Sangh (first known as the All-India Anti-Untoucha-
bility League, and subsequently as the Servants of
Untouchables Society) was functioning from the end
of 1932.

Congressmen like Jawaharlal had however
become impatient at the turn of events ; for, according
to them, this amounted to side-tracking the struggle
for Swaraj on the political plane. There was a significant exchange of letters between him and Gandhi
in September 1933. Jawaharlal wanted the latter
to define clearly his political objective ; for, as he
said, only a truly inspiring political ideal could enlist
the support of the masses in the national struggle. In
reply, Gandhi wrote that once having fixed the goal,
he was not much interested in its repetition ; but only
in devising means of its progressive realization.
That goal, as we know, was set forth in the *Hind
Swaraj or Indian Home Rule* of 1908 as an exploitation-free society in which the supreme instrument of
defending just rights lay within the grasp of the
common unarmed individual. The clearest appreciation of the goal, wrote Gandhi, would fail to carry
us there if we do not adopt means suited to the end
in view. In a similar context, he had previously
written that he did not want to see the distant view,
for one step was enough for him.

These explanations did not however carry conviction to numerous political workers. But they did
not yet feel self-confident enough to take over full
charge of leadership in the Congress in place of
Gandhiji. And thus, with Jawaharlal's blessings,
the Congress Socialist Party was formally initiated

in October 1934. The first conference of Congress-men with socialistic tendencies was held in May 1934, according to the report of the Organizing Secretary, Shri Jaiprakash Narayan. The object of the Party, among other things, was stated thus : 'We as a Party must participate in the activities of the Congress and consider them our own, except where we disagree with a particular policy of the Congress. At the same time, we must exercise our right as a minority to propagate our views within the Congress, to work along our lines, to criticize and even oppose such policies of the Congress as appear to us to be not in the interests of the masses.'

The Organizing Secretary moreover said : 'The National Congress is the only political organization which has led major struggles against the British imperialism in this country and there is no reason to expect that it will abandon its anti-imperialist task at this stage. I do not imply that the Congress, as it is, is competent to overthrow imperialism. That exactly is our task. We must so develop the Congress that it does become such a body. The alternative of forming such a body outside the Congress means sheer and foolish waste of energy if it were possible to do so. I have not the slightest doubt, that it is possible for us to so influence and change the Congress, as to make it a real anti-imperialist body.'

In the meanwhile, the Yeravda Pact and Gandhi's repeated endeavours to accomodate just Muslim demands led to important developments in a contrary

direction. Gandhi's attitude to the question of
communal relations is first set forth in the following
quotation.

As a Satyagrahi, I believe in the absolute
efficacy of full surrender. Numerically the Hindus
happen to be the major community. But even if
the Hindus were in a minority, as a Satyagrahi
and Hindu, I should say that the Hindus would
lose nothing in the long run by full surrender.
To this argument a retort has thoughtlessly
been made, 'Why then do you not advise India to
surrender to the English ? Give them the
domination they want and be happy.' This hasty
retort ignores the vital fact that I have not
advised surrender to the bayonet. In the code of
the Satyagrahi there is no such thing as surrender
to brute force. Or the surrender then is
a surrender of suffering and not to the wielder
of the bayonet. A Satyagrahi's surrender has to
come out of his strength, not out of weakness.
The surrender advised by me is not of honour
but of earthly goods.—(*YI*, 30-4-31, 92.)

It would be a great thing, a brave thing, for
the Hindus to achieve this act of self-denial.

—(*YI*, 12-3-31, 36.)

Now, this solicitude for Muslim interests, although
it was for the sake of national unity, as well as the
endorsement of the Yeravda Pact, in which, according
to some, injustice had been done to the rights of the
Hindu community on the basis of its numerical
position, led to another kind of division within the

Congress. The Congress Nationalist Party came into being ; while outside, one section of nationalist India organized itself under the Hindu Mahasabha. The Congress Nationalist Party has now ceased to function ; while the Hindu Mahasabha has earned for itself a strong hold among educated Hindus throughout the country.

On a close comparison, the nationalism of the Hindu Mahasabha is found to be of a different order from that of the Indian National Congress. The former contemplates a balance between upper class interests with those of the masses, while in the conception of the latter, as enunciated by Gandhi in England, the interest of the masses will be supreme, others would exist in so far as they subserve the interests of labouring humanity. There is another point of difference also ; but this is not so much with the Congress as with the ideas of Gandhi himself. In the latter's conception of the State, the centre of authority will be changed in a new direction altogether. Whereas power today flows from the centre to the periphery, in a society organized in terms of non-violent strength, it will vest principally with the people. The latter will live in, more or less, self-sufficient groups enjoying a large measure of economic and political autonomy.

As this crystallization of opinions and interests proceeded in Indian politics, Gandhi broke his formal connection with the Congress ; he ceased to be even an ordinary member of the institution. Explaining the reason many years later, he wrote :

It was in 1935 that I was successful in my attempt to sever all formal connection with the Congress. There was no coolness between the Congress Working Committee members and myself. But I realized that I was cramped and so were the members, whilst I was officially connected with the Congress. The growing restraints which my conception of non-violence required from time to time were proving too hard to bear. I felt therefore that my influence should be strictly moral. I had no political ambition. My politics were subservient to the demands of truth and non-violence, as I had defined and practised for practically the whole of my life. And so I was permitted by the fellow members to sever the official connection even to the extent of giving up the four-anna membership. It was understood between us that I should attend the meetings of the Working Committee only when the members required my presence for consultation in matters involving the application of non-violence or affecting communal unity.

—(*GC*, 100.)*

Gandhi after 1923 and 1934

A comparison may now be drawn between the present period following the Civil Disobedience Movement with a similar one after the Non-co-operation Movement. During the years of Non-co-operation, Gandhi had been regarded as a saint rather than as an ordinary statesman. He was capable of

---

*For full contemporary statements, see *H.C*, I, 568, 579.

working political miracles ; and even the best among
men were not always free from a thin strain of such
bias. As a matter of fact, Non-co-operation had served
to release the spirit of the people, as a whole, after a
prolonged period of psychological repression. The
mental reaction had been of the nature of a religious
conversion ; and mass demonstrations had served to
generate the same type of emotional surge as is
usually associated with Revivalist meetings ; only
they were of a more subdued nature because of the
risks involved in disobedience to State ordinances.
The emotional content of the Movement had consequently overshadowed its economic, social or political
implications. This is one of the principal reasons
why Gandhi's constructive programme had been
carried out more as part of a religious routine rather
than a new social experiment whose results had to
be watched with scientific care. Another reason,
already referred to, is that during the ebb which
followed 1924, the followers of Gandhi felt isolated
and cramped between those who advocated Council-
entry on the one hand, and those who prepared for
violent revolution on the other. Pressed between
these two forces, they stuck to their own constructive
programme and struggled ahead with it, often as a
mark of loyalty to their leader and consequently
without allowing their personal experiences to
reshape the programme accordingly. Constructive
work, therefore, yielded results more satisfactory
to the worker personally, as it helped him to transform
his character and bring his life in tune with the life
of the masses. This encouraged orthodoxy ; but,

so far as the organization and stimulation of self-consciousness and self-reliance among the labouring people themselves was concerned, it failed of its purpose ; because that aim was frequently lost sight of.

But after the Civil Disobedience Movement of 1930-34, one great thing happened. Gandhi's advocacy of the Untouchables' cause, his solicitude for Muslim sentiments, were both subjected to hostile criticism ; while socialists submitted his economic programme to keen examination. As a result, Gandhi lost much of his super-human glamour ; in fact, the idol of Gandhi, current so long, was now dethroned and he was definitely secularized. Instead of remaining a miracle worker, he was brought down to the level of a great moral and political leader of mankind, which he truly is. People began to realize that Gandhi could only show the way, but it was up to the people themselves to march if they wanted to win the prize ; and in that march, Gandhi wanted everyone to develop and follow his own light rather than surrender reason even to the highest in the land. In other words, reason and critical examination began to take the place of ortho- doxy ; and there is reason to believe, that none felt happier than Gandhi himself on account of these developments. Gandhi indeed remarked once that he felt sure of his ground when people spat upon him, but he did not know where he stood when they praised him.

In Gandhi himself also, these critical years wrought some amount of significant change. His frequent contact with those who did not believe in non-violence but in violence, his contact with independent thinkers like Jawaharlal, for whom he has ever retained the warmest corner in his heart, the passion with which many Muslims and some Hindus disavowed him, gave him a clearer indication of how things were shaping themselves in the country. The effect upon his own self, sensitive as he is to even slight changes in the environment, must have been deep. This we can infer from a change which came about in his 'theological' belief. Whereas he used to say formerly that 'God is Truth', from a little before 1931, he began to say, 'Truth is God'. The distinction, though subtle, is of a very significant character. With this changed creed, he could easily accommodate as fellow-seekers those who looked on Humanity or any other object as their god, and for which they were prepared to sacrifice their all. By enthroning Truth on the highest pedestal, Gandhi thus truly became a catholic, and lost all trace of separateness from every other honest man who worshipped gods other than his own.

These then were some of the significant signs of change in the evolution of India's political experiences during the years now under review.

Systematization of Constructive Activities

Gandhi's intensive campaign against the social stain of untouchability continued unabated ; but he now began to devote more attention to the all round development of rural economic and cultural life. The All-India Village Industries Association was founded with its headquarters at Wardha on 26th October

1934, and throughout the years 1935 and 1936, the weekly paper *Harijan* came out full of details regarding cheap balanced diets, new and more efficient methods of oil-pressing, carding cotton, the propagation of Hindustani as the common language of national intercourse, and so on. A new orientation took place in the activities of the All-India Spinners' Association in October 1935. Gandhi now desired that the production of khadi should be reorganized in such a manner as to fetch a minimum living wage to spinners and this he suggested was to be eight annas for a working day of eight hours. Spinners were moreover to be encouraged to spin for consumption rather than for sale.

The Gandhi Seva Sangh which had been established earlier to help Congressmen wholly engaged in constructive work with personal financial assistance, was now developed into a larger organization. The most significant feature was that Gandhi wanted all constructive workers to keep sedulously away from elective posts within the Congress. Only then could they do their work with full efficiency, and also secure the co-operation of millions of their countrymen who might be less interested in active politics than in the true economic regeneration of the masses. Unless such a living interest could be created by whole-time constructive workers, freedom of the masses, whether economic or political, would remain a dream either through violence or non-violence.

Working the Reforms

The depression which had set over the country at

the end of 1934 still continued, although it showed signs of lifting in the numerous political or social developments which were taking place in the country. In the meanwhile, the new constitution was forced upon India by the British Government. The franchise was undoubtedly broader than before, but disproportionate importance was given in it to vested economic interests, while little real power was transferred to the elected representatives of the people. The Viceroy was endowed with power to set aside any recommendation of the legislative bodies when he thought fit. He himself was not responsible to the people of India but to the British Parliament ; and he was thus in enjoyment of a position unequalled by crowned heads or even chosen representatives of the people in any other part of the world.

In spite of such severe shortcomings in the Constitution, the Congress ultimately decided to run the elections in February 1937. The result was a sweeping majority in eight out of British India's eleven Provinces. In March 1937, the Congress authorized acceptance of office, but ministries were not to be formed unless assurance was forthcoming from the Provincial Governors that they would not exercise their special statutory powers against the will of the people's representatives. This having been duly received, Congressmen gradually formed their own ministries ; and, as there was now no distinction between ordinary Congressmen who had suffered again and again in jail and those who went into office, the feeling gained ground among the common people that, after all, we could have our own men to run the business of government. The Congress Parliamentary Board was formed in order to co-ordinate and guide the work in various Provinces and Gandhiji's personal guidance and advice were, of course, always available.

The latter wrote :

The Government of India Act is universally regarded as wholly unsatisfactory for achieving India's freedom. But it is possible to construe it as an attempt, however limited and feeble, to replace the rule of the sword by the rule of the majority. The creation of the big electorate of three crores of men and women and the placing of wide power in their hands cannot be described by any other name. Underlying it is the hope that what has been imposed upon us we shall get to like, i.e. we shall really regard exploitation as a blessing in the end. The hope may be frustrated if the representatives of the thirty million voters have a faith of their own and are intelligent enough to use the powers (including the holding of offices) placed in their hands for the purpose of thwarting the assumed intention of the framers of the Act. And this can be easily done by lawfully using the Act in a manner not expected by them and by refraining from using it in the way intended by them.

Thus the Ministries may enforce immediate prohibition by making education self-supporting instead of paying for it from liquor revenue. This may appear a startling proposition, but I hold it perfectly feasible and eminently reasonable. The jails may be turned into reformatories and work-shops. They should be self-supporting and educational instead of being spending and punitive departments. In accordance with the Irwin-Gandhi Pact, of which only the Salt Clause remains still alive, salt should be free for the poor man, but it is not; it can now be free in Congress Provinces at least. All purchases of cotton should be in khadi. The attention should now be devoted more to the villages and the peasantry than to the cities. These are but illustrations taken at random. They are perfectly lawful, and yet not one of them has as yet even been attempted.—(*H*, 17-7-37, 180.)

Seeing that the Congress has gone to the farthest limit and has accepted office, let every Congressman note the power it has taken. Whereas formerly the Ministries were amenable to control of the Governors, now they are under the control of the Congress. They are responsible to the Congress. They owe their status to the Congress. The Governors and the Civil Service though irremovable are yet answerable to the Ministers. The Ministers have effective control over them up to a point. That point enables them to consolidate the power of the Congress, i.e. the people. The Ministers have the whip hand so long as they act within the four corners of the Act, no matter how distasteful their action may be to the Governors. It will be found upon examination that so long as the people remain non-violent, the Congress Ministers have enough freedom of action for national growth.

Congressmen should also realize that there is no other political party in the field to question the authority of the Congress. For the other parties have never penetrated the villages. And that is not a work which can be done in a day. So far, therefore, as I can see a vast opportunity is at the disposal of the Ministers in terms of the Congress objective of Complete Independence, if only they are honest, selfless, industrious, vigilant, and solicitous of the true welfare of the starving millions. No doubt there is great validity in the argument that the Act has left the Ministers no money to spend for the nation-building departments. But this is largely an illusion. I believe with Sir Daniel Hamilton that labour, and not metal, is real money. Labour backed by paper is as good as, if not better than, paper backed by labour. Here are the sentiments of an English financier who has held high office in India. 'The worst legacy we have left to India is a high-grade Service. What has been done cannot be undone. I should now start something independent. Whatever is being done today with "money motive" should in future be based on "service motive". Why should teachers and doctors be paid high salaries ? Why cannot most of the work be done on a co-operative basis ? Why should you worry about capital when there are seven hundred million hands to toil? If things are done on a co-operative basis, which in other words is modified socialism, money would not be needed, at least not in large quantity?' I find this verified in little Segaon. The four hundred adults of Segaon can easily put ten thousand rupees annually into their pockets if only they would work as I ask them. But they won't. They lack co-operation, they do not know the art of intelligent labour, they refuse to learn anything new. Untouchability blocks the way. If someone presented them with one lac of rupees, they would not turn it to account. They are not responsible for this state of affairs. We the middle class are. What is true of Segaon is true of other villages. They will respond by patient effort as they are responding in Segaon though ever so slowly. The State, however, can do much in this direction without having to spend a single pie extra. The State officials can be utilized for serving the people instead of harassing them. The villagers may not be coerced into doing anything. They can be educated to do things which enrich them morally, mentally, physically and economically.—(H, 24-7-37, 188.)

When the Congress entered office, the programme of mass uplift was taken up in earnest, and a fair amount of progress was made during the two years and odd months in which office was altogether held. Substantial relief was secured to the peasantry by a revision of laws relating to tenancy and debts in the U. P., Bombay and Orissa and through prohibition in both Bombay and Madras.*

In spite of their achievements, the impression left was that the Congress Ministries did not do all that could have been done. In some places, force was called upon to quell communal or labour disturbances. This called forth Gandhiji's severe criticism, for he wanted the Ministers and other Congressmen to tackle every situation non-violently, and if necessary to lay down their lives in the attempt. In a few cases, Ministers became more readily involved in settling middle class unemployment problems, than in the chronic and extreme forms of underemployment prevailing among the toiling millions. In April 1938, 'Jawaharlal wrote Gandhi about his distress regarding "the turn of events taken in Congress politics. They are trying to adapt business far too much to the old order and trying to justify it. We are apt to be misled by the illusion that we possess power." '—(*Gandhiji*, 464.)

Thus, although, on the whole, the results of office acceptance were not disappointing, but definitely encouraging in parts, it should be pointed out that the real weakness revealed by this venture lay in the fact that Congressmen were found prone to slide back into power politics. It was also clear that the masses had not yet been organized to the extent when they could check abuse of power among their representatives at the Centre.

* See H. C. Mookerjee : *Congress and the Masses* (1945). and Professor Horace Alexander : *Congress Rule in India* issued by the Fabian Research Bureau, 1938.

However as that may be, the period of two years and few months was too short for any real test of Congressmen's organizational powers. In the meanwhile, the World War began in September 1939 ; and it very soon became evident that the wishes of the people's representatives would be of no avail when they came into conflict with immediate Imperial interests. When this was duly realized, the Congress felt that any further continuance in office would serve no useful purpose. The Ministers were accordingly called back in October 1939, when Gandhi advised every Congressman to devote himself whole-heartedly and energetically to making the villages self-sufficient with regard to food and clothing in order to tide over the difficult times which, he foresaw, were lying not very far ahead.

Congress 1939-42

Late in July 1939, Gandhi had tried to send the following appeal addressed to Hitler :

Friends have been urging me to write to you for the sake of humanity. But I have resisted their request because of the feeling that any letter from me would be an impertinence. Something tells me that I must not calculate and that I must make an appeal for whatever it may be worth.

It is quite clear that you are today the one person in the world who can prevent a war which may reduce humanity to the savage state. Must you pay that price for an object, however worthy it may appear to you to be ? Will you listen to the appeal of one who has deliberately shunned the method of war not without considerable success ?

Anyway I anticipate your forgiveness, if I have erred in writing to you. —(*H*, 9-9-39, 265.)

When the war actually broke out on the 3rd of September 1939, Gandhi expressed his sympathy for the anti-Axis powers, when he said :

I have come to the conclusion that Herr Hitler is responsible for the war. I do not judge his claim. It is highly probable that his right to incorporate Danzig in Germany is beyond question, if the Danzig Germans desire to give up their independent status. It may be that his claim to appropriate the Polish Corridor is a just claim. My complaint is that he will not let the claim be examined by an independent tribunal. —(*H*,16-9-39, 272.)

The Working Committee met immediately after at Wardha and invited 'the British Government to declare in unequivocal terms what their war aims were in regard to democracy and imperialism and the new order that was envisaged, in particular, how these aims were going to apply to India and to be given effect to in the present.' The Resolution also stated :

The Congress has further laid down that the issue of war and peace for India must be decided by the Indian people, and no outside authority can impose this decision upon them, nor can the Indian people permit their resources to be exploited for imperialist ends. Any imposed decision, or attempt to use India's resources, for purposes not approved by them, will necessarily have to be opposed by them. If co-operation is desired in a worthy cause, this cannot be obtained by compulsion and imposition, and the Committee cannot agree to the carrying out by the Indian people of orders issued by external authority. Co-operation must be between equals by mutual consent for a cause which both consider to be worthy. The people of India have, in the recent past, faced great risks and willingly made great sacrifices to secure their own freedom and establish a free democratic state in India, and their sympathy is entirely on the side of democracy and freedom. But India cannot associate herself in a war said to be for democratic freedom when that very freedom is denied to her, and such limited freedom she possesses taken away from her.

A free democratic India will gladly associate herself with other free nations for mutual defence against aggression and for economic co-operation. She will work for the establishment of a real world order based on freedom and democracy, utilizing the world's knowledge and resources for the progress and advancement of humanity.

—(CB, 25-9-39, 9-11.)

This however was not an attitude with which Gandhi could fully agree. Shortly after, he consequently wrote :

Though I have failed with the Working Committee in persuading them, at this supreme moment, to declare their undying faith in non-violence as the only sovereign remedy for saving mankind from destruction, I have not lost the hope that the masses will refuse to bow to the Moloch of war but will rely upon their capacity for suffering to save the country's honour.

—(*H*, 30-9-39, 285.)

My line is cast. Whether I act as a humble guide of the Working Committee or, if I may use the same expression, without offence, of the Government, my guidance will be for the deliberate purpose of taking either or both along the path of non-violence, be the step ever so imperceptible. I would not serve the cause of non-violence, if I deserted my best co-workers because they could not follow me in an extended application of non-violence. I therefore remain with them in the faith that their departure from the non-violent method will be confined to the narrowest field and will be temporary.

—(*H*, 30-9-39, 288.)

The Congress (he said) will be lost in the crowd if it wears the same old outworn armour that the world is wearing today.

—(*H*, 14-10-39, 304.)

The Working Committee Manifesto was answered by the Viceroy in a statement which, according to Gandhi, 'simply shows that the old policy of divide and rule is to continue. The Congress will have to go into the wilderness again before it becomes strong and pure enough to reach its objective.'—(*H*, 21-10-39, 309.)

Accordingly, the Working Committee met once more at Wardha and Ministers in the Provinces were asked to tender their resignation. This fact has already been referred to. But some, like Mr. M. N. Roy, questioned the wisdom of the step, holding that it was necessary for the Ministers to continue in office for 'the very useful purpose of defending the maximum possible civil liberties against the operation of the Defence of India Act.' 'The Working Committee (Mr. M. N. Roy wrote to Gandhiji) is being driven in the direction of a struggle for which, you are so decidedly of the opinion, the country is not prepared.'—(*H*, 18-11-39, 342.)

After the fall of France, the Congress revised its position and with rare independence of judgment absolved Gandhiji from the charge with which he had been entrusted of leading the country in civil resistance.

The Working Committee meeting was held at Wardha in June 17-21, 1940 when a statement on the political situation was issued, which said in part :

While the Working Committee hold that the Congress must continue to adhere strictly to the principle of non-violence in their struggle for independence, the Committee cannot ignore the present imperfections and failings in this respect of the human elements that they have to deal with, and the possible dangers in a period of transition and dynamic change, until the Congress has acquired non-violent control over the people in

adequate measure and the people have imbibed
sufficiently the lesson of organized non-violence.
The Committee have deliberated over the problem
that has thus arisen and have come to the conclusion that they are unable to go the full length
with Gandhiji. But they recognize that he
should be free to pursue his great ideal in his own
way and therefore absolve him from responsibility for the programme and activity which
the Congress has to pursue under the conditions
at present prevailing in India and the world in
regard to external aggression and internal dis-
order.—(*CB*, 18-7-40, 6.)

The Working Committee then made a conditional
offer in its Resolution, dated July 7, 1940, of
'throwing in full weight in the efforts for the
effective organization of the Defence of the country',
if a National Government was constituted at the
Centre without delay. This resolution was ratified
subsequently at Poona on July 27, 1940.—(*CB*, 18-7-
40, 9 and *CB*, 7-9-40, 6.)* On this Gandhi wrote :

The help that the Congress in its latest
resolution promises to give is material and for
a consideration, eminently just, no doubt, but it
is not and cannot be unconditional. I do not
suggest that this position is either untenable or
morally wrong. The Resolution has dignity because it is the considered opinion of the majority.
But by passing it the Congress has, in my opinion,
surrendered the prestige it had or was supposed
to have. Many Congressmen say that while

* See appendix to this chapter.

they firmly believed that they could attain
Swaraj through non-violence, they had never
meant it to be understood that they could retain
it also through non-violence. The entire outside
world, however, believed that the Congress was
showing the golden way to the abolition of war.
No one outside India ever dreamed that, if the
Congress could wrest Independence from a mighty
power like Britain purely through non-violence,
it would not be able to defend it also by the
same means.—(*H*, 18-8-40, 249.)

The Poona offer of the Congress did not however
succeed in eliciting favourable response from the
Government, and so within a short time, Gandhi's
services were once more requisitioned for leading
the country in civil resistance. This happened in
Bombay on the 16th of September 1940.

The new Resolution stated :

In order to end the deadlock in India and
to promote the national cause, in co-operation
with the British people, the Working Committee,
even at the sacrifice of Mahatma Gandhi's co-
operation, made a proposal to the British Government in their Delhi Resolution of July 7,
which was subsequently approved by the A. I.
C. C. at Poona. This proposal was rejected by
the British Government in a manner which left
no doubt that they had no intention to recognize
India's independence, and would, if they could,
continue to hold this country indefinitely in
bondage for British exploitation. This decision

of the British Government shows that they will impose their will upon India, and their recent policy has further shown that they will not even tolerate free expression of public opinion in condemnation of their associating India in the war against Germany, against the will of a vast body of the people of India, and of exploiting her national resources and man-power for this purpose.

The A. I. C. C. cannot submit to a policy which is a denial of India's natural right to freedom, which suppresses the free expression of public opinion and which would lead to the degradation of her people and their continued enslavement. By following this policy the British Government have created an intolerable situation, and are imposing upon the Congress a struggle for the preservation of the honour and the elementary rights of the people. The Congress is pledged under Gandhiji's leadership to non-violence for the vindication of India's freedom. At this grave crisis in the movement for national freedom, the All India Congress Committee, therefore, requests him to guide the Congress in the action that should be taken. The Delhi resolution, confirmed by the A. I. C. C. at Poona, which prevented him from so doing, no longer applies. It has lapsed.—(*CB*, 24-10-40, 4.)

At the same meeting of the A. I. C. C. Gandhi who was present by invitation, unfolded his plan of action thus :

I do not want to hurl civil disobedience or anything in the face of the Government without making my meaning clear. In order completely to clarify our position, I propose to approach the Viceroy with a request that he will be good enough to see me, and I have no doubt that he will. I shall strain every nerve to avoid Satyagraha in your name. What shape it will take, when it comes, I do not know. But I know that there will be no mass civil disobedience, because mass civil disobedience is not required for this occasion.—(*H*, 29-9-40, 304.)

Gandhi began correspondence with the Viceroy in which all the demand that was made on behalf of the Congress was for freedom of speech and pen. In his interview with the Viceroy, he explained the whole position very clearly.

I told His Excellency in the plainest words possible that the Congress had no desire to mount to power at the expense of a single national interest. It seeks no power save for the whole nation. Therefore he will have no opposition from the Congress if he forms a cabinet composed of representatives of different parties. The Congress would be content to be in opposition so far as the war effort is concerned and so long as the machinery of Government has to subserve Imperialist ends. The immediate issue is not independence. The immediate issue is the right of existence, i.e. the right of self-expression which, broadly put, means free speech. This the

Congress wants not merely for itself, but for all, the only restraint being complete observance of non-violence.—(*H*, 13-10-40, 324.)

When negotiations failed, Gandhi started Individual Civil Disobedience with Satyagrahis who were chosen from all provinces of India. These Satyagrahis were to march from their respective stations on foot towards Delhi while they repeated the following slogan before the people whom they met :

It is wrong to help the British war effort with men or money. The only worthy effort is to resist all war with non-violent resistance.

—(*CB*, 8-1-42, 87.)

In his instruction to Satyagrahis, Gandhiji said :

Congressmen should make it clear in their speech and their action that they are neither pro-fascists nor pro-Nazis but that they are opposed either to all war or at least to the war conducted on behalf of British Imperialism. They sympathise with the British in their effort to live but they want also to live themselves as members of a fully free nation. They must not therefore be expected to help Britain at the cost of their own liberty. They bear ill will to no nation. They want to play their part in establishing lasting peace in the world.

—(*CB*, 8-1-42, 89.)

Within about one year from October 1940, when Shri Vinoba, the first Satyagrahi started the campaign, 23,223 persons were sent to prison all over India, and fines to the exent of nearly five lacs and a half rupees were imposed. On October 30th, 1941,

Gandhi reviewed the whole situation and issued a very important statement (*CB*, 8-1-42, 46.) The *Harijan* had already been suspended after the issue of November 10th, 1940, for the Government would not allow any news about Satyagraha being published without previous censoring.

In that statement, Gandhi said that he had come to realize that Congressmen who had joined in the Satyagraha were mostly not opposed to war because of their faith in non-violence, but because they wanted to force the British Government to yield favourable terms so that they might join in the war against the Axis Powers. But, as he was opposed to all war, and that in terms of non-violence, it was not possible for him to carry on Individual Civil Disobedience any more in the name and on behalf of the Congress. The Satyagraha was accordingly withdrawn, and Gandhi immediately devoted himself to the organization of the country in terms of non-violence with rare energy.

The *Harijan* was started once again on 18-1-42, and he placed before the country a fuller programme of constructive activities, because that alone could save the nation from the very dark days which were looming ahead. (See for instance *H*, 12-4-42, 112.) He wrote in the first issue of the *Harijan* :

My resistance to war does not carry me to the point of thwarting those who wish to take part in it. I reason with them. I put before them the better way and leave them to make the choice.—(*H*, 18-1-42, 4.)

Rangoon fell early in March 1942, and the British Government sent Sir Stafford Cripps to India with an offer of political settlement because, as the British Government stated, 'The crisis in the affairs of India arising out of the Japanese advance has made the British wish to rally all the forces of Indian life to guard their land from the menace of the invader'. (See *Gandhiji*, 473.) The terms were found unacceptable by all parties in India without exception, with the result that Cripps had to go back home disappointed, after a month's sojourn in the country.

The political horizon was dark all around ; and in a frantic effort to save the Empire even without the co-operation of the nationalist forces in the country, the Government plunged the people into economic destitution by buying up all its resources and diverting every available labour for war purposes by a disastrous form of monetary policy. The famine of 1943 was foredoomed to come ; for it did not lie within the powers of a Government interested in the preservation of its imperial interests to marshall the willing co-operation of the people of India in order to stem its tide. The latter were no longer interested in preserving the chains which held them in subjection. This was the mental state of common people. Gandhi described the situation in his letter to Generalissimo Chiang Kai-Shek in August 1942 in the following terms :

Many, like me, feel that it is not proper or manly to remain in this helpless state and allow events to overwhelm us when a way to effective action can be open to us. They feel, therefore, that every possible effort should be made to ensure independence and that freedom of action which is so urgently needed. This is the origin of my appeal to the British power to end immediately the unnatural connection between Britain and India.

Unless we make that effort, there is grave danger of public feeling in India going into wrong and harmful channels. There is every likelihood of subterranean sympathy for Japan growing simply in order to weaken and oust British authority in India. This feeling may take the place of robust confidence in our ability never to look to outsiders for help in winning our freedom. We have to learn self-reliance and develop the strength to work our own salvation. This is only possible if we make a determined effort to free ourselves from bondage. That freedom has become a present necessity to enable us to take our due place among the free nations of the world.—(*GC*, 232.)

Let me sum up my attitude (Gandhi said while discussing the question with a friend). One thing and only one thing for me is solid and certain. This unnatural prostration of a great nation—it is neither 'nations' nor 'peoples'—must cease if the victory of the Allies is to be ensured. They lack the moral basis. I see no difference between the Fascist or Nazi powers and the Allies. All are exploiters, all resort to ruthlessness to the extent required to compass their end.

America and Britain are very great nations, but their greatness will count as dust before the bar of dumb humanity, whether African or Asiatic. They and they alone have the power to undo the wrong. They have no right to talk of human liberty and all else unless they have washed their hands clean of the pollution. That necessary wash will be their surest insurance of success, for they will have the good wishes—unexpressed but no less certain—of millions of dumb Asiatics and Africans. Then, but not till then, will they be fighting for a new order.—(*H*, 14-6-42, 188.)

To the Japanese people, he addressed a letter which was published in the *Harijan* of July 26, 1942, in which he said :

The end and aim of the movement for British withdrawal is to prepare India, by making her free, for resisting all militarist and imperialist ambition whether it is called British Imperialism, German Nazism, or your pattern. If we do not, we shall have been ignoble spectators of the militarization of the world inspite of our belief that in non-violence we have the only solvent of the militarist spirit and ambition. Personally I fear that without declaring the Independence of India the Allied Powers will not be able to beat the Axis combination which has raised violence to the dignity of religion. The Allies cannot beat you and your partners unless they beat you in your ruthless and skilled warfare. If they copy it their declaration that they will save the world for democracy and individual freedom must come to naught. I feel that they can only gain strength to avoid copying your ruthlessness by declaring and recognizing now the freedom of India, and turning sullen India's forced co-operation into freed India's voluntary co-operation.

To Britain and the Allies we have appealed in the name of justice, in proof of their professions, and in their own self-interest. To you I appeal in the name of humanity. It is a marvel to me that you do not see that ruthless warfare is nobody's monopoly. If not the Allies some other power will certainly improve upon your method and beat you with your own weapon. Even if you win you will leave no legacy to your people of which they could feel proud. They cannot take pride in a recital of cruel deeds however skilfully achieved.

Even if you win it will not prove that you were in the right, it will only prove that your power of destruction was greater. This applies obviously to the Allies too, unless they perform *now* the just and righteous act of freeing India as an earnest and promise of similarly freeing all other subject peoples in Asia and Africa.

Our appeal to Britain is coupled with the offer of Free India's willingness to let the Allies retain their troops in India. The offer is made in order to prove that we do not in any way mean to harm the Allied cause, and in order to prevent you from being misled into feeling that you have

but to step into the country that Britain has
vacated. Needless to repeat that if you cherish
any such idea and will carry it out, we will not
fail in resisting you with all the might that our
country can muster. I address this appeal to you
in the hope that our movement may even influence
you and your partners in the right direction and
deflect you and them from the course which is
bound to end in your moral ruin and the reduction of human beings to robots.

The hope of your response to my appeal is
much fainter than that of response from Britain.
I know that the British are not devoid of a sense
of justice and they know me. I do not know you
enough to be able to judge. All I have read tells
me that you listen to no appeal but to the sword.
How I wish that you are cruelly misrepresented
and that I shall touch the right chord in your
heart. Anyway I have an undying faith in the
responsiveness of human nature. On the strength
of that faith I have conceived the impending
movement in India, and it is that faith which has
prompted this appeal to you.—(*H*, 26-7-42, 240.)

Gandhi's Quit-India proposal and the possibility
of a nation-wide civil resistance movement raised
unusual interest, and numerous foreign and Indian
correspondents flocked round him in order to understand fully the implications of the proposal. The
following passages culled from the *Harijan* will
illustrate clearly his own stand as well as that of the
Indian National Congress, where it happened to differ
from his own.

'You desire to have India's freedom in order to help the Allies,' was Mr. Edgar Snow's question, and the last question. 'Will Free India carry out total mobilization and adopt methods of total war ?'

'That question,' said Gandhiji, 'is legitimate but it is beyond me. I can only say Free India will make common cause with the Allies. I cannot say that Free India will take part in militarism or choose to go the non-violent way. But I can say without hesitation that if I can turn India to non-violence I will certainly do so. If I succeed in converting 40 crores of people to non-violence, it will be a tremendous thing, a wonderful transformation.'

'But you won't oppose a militarist effort by civil disobedience ?' Mr. Snow pertinently asked.

'I have no such desire. I cannot oppose Free India's will with civil disobedience, it would be wrong.'—(H, 19-7-42, 234.)

'But,' asked a friend, 'have we not to see that the remedy may not be worse than the disease ? There will be, in the course of the resistance, in spite of all our will to prevent them, clashes and resultant anarchy. May not that anarchy be worse than the present anarchy which you have called ordered anarchy ?'

'That is a very proper question. That is the consideration that has weighed with me all these 22 years. I waited and waited until the country should develop the non-violent strength necessary to throw off foreign yoke. But my attitude has now undergone a change. I feel that I cannot afford to wait. If I continue to wait I might have to wait till doomsday. For the preparation that I have prayed for and worked for may never come, and in the meanwhile I may be enveloped and overwhelmed by the flames that threaten all of us. That is why I have decided that even at certain risks which are obviously involved, I must ask the people to resist the slavery. But even that readiness, let me assure you, depends on the non-violent man's unflinching faith. All I am conscious of is that there is not a trace of violence in the remotest corner of my being, and my conscious pursuit of *ahimsa* for the last 50 years cannot possibly fail me at this crisis. The people have not my *ahimsa*, but mine should help them. There is ordered anarchy around and about us. I am sure that the anarchy that may result because of the British withdrawal or their refusal to listen to us and our decision to defy their authority will in no way be worse than the present anarchy. After all, those who are unarmed cannot produce a frightful amount of violence or anarchy, and I have a faith that out of that anarchy may arise pure non-violence. But to be passive witness of the terrible violence that is going on, of the terrible anarchy that is going on in the name of resisting a possible foreign aggression, is a thing I cannot stand. It is a thing that would make me ashamed of my *ahimsa*. It is made of sterner stuff.—(*H*, 7-6-42, 184.)

'Would a Free India declare war against Japan ?'

'Free India need not do so. It simply becomes the ally of the Allied Powers, simply out of gratefulness for the payment of a debt, however overdue. Human nature thanks the debtor when he discharges the debt.'

'How then would this alliance fit in with India's non-violence ?'

'It is a good question. The *whole* of India is not non-violent. If the whole of India had been non-violent, there would have been no need for my appeal to Britain, nor would there be any fear of a Japanese invasion. But my non-violence is represented possibly by a hopeless minority, or perhaps by India's dumb millions who are temperamentally non-violent. But there too the question may be asked : "What have they done ?" They have done nothing, I agree ; but they may act when the supreme test comes, and they may not. I have no non-violence of millions to present to Britain, and what we have has been discounted by the British as non-violence of the weak. And so all I have done is to make this appeal on the strength of bare inherent justice, so that it might find an echo in the British heart. It is made from a moral plane, and even as they do not hesitate to act desperately in the physical field and take grave risks, let them for once act desperately on the moral field and declare that India is independent today, irrespective of India's demand.—(*H*, 14-6-42, 187.)

Q. Would that Indian national Government permit the United Nations to use Indian territory as a base of military operations against Japan and other Axis powers ?

A. Assuming that the national Government is formed and if it answers my expectations, its first act would be to enter into a treaty with the United Nations for defensive operations against aggressive powers, it being common cause that India will have nothing to do with any of the Fascist powers and India would be morally bound to help the United Nations.

Q. What further assistance would this Indian national Government be ready to render the United Nations in the course of the present war against the Fascist aggressors ?

A. If I have any hand in guiding the imagined national Government, there would be no further assistance save the toleration of the United Nations on the Indian soil under well-defined conditions. Naturally there will be no prohibition against any Indian giving his own personal help by way of being a recruit $\frac{or}{and}$ of giving financial aid. It should be understood that the Indian army has been disbanded with the withdrawal of British power. Again if I have any say in the councils of the national Government, all its power, prestige and resources would be used towards bringing about world peace. But

of course after the formation of the national
Government my voice may be a voice in the
wilderness and nationalist India may go war-mad.
—(H, 14-6-42, 188.)

Q. But what about your non-violence ? To
what extent will you carry out your policy after
freedom is gained ?

A. The question hardly arises. I am using
the first personal pronoun for brevity, but I am
trying to represent the spirit of India as I conceive it. It is and will be a mixture. What
policy the national Government will adopt I
cannot say. I may not even survive it much as
I would love to. If I do, I would advise the
adoption of non-violence to the utmost extent
possible and that will be India's great contribution
to the peace of the world and the establishment
of a new world order. I expect that with the
existence of so many martial races in India, all
of whom will have a voice in the government of
the day, the national policy will incline towards
militarism of a modified character. I shall
certainly hope that all the effort for the last
twenty-two years to show the efficiency of non-
violence as a political force will not have gone in
vain and a strong party representing true non-
violence will exist in the country. In every case
a free India in alliance with the Allied Powers
must be a great help to their cause, whereas India
held in bondage as she is today must be a drag

upon the war-chariot and may prove a source of real danger at the most critical moment.

—(*H*, 21-6-42, 197.)

The vast majority won't be believers in non-violence. The Congress does not believe in non-violence as a creed. Very few go to the extreme length I do. The Maulana and Pandit Nehru 'believe in offering armed resistance.' And I may add so do many Congressmen. Therefore, whether in the country as a whole or in the Congress, I shall be in a hopeless minority. But for me even if I find myself in a minority of one my course is clear. My non-violence is on its trial. I hope I shall come out unscathed through the ordeal. My faith in its efficacy is unflinching. If I could turn India, Great Britain, America and the rest of the world including the Axis Powers in the direction of non-violence I should do so. But that feat mere human effort cannot accomplish. That is in God's hands. For me, 'I can but do or die'.—(*H*, 9-8-42, 262.)

The above passages show very clearly how Gandhi was led to formulate the Quit-India Demand and plan a civil resistance movement if it was not conceded. All this was done in accordance with the reality of the Indian situation. By this means he proposed to canalize the rising tide of bitterness against the ruling power into a healthy direction ; otherwise there was every likelihood of its breaking forth in the form of a cowardly welcome to Japanese forces, which would have been nothing short of a national disaster, in the opinion of Gandhiji. The latter's remarkably statesmanly proposal galvanized the spirit of the nation, and the All India Congress Committee accordingly passed its fateful resolution at Bombay on the 8th of August 1942. Only a small number of Communist Congressmen opposed, but the rest of that vast gathering voted in a body and placed full powers in the hands of Gandhi.

On the 7th of August 1942, Gandhi said in course of his speech :

Never believe that the British are going to lose the war. I know they are not a nation of cowards. They will fight to the last rather than accept defeat. But suppose, for strategic reasons they are forced to leave India as they had to leave Malaya, Singapore and Burma, what shall be our position in that event ? The Japanese will invade India, and we shall be unprepared. Occupation of India by the Japanese will mean too the end of China and perhaps Russia. I do not want to be the instrument of Russia's or China's defeat. Out of this agony has emerged the proposal for British withdrawal. It may irritate the Britishers today and they may even look upon me as their enemy. But some day they will say that I was their true friend.—(*GC*, 141.)

When the resolution was passed, he said in course of the concluding English speech on 8th August 1942 :

I have been the author of the non-embarrassment policy of the Congress and yet today you
find me talking in strong language. My non-
embarrassment plea, however, was always qualified
by the proviso, 'consistently with the honour
and safety of the nation'. If a man holds me by
the collar and I am drowning, may I not struggle
to free myself from the stranglehold ?   Therefore
there is no inconsistency between our earlier
declarations and our present demand.   I have
always recognized a fundamental difference
between Fascism and the Democracies, despite
their many limitations, and even between Fascism
and British imperialism which I am fighting.
Do the British get from India all they want ?
What they get today is from an India which
they hold in bondage. Think, what a difference
it would make if India were to participate in the
war as a free ally.   That freedom, if it is to come,
must come today.   For she will utilize that
freedom for the success of the Allies, including
Russia and China.   The Burma Road will once
more be opened, and the way cleared for
rendering really effective help to Russia.

Englishmen did not die to the last man in
Malaya or on the soil of Burma. They effected
instead, what has been described as a 'masterly
evacuation'.   But I cannot afford to do that.
Where shall I go, where shall I take the forty
crores of India ?   How is this mass of humanity
to be set aflame in the cause of world deliverance

unless and until it has touched and felt freedom ?
Today there is no life in them. It has been
crushed out of them. If lustre has to be
restored to their eyes, freedom has to come not
tomorrow but today. Congress must therefore
pledge itself to do or die.—(*GC*, 141.)

The next morning, however, the whole of
Congress India found itself behind prison bars.

From jail, Gandhi tried to explain once more the
genesis of the Quit-India Resolution and to justify
the Congress, in a series of letters addressed to the
Government of India and to Lord Samuel who had
wrongly represented the Congress position in the
British Parliament. These letters published in the
form of a book will remain a most important historical document not only with regard to the Congress
case, but also as it reveals how Gandhi has been
consistently trying to work out his plan of non-
violence through the limitations which the contemporary social atmosphere presented to him, in the
midst of a period of extraordinary confusion of ideals
through which the world was passing in those days.

The first letter which he wrote to the Viceroy was
less than a week after his arrest. He wrote :

The Government of India were wrong in
precipitating the crisis. The Government resolution justifying the step is full of distortions and
misrepresentations. That you had the approval
of your Indian 'colleagues' can have no significance, except this that in India you can always
command such services. That co-operation is an

additional justification for the demand of withdrawal irrespective of what people and parties
may say.

The whole Congress movement was intended
to evoke in the people the measure of sacrifice
sufficient to compel attention. It was intended
to demonstrate what measure of popular support
it had.

The declared cause is common between the
Government of India and us. To put it in the
most concrete terms, it is the protection of the
freedom of China and Russia. The Government
of India think that freedom of India is not necessary for winning the cause. I think exactly the
opposite. I have taken Jawaharlal Nehru as my
measuring rod. His personal contacts make him
feel much more the misery of the impending ruin
of China and Russia than I can, and may I say
than even you can. In that misery he tried to
forget his old quarrel with imperialism. He
dreads much more than I do the success of
Nazism. I argued with him for days together.
He fought against my position with a passion
which I have no words to describe. But the
logic of facts overwhelmed him. He yielded
when he saw clearly that without the freedom
of India that of the other two was in great
jeopardy.—(GC, 15,17,19.)

To Lord Samuel, he addressed a letter on the
15th of May 1943, which was however not permitted
to reach its destination by the Government. There
he said :

Neither the Congress, nor any other organization can possibly kindle mass enthusiasm for the Allied cause without the present possession of independence, to use your own expression either *de jure* or *de facto*. Mere promise of future independence cannot work that miracle. The cry of 'Quit India' has arisen from a realization of the fact that if India is to shoulder the burden of representing, or fighting for the cause of mankind, she must have the glow of freedom now. Has a freezing man ever been warmed by the promise of the warmth of sunshine coming at some future date ?   —(*GC*, 99.)

To the Additional Secretary of the Government of India, Home Deparment, he wrote on the 15th of July 1943 :

Young and impatient Congressmen and even elder men have not hesitated at times to press me to hasten the mass movement. But I, who knew better, always restrained their ardour, and I must gratefully admit that they gladly submitted to the restraint.—(*GC*, 120.)

Again,

There is no necessary inconsistency between the genuine belief that an acceptance of the Congress demand would help the cause of the United Nations, i.e. of democracy all the world over and a mass movement (which moreover was merely contemplated) to paralyse the administration on non-acceptance of the Congress demand. It is submitted that the attempt 'to paralyse the administration' on non-acceptance proves the genuineness of the demand. It sets the seal on its genuineness by Congressmen preparing to die in the attempt to paralyse an administration that thwarts their will to fight the combine against democracy.

For me, I am as much opposed to all war today as I was before a year or more. I am but an individual. All Congressmen are not of that mind. The Congress will give up the policy of non-violence today, if it can achieve India's freedom by so doing. And I would have no compunction about inviting those who seek my advice to throw themselves heart and soul into the effort to help themselves and thus deliver from bondage those nations that are wedded to democracy. If the effort involves military training, the people will be free to take it, leaving me and those who think with me to our own non-violence. I did this very thing during the Boer War, and in the last war. I was a 'good boy' then, because my action harmonized with the British Government's wishes. Today I am the arch enemy, not because I have changed but because the British Government which is being tried in the balance is being found wanting. I helped before, because I believed in British good faith. I appear to be hindering today because the British Government will not act up to the faith that was reposed in them. My answer to the two questions propounded by the author may sound harsh, but it is the truth, the whole truth and nothing but the truth as God lets me see it.

—(*GC*, 164.)

Gandhi and Congressmen

We have tried to present the reader with rather full evidence in order to show how Gandhi was directing the Congress ever since the beginning of the war, and what was also the exact relation subsisting between him and the institution. Politically, he has never acted except through the Congress ; and, on the other hand, his 'association enables the Congress to pursue the technique of corporate non-violent action.'—(*H*, 2-12-39, 357.)

Gandhi has consistently tried to give due expression to the feelings of the nation in respect of freedom, and this has been along the path of non-violence. Occasionally, Congressmen have become impatient of his methods ; but it has ever been Gandhi's belief that without an economic system based upon non-violence, the isolated exercise of non-violence in the political sphere is bound to end in failure. That has been the reason why he has tried to harness the energy and enthusiasm of the nation along constructive lines. And when the average Congressman has failed him, he has founded expert bodies, under the auspices of the Congress, very often, but working in an autonomous manner, to carry on that part of the programme. Thus the All-India Village Industries Association, the Harijan Sevak Sangh, the Go-seva Sangh, have all come into being one by one.

When the moment of political action has come, Gandhi has never hesitated to take up the responsibility with which the nation has entrusted him. But the demands he has made in respect of non-violence have grown more and more stringent as the nation's strength and spirit of resistance have also shown signs of progress. Indeed it is Gandhi's firm belief that the insistence on non-violence has actually helped the nation to grow from strength to strength ; for violence on the part of the masses would surely have led to defeat and demoralization on their part. Non-violence, according to him, knows no defeat. With his eye upon the organization and development of the masses, he has therefore held fast to the supreme instrument of non-violence. Lately he has written :

Granted that India produced sufficient arms and ammunition and men who knew the art of war, what part or lot will those who cannot bear arms have in the attainment of Swaraj ? I want Swaraj in the winning of which even women and children would contribute an equal share with physically the strongest. That can be under ahimsa only. I would, therefore, stand for ahimsa as the only means for obtaining India's freedom even if I were alone.—(*H*, 3-3-46, 27.)

And so I plead for non-violence and yet more non-violence. I do so not without knowledge but with sixty years' experience behind me.—(*H*, 24-2-46, 20.)

The accumulated experience of the past

thirty years, fills me with the greatest hope that in the adoption of non-violence lies the future of India and the world.   It is the most harmless and yet equally effective way of dealing with the political and economic wrongs of the down-trodden portion of humanity. I have known from early youth that non-violence is not a cloistered virtue to be practised by the individual for his peace and final salvation, but it is a rule of conduct for society if it is to live consistently with human dignity and make progress towards the attainment of peace for which it has been yearning for ages past.—(*GC*, 170.)

In the end, we shall try to describe the relation between Gandhi and Congressmen, through whom he tries to organize his non-violence, by means of a simile, however imperfect our effort may turn out to be.

The life of Gandhi and of Congressmen are like two rivers which flow side by side towards a common goal, viz. the economic and political freedom of the toiling millions of India.   Of these, the stream which represents non-violence descends pure and undefiled from the height of the mountains.   The main stream is enormous in volume compared to it.   The latter has coursed over vast plains, which lay unwatered for ages, and has thus gathered the dust of centuries within its waters.   In times of flood, the two streams, which flow within common banks, coalesce ; but when the floods are low, the big river courses in slow measure, a little away from the clear stream which comes from the mountains. But one feels, that the more the former draws its supply from the latter, the better will it be able to quench the thirst for parched humanity.

The more, therefore, Congressmen are able to work according to the method of non-violence in the reorganization of their economic as well as political life, the better will it be not only for India but for the whole human race.

APPENDIX

As we have seen already, the Congress temporarily parted company with Gandhiji after the A.I.C.C. meeting at Poona in July, 1940. The relation between the latter and the Congress was set forth brilliantly in the speech delivered by the Congress President on the occasion. It is given below in part.

'Before commencing the proceedings Maulana Abul Kalam Azad made a statement explaining the two official resolutions as also the circumstances leading up to the A.I.C.C. meeting at Poona. A summary is given below.

'It is hardly four months and two weeks since we met at Ramgarh but during this short period the world had changed almost out of recognition. This change was not only in respect of outward form but it had almost brought about a revolution in ideas and beliefs. It would not be possible for us not to be affected by all that has happened and, therefore, it becomes our duty to review our own position and take stock of the situation with a view to seeking what changes we should make in our own attitude.

'Two important decisions of the Congress Working Commitee are to be placed before you. One of these is known as the Wardha Statement. Although there is nothing new in it, as it relates to the basic policy of the Indian National Congress, it becomes our duty to consider it as this House represents the Congress.

'It was not at the Wardha meeting in June last that Mahatma Gandhi raised the question of non-violence for the first time. He had raised it two years ago. In September 1938 the All India Congress Committee met at Delhi. At this meeting of the Congress Working Committee Mahatma Gandhi raised the issue of extending the principle of non-violence which the Congress had followed in regard to its internal policy for the last twenty years to other spheres.

'Mahatma Gandhi wanted the Congress at this stage to declare that a free India would eschew all violence and would have no army to defend the country against aggression. The Congress should thus depend entirely upon non-violence for the purpose of dealing with internal disorders and external aggression. Mahatma Gandhi felt that he had to give the message of non-violence to the world and if he could not persuade his own countrymen to accept it, it would be difficult for him to preach it to others. The Congress Working Committee felt

itself unable to accept this position and explained its
difficulties to Mahatma Gandhi. The issue however
did not assume any serious proportions then as the
Munich Agreement postponed war.

'The question was again raised by Mahatma
Gandhi when war broke out in September last. In
November last when Gandhiji went to interview the
Viceroy he asked me and other members of the
Working Committee to relieve him of the responsibility of guiding the Congress policy and leave him
free to pursue in his own way the policy of non-
violence. The Committee, however once again
persuaded Mahatma Gandhi to postpone decision.
At Ramgarh Mahatma Gandhi raised this question
for the third time. On this occasion Mahatma
Gandhi also referred to other weaknesses in the
Congress organization and expressed a desire to be
relieved of responsibility. This came as a shock to
the Working Committee and if I had not practically
forced Mahatma Gandhi to postpone decision of the
issue once again, a crisis would have arisen as early
as at Ramgarh.

'You will thus see that this issue has been hanging
fire for over two years and when we met in Wardha
in June last Mahatma Gandhi wanted the Committee
to make up its mind once for all, as the international
situation had become delicate and he felt that a
decision on such a vital issue could not be postponed
any longer. Even then I tried to persuade Mahatma
Gandhi once again to postpone the matter as I knew
the dangers and the difficulties of a decision. There
is not a soul in the Congress who is not anxious to

go the whole length with Mahatma Gandhi, if he can help it ; but we cannot close our eyes to hard facts. We know that arms and ammunitions have not been able to save the freedom of France, Holland, Belgium and Norway but we also know that human nature even after realizing the futility of armed resistance is not prepared to give up force. We had not the courage to declare that we shall organize a State in this country without an armed force. If we did it would be wrong on our part. Mahatma Gandhi has to give the message of non-violence to the world and, therefore, it is his duty to propagate it but we have to consider our position as the representatives of the Indian Nation meeting in the Indian National Congress. The Indian National Congress is a political organization pledged to win the political independence of the country. It is not an institution for organizing world peace'.—(*CB*, 7-9-40, 2.)

Later on, as we have already seen, the Congress entrusted Mahatma Gandhi at Bombay with the responsibilty of leading the campaign of civil resistance. Describing the first step of that of Individual Civil Disobedience, Gandhiji wrote :

'Let me repeat the issue. On the surface, it is incredibly narrow—the right to preach against war as war or participation in the present war. Both are matters of conscience for those who hold either view. Both are substantial rights. Their exercise can do no harm to the British if their pretention that to all intents and purposes India is an independent country is at all true. If India is very much a dependency in fact, as it is in law, whatever the British get from India can never be regarded as voluntary, it must be regarded as impressed. This battle of life and death cannot be won by impressed levies however large. They may win if they have the moral backing of an India truly regarded as free.

'Non-violent Congress cannot wish ill to Britain. Nor can it help her through arms, since it seeks to gain her own freedom, not through arms but through unadulterated non-violence. And the Congress vanishes if, at the crucial moment, it suppresses itself for fear of consequences or otherwise by ceasing to preach non-violence through non-violent means. So when we probe the issue deep enough we discover that it is a matter of life and death for us. If we vindicate that right all is well with us. If we do not, all is lost. We cannot then win Swaraj through non-violent means.

'I know that India has not one mind. There is a part of India that is war-minded and will learn the art of war through helping the British. The Congress has no desire therefore to surround ammunition factories or barracks and prevent people from doing what they like. We want to tell the people of India that if they will win Swaraj through non-violent means, they may not co-operate militarily with Britain in the prosecution of the war.

'This right of preaching against participation in the war is being denied to us and we have to fight against the denial. Therefore while that right will be exercised only by those whom I may select for the purpose all the other activities of the Congress will continue as before unless the Government interfere with them.

'A question has been asked why, if I attach so much importance to quality, I do not offer civil resistance myself. I have already said that unlike as on previous occasions I do not wish to do so for the very good reason that my imprisonment is likely to cause greater embarrassment to the authorities than anything else the Congress can do. I want also to remain outside to cope with any contingency that may arise. My going to jail may be interpreted as a general invitation to all Congressmen to follow suit. They will not easily distinguish between my act and speech. Lastly I do not know how things will shape. I myself do not know the next step. I do not know the Government plan. I am a man of faith. My reliance is solely on God. One step is enough for me. The next He will make clear to me when the time for it comes. And who knows that I shall not be an instrument for bringing about peace not only between Britain and India but also between the warring nations of the earth. This last wish will not be taken for vanity by those who believe that my faith is not a sham but a reality greater than the fact that I am penning these lines'. —(*CB*, 8-1-42, 5.)

At the end of the Individual Civil Disobedience Movement, Gandhiji issued a review of the situation, in course of which he wrote :

'It is true that some of those who have been discharged are reluctant to go back. There is no shame

or harm in unavoidable delay. Hypocrisy and camouflage must be avoided at all cost. In Satyagraha
there is no waste of men or time or labour provided
that *Satya* is adhered to in its entirety. I can otherwise utilize the services, as true soldiers of Truth,
of men and women, who will whole-heartedly carry
out instructions. Thus those who cannot for some
just reason court imprisonment, should engage themselves in corporate constructive activity. Difficulty
arises because many Congressmen though they profess
to believe in C.D. have no faith in the constructive
programme. I must proclaim from the housetop for
the thousandth time that constructive programme is
an integral part of the national movement and
therefore also of the C.D. C.D. without the backing
of the constructive programme is criminal and a waste
of effort. All cannot go to jail. But all must work the
constructive programme. Even in armed conflict
armies are powerfully helped by the civil population.
Imagine the fate of the British forces, if their effort
was not co-ordinated with that of the civilians. I
was therefore delighted that there was a wide response from the prisoners and the other Congressmen
this time in the matter of spinning during the spinning carnival. I dare to believe that if Congressmen
were enthusiastic believers in communal unity
and removal of untouchability and the like, there
would be no communal discord and there would be
no antagonism such as it is from Harijans. We are
the makers of our own destiny.

'It has been somewhat justly said that if I am a
good general, I must not grumble about my men.

For I must choose them from the material at my disposal. I plead guilty. But I have qualified my admission by the adverb 'somewhat', for I laid down the conditions from the very inception of the programme of non-violence. My terms were accepted. If from experience it is found that the terms cannot be worked, I must either be dismissed or I must retire. I retired but to no purpose. The bond between Congressmen and me seems to be unbreakable. They may quarrel with my conditions but they will not leave me or let me go. They know that however unskilled a servant I may be, I will neither desert them nor fail them in the hour of need. And so they try though often grumblingly, to fulfil my condition. I must then on the one hand adhere to my conditions so long as I have a living faith in them, and on the other take what I can get from Congressmen, expecting that if I am true, they will someday fulfil all my conditions and find themselves in the enjoyment of full independence such as has never before been seen on earth'. —(*CB*, 8-1-42, 48.)

IS SATYAGRAHA PLAYED OUT ?

Mr. M. N. Roy has made out a strong case against Satyagraha as a means of gaining Swaraj in terms of the masses in India. His arguments may be briefly summarized thus :

1. Gandhiji imposes certain conditions for the resumption of civil disobedience which are impossible to fulfil : charkha must be there in every Indian home ; non-violence has to be observed in thought, word and deed. So civil disobedience is practically permanently suspended, it is never going to come again.

2. Gandhism succeeded in 1919 because it fulfilled a historical necessity. We were under repression for a long time, there was not self-confidence enough for an armed rebellion. So the passive resistance movement became popular ; 'it did not risk an open attack, but there was the perspective of defeating the enemy by refusing to have anything to do with him'. The Non-co-operation Movement was thus useful in giving expression to the mixed feelings of revolt and lack of self-confidence which existed at that time. But after 1921, the masses moved forward. The C. D. Movement came, but was repressed by Gandhi on the score of violence. The movement in the States today is also being suppressed on the same account. That means there is a conflict between the revolutionary urge of the masses and Gandhi's leadership

with its particular methods. The masses are today not entirely self-confident, hence his remaining popularity. But things are so shaping themselves that their revolutionary fervour will grow, their confidence in action will also grow, and then they will be able to dispense with the method of non-violent non-co-operation.

Gandhi's methods do not show growth ; they do not adjust themselves to the growing force of revolutionary mentality among the Indian masses. So it ought to be discarded.

Now, this is a strong case, if all of it could be taken as true. So far as the popularity of the movement is concerned, I believe Mr. M. N. Roy has said the right word. But has he stated the correct thing with regard to Satyagraha ? We have a different view ; and because we hold that view, we stick to the method of Satyagraha in spite of reverses. Let us state the reasons briefly for whatever they may be worth.

Satyagraha requires a large amount of mass organization. Gandhi may set certain ideal conditions for its fulfilment ; but we find that in working for those conditions we organize the masses to a very great extent, even if we cannot reach the absolute ideal. Khadi and Harijan work or the spread of primary education has given some political workers in Bengal a means of coming into intimate contact with the masses, a contact which would otherwise have been difficult to establish. From such positions of advantage, workers have often also taken the opportunity of engaging in non-violent action on economic issues, when an opportunity presented itself.

The non-violent method requires us to organize the masses in such a manner that, in the final stages of non-co-operation, they will be able to carry on work without outside aid. They will be trained to remain calm in the face of confiscation of their holdings or the forced sale of their cattle and other belongings. We hope to evoke that measure of courage and determination among them ; so we work along the non-violent way.

We also hold that it will be enough for our purpose if the masses are substantially organized, and remain non-violent in action. On the mental side, we try to explain to them that they must not hate the man who works the imperialist system. He is as much a victim of the system as we are ; so there is no reason for personal hatred. And if we can generate this absence of hatred, even if we cannot generate active love for the enemy, it will be enough for our purpose ; such are Gandhi's specific instructions.

We have faith that long before every man is non-violent in thought, word and deed, Swaraj will come to India. For the Congress worker, however, a higher standard is necessary than that for the masses. The ideal conditions may be necessary for *moksha*, but a lesser measure will do for gaining India's Swaraj. We need not, however, on that account lower the ideal.

This faith is there in us. So when Gandhi suspends movements in Orissa or perhaps also in Travancore, and spreads us out in the villages for intensive constructive work, we only believe he wants us to establish more intimate mass contact as a prelude to direct action in the future. We do not believe that he suspends the Satyagraha movement there for all time to come. Mr. M. N. Roy says, this suspension is really permanent. We think otherwise ; but that is a matter of opinion. And it is because we hold a different opinion that we obey Gandhi even when we may fret for immediate direct action.

But this does not necessarily spring from a blind faith in Gandhi. The Salt Movement came after Non-co-operation, the Civil Disobedience Movement followed the Salt Movement, and some other movement may come again in its due time. And in course of these movements, we have noticed also how the masses have grown more and more fearless, more and more politically conscious. The above movements have given a concrete expression to the revolutionary urge of the masses ; but we do not think they were suppressed at the critical moment. We believe Gandhi has often ordered a retreat for reasons other than the fear of mass violence. In his words : 'Whenever I have suspended civil disobedience I have done so not by reason of any outbreak of violence, but upon the discovery of such violence as has been initiated or encouraged by Congressmen who should have known better'. (*YI*, 29-10-25, 368.) For he holds : 'No organization can be run with success if its members, especially its officers, refuse to carry out its policy and hold on to it in spite of opposition to it'. (*YI*, 28-8-24, 285.) This is not an impossible condition which he imposes upon Congress workers. So we believe that Gandhi has often ordered a retreat before the actual routing took place, and this for organizational defect rather than for fear of mob-violence.

Mr. Roy may say that this reveals lack of self-confidence in us as regards the fighting capacity of the masses. But unfortunately we have had the experience of the masses retreating even though they promised to sacrifice their all in the face of repression. Even violence is not always necessarily successful. Sometimes a hasty step has been known to lead to defeat in the end, whose effects it has been extremely difficult to overcome. It is wrong to under-estimate the strength of the fighters, but it is also wrong to over-estimate it. It is because we consider Gandhi to be a wise general, that we are loyal to him.

But there is another more fundamental reason why we prefer the Gandhian method. And that loyalty to non-violent non-co-operation has come, not from any lurking cowardice within us, but from a particular intellectual judgement. If we win by violence and capture the State, then the party which wins may like to use violence against everyone who disagrees with it. This leads not to democracy but to authoritarianism. By false propaganda among the masses also, it may keep them in darkness and maintain its own position of authority. In the

Gandhian way, the authority of the State is not centralized to the same extent as in the declared way of socialism. Moreover, in the way of non-violent non-co-operation, the State can be won only when the masses have become self-conscious and self-reliant. And if they succeed in the non-violent way, then they will also succeed in keeping abuses of State power in check.

It is this hope ultimately which keeps us loyal to non-violence, even when the prospects of Satyagraha are admittedly dark on all sides. Mussolini claims that the masses are on his side. Hitler too does the same. Stalin surely does that, and in the name of mass-interest drives away all who differ from him. Krupskaya shared hardly any better fate. It is this blind condition of the masses in Europe, who cannot be accused of non-violence in any shape or form, which keeps us in doubt about the usefulness of violence. This is what ultimately leads us to hold on to non-violence intellectually as a better guarantee of democracy than violence, even when we are temperamentally otherwise. But we hope to rule our lives by intellect and not by emotion.

SATYAGRAHA : A DEAD WEAPON

By V. G. Kulkarni

Mr. Nirmal Kumar Bose has attempted to make out a case in favour of "Satyagraha as a means of gaining Swaraj in terms of the masses in India." The article has been written as a reply to Comrade M. N. Roy who, "has made a strong case against Satyagraha." However, the arguments advanced appear not by way of replies to the various points raised by Roy for the purpose, but rather independent of them. In the present most critical period of our struggle for freedom such a discussion of the very "sheet anchor" of the Gandhian Way is most welcome and particularly so when the discussion is carried on a higher level without bringing in persons or personalities, on the merits of the case itself.

Mr. Bose's arguments can be briefly summarized as follows. That Swaraj can be won by non-violent non-co-operation, i. e. Satyagraha. (He nowhere tells how that can be done.) That mass organization is necessary for the purpose and the constructive programme of khadi, Harijan work, spread of primary education etc. are means for establishing mass contact. The masses will be organized in such a way as, in the final stages of non-co-operation, will do without outside aid and will be courageous enough to stand the worst repression. "On the mental side", proceeds Mr. Bose, "they (the masses) must not hate the man who works the imperialist system. As he also is a victim of the same system, it will be enough, if absence of hatred is generated towards the "enemy."

"When Gandhi suspends movements···we only believe he wants us to establish more intimate mass contact as a prelude to direct action. He does not suspend the movement permanently. Whenever he has done so in the past, he has done so not for the fear of mob-violence but for organizational defects. This *faith* is there in us and because we consider Gandhi a wise general, that we are loyal to him."

Lastly comes the "more fundamental reason why we prefer the Gandhian method. If we win by violence and capture the State, then the party which wins may like to use violence. The State can be won non-violently and then alone the abuses of State power can be checked. This is what ultimately leads us to hold on to non-violence intellectually.···"

In the beginning it is necessary for us to state that the common objective is "Swaraj in terms of the masses" and that Swaraj means "winning of State." Once our objective is thus made clear it will be possible to find out whether or not any particular method of struggle will lead us thereto or fall short thereof.

I stretched my eyes and eked my brain to find out whether any way towards the realization of our goal, winning of State, was indicated by Mr. Bose. Except for the declaration that the State can be won by the masses when they become self-conscious etc. nothing more has been stated. Granting that the masses become self-conscious and are sufficiently courageous, how will that bring State power to them ? Self-consciousness and courage are necessary but this psychological equipment will not alone be able to achieve concrete material results which need positive action on the part of the masses. Non-co-operation is a negative weapon incapable of yielding positive results. It will be idle to conceive that the power will come to the masses of itself. Such an idea about State power betrays gross ignorance about the character of the State. State is an organization, created by the dominant classes controlling the means of production in a given phase of society, to safeguard their own interests. It is a system, as admitted by Mr. Bose, an imperialist system for our present purposes. Obviously the system holds its existence by force. Our objective is to get rid of this system. The main question that concerns us is how to do that ?

The usual argument advanced by the advocates of Satyagraha is that, State power can be transferred to the people by the imperialists. This will be achieved by converting the hearts of the enemy by "suffering and sacrifice of the people". But for Mr. Bose this usual argument does not seem to weigh much as he has chosen not to advance it. According to Gandhian tenets all advocates of Satyagraha must believe in possibility of converting the heart of the enemy.

But Mr. Bose states that it is necessary to generate the absence of hatred towards enemy. Somehow he harbours certain misunderstandings that the persons as such, running the imperialist system are held as the enemy. What has led him to hold such utterly mistaken notions, it is difficult to say. But I may tell him that no revolutionary, no politically advanced person will entertain such stupid notions. The imperialist system is the enemy. The individual or group of individuals roped therein are merely incidental, as they may change and do change from time to time. But at the same time they are not victims, as Mr. Bose thinks, but are the conscious supporters of it to safeguard their interests, for which it has been created. If Mr. Bose says that it is not the individual but the system responsible for all the mischief and needs it to be scrapped, what is the way to realize the idea ? Obviously, Mr. Bose may not suggest "absence of hatred" towards the system, the real enemy. There can be no other extreme form of hatred than to work for the removal of a thing out of its existence. And if Mr. Bose does not mean reforming imperialist system, he must work to end it.

Is it necessary to point out that the imperialist system is based on force ? As a matter of fact no State can exist without force ; it is an embodiment of force. Can it, therefore, be removed out of existence without applying force ? Obviously not. It can be removed, it can be defeated only by the creation of superior forces. It has no heart to melt or decide to commit suicide. It knows one thing, to exist, to strive to exist at all costs till it is destroyed by those interested in its destruction. Can Mr. Bose point out any other way to do away with this universally condemned system ?   Let Mr. Bose show, if any.

Mr. Bose raises the bogey of violence as the "more fundamental" reason why he and others stick to non-violence. It would have been surprising if that would not have been raised.   Because violence breeds violence, it is to be tabooed.   Comrade Roy has times without number declared that to presume non-violence and violence as the only two alternatives is utterly mistaken. Those who are opposed to non-violence are not advocates of violence as such.   They abhor violence more than anybody else.   But they are opposed to place the means higher than the end itself.   And consequently do not want to make any irrelevant conditions for the realization of the goal. Gandhian way does that, places the means above the end, makes the end itself unrealizable.   And as the imperialist system holds itself on force, it can be removed by the creation of superior forces only.   As a matter of fact, in the process of this creation of superior forces, the forces of democracy, violence should have no place. Really speaking nowhere does it come in.   But the rise of the forces of democracy signalizes a challenge to the very existence of the imperialist system and therefore it launches a counter-offensive.   Here comes the question of violence. The otherwise peaceful march of the democratic forces is attempted to be crushed violently by the imperialist system. So it is not violence as is wrongly termed, but is the application of force necessary to put down the imperialist

opposition *which is violent*. The tragic history of
Spain should be instructive to us. The forces of
democracy triumphed peacefully. They held the
Parliament, the Spanish Diet, without shedding
a single drop of blood. But the old economic
system which was threatened of extinction revolted
and ultimately defeated democracy *violently*. It is
therefore plain that if you want to fight imperialist
system out of its existence you must be prepared
to apply force necessary for the purpose. It is
another thing how much force will be needed and at
what stage of the struggle it will have to be applied.
But to rule out of order any application of force
is to refuse to march on the only road leading
towards the goal.

The entire basis of Mr. Bose's argument is the
faith in the infallibility of Gandhiji. He has unhesitatingly declared so. He has said that they *believe*
so and so, and *hope* that certain things will
happen and hence loyalty to Gandhiji and non-
violence. But still he concludes that "we hope to
rule our lives by the intellect and not by emotion."
Unfortunately, it is not intellect but faith, I dare say
blind faith, on the authority of Gandhiji himself.
"It is impossible", said Gandhiji, "that a thing essentially of the soul can ever be imparted through the
intellect. It is just like trying to impart faith in God
through the intellect. It cannot be as it is a matter of
heart....*The intellect, if anything, acts as a barrier
in matters of faith.*" (*Harijan*, dated 18-6-38,153.)
"He or she must have a living faith in non-violence.
This is impossible without living faith in God." "If

the Congress can give such a demonstration, (of the virtue of non-violence and the sincerity of their conviction about it.—Author)...the Congress can achieve its goal without a violent struggle, and also without civil disobedience." (*Harijan*, dated 23-10-37, 308.) No further comment is necessary to prove that the whole Satyagraha movement is based on faith. No use arguing about the intellectual appreciation or evaluation of it. I am constrained to repeat what Pandit Nehru said, "I do not see how political movement can be guided in this way." "No great movement can be carried on this basis ; certainly not democratic movement." After laying down certain impossible conditions arbitrarily, to talk of free thinking is either idle or sheer hypocrisy.

The Satyagraha movement has played a useful function when it served to open the channel of popular discontent against imperialism. It simply opened it and stirred it, but did not indicate the way towards the declared aim of destroying the Satanic Government. The semi-religious appeal was useful to stir up the people when there was not sufficient consciousness and the discontent was in its elementary form. It did aim at a conscious revolt against imperialism. But times have changed. There is a tremendous advance in mass consciousness. "Fretting for immediate direct action", even by those refusing to discard Gandhism, is the surest sign of the volume of growing discontent at the bottom. The States People's movement, the workers' and peasants' struggle developing throughout the length and breadth of the country are sufficient proofs for the unprejudiced. Non-violent non-co-operation and civil resistance, these negative weapons, have had their days. But the masses today will not stop at this negative attitude of "suffering and sacrifice" but aim at positive economic and political results. So there is a clash of ideas. Not that the advocates of Satyagraha see this. But they are afraid of violence. Gandhiji breathes violence in the air and considers the atmosphere utterly uncongenial for starting any struggle. It is not the fear of violence, but the onward march of the democratic forces, which will sweep away everything that comes in, even the illogical and irrelevant Gandhian inhibitions, towards the realization of their goal, the capture of power. That is force in action. Gandhism is the negation of this kind of development. Gandhian leadership is conscious of these possible developments and hence the virtual indefinite suspension of Satyagraha. The suspension can therefore, be treated as permanent. The conditions recently laid down by Gandhiji on starting the struggle are beyond fulfilment, besides overruling any form of mass Satyagraha (*Harijan*, New Technique in Action, dated 10-6-39). Such being the case, will it be unfair on the part of revolutionaries to persume that Satyagraha as a weapon in the struggle for freedom, has exhausted its potentialities and also looking to the dynamic situation, pregnant with immense potentialities of mass revolutionary out-breaks, not to be circumvented by the Gandhian limitations, will never be resumed ? Any resumption of Satyagraha, therefore is rendered too remote.

These and such other considerations led Comrade Roy boldly to advocate that the *Bramhastra* is no more useful for our struggle for democratic freedom and as such must be discarded in favour of higher forms of struggle consciously leading towards the capture of power. And those people who refusing to recognize this reality stubbornly sit tight, preventing the march forwards, must also share the same fate.

OUR DIFFERENCES

The way in which Mr. V. G. Kulkarni has tried to show the hollowness of the Satyagrahi's case and establish the socialist one in his article 'Satyagraha : a Dead Weapon' is hardly tainted by considerations other than purely scientific ; and as I read it, our points of agreement and of difference came up all the more clearly before my mind. When two persons draw different conclusions from exactly the same series of facts, it only means that any further talking can never convince each other. Perhaps it is good at such moments to state clearly how we stand in relation to one another.

Let none of us claim that all truth is on his side ; both have our premises to start with. And so far as the premises are concerned, both are logically equally assailable. Whatever a socialist may say about science, his fundamentals are not so much matters of science as of faith ; and the same is true of Satyagraha. I shall take an example. Socialists believe that ultimately victory will come to the working classes. Personally, I have found no justification for this belief in science. As a result of fighting one another, mankind may die out like any of the extinct reptiles without victory ever coming to any one side. The only justification for the belief lies in faith. Similarly, when a Satyagrahi believes that it is possible to replace a world guided by habit by one guided by will, I know it is not science but faith. But I admit the fact that even these faiths of the socialists and of the Satyagrahis do work wonders as long as they are there. They can change the face of humanity although they have no foundation in cold science.

Recognizing this fact as such, I can only refuse to try to change the faith of another man who works best under a different mental atmosphere than what I require for myself. I shall therefore try to enunciate clearly those points of agreement and of difference as have cropped up in course of the two articles in question, before we part company in a friendly spirit. Unfortunately, I do not know if this will be mutual ; at least there will be no lack of it on my part.

1. We agree with Mr. Kulkarni when he says that the State is based on force, and the imperialist State has got to be destroyed by superior exercise of force. The difference lies in the fact that we hold such force can be exercised during the operation of non-violent non-co-operation, which he believes is all bunkum.

2. We quite agree that the State has no soul, and cannot be changed like a human being ; one State has to be replaced by another. Our attitude towards the capitalist State is one of hatred, we want to end it. But we try not to extend this hatred towards those who work the imperialist system, those who, according to Mr. Kulkarni are 'conscious supporters of it to safeguard their interests, for which it has been created.'

We differ from one another clearly in the attitude we bring to bear upon the upholders of imperialism, but are completely in agreement so far as our attitude towards the capitalist State is concerned.

3. Mr. Kulkarni draws a distinction between violence used for selfish ends, as by capitalists, and violence used for defensive purposes, as by the working classes. He holds that the two are different in kind. The former knows no end, while the latter ends when victory is achieved.

We have not the faith that it will end, for the final victory may never come. Violence used for defensive purposes has also been known historically to cause degeneration within the erstwhile exploited or within a party operating on behalf of the exploited. The present Comintern does not seem to be an exception to this rule.

So we prefer to emphasize non-violence as a corrective against violence. Just as Mr. Kulkarni has the faith that defensive violence of the working classes will end the moment complete victory is attained, so also we have the faith that non-violence alone can root out violence, nothing else can.

4. One point which has not been raised by any of us previously may perhaps be profitably discussed here. While reading the *State and Revolution*, it was clear, Lenin recognized that man lives more by habit than by will. So he decided to base his revolutionary tactics upon a radical change of habits, to start with.

But we believe that the good attained in this

manner is temporary. In order to make it permanent, such a plan requires the continuous existence
of a political party, which will keep these habits
at the proper moral level. Otherwise men are
likely to slide back into capitalistic habits once
more. But where is the certainty that the
organization of true men itself will not degenerate?
Many churches—I use the word advisedly—have
been known to degenerate even when they started
with the best of intentions. The belief that the
Comintern itself will never degenerate is not based
on science, but on faith. But it is not worthless
on that account. Let Mr. Kulkarni have that faith;
we shall have our own.

We believe it is better to build upon will than
upon habit for effecting a comparatively more permanent cure. In Satyagraha, a man puts his
reliance not so much upon an organization of Satyagrahis as upon the principle of non-violence, and
in the last heat he has to depend upon himself. It
stimulates the will at the expense of habit. Whether
Satyagraha can operate successfully where large
masses of mankind are concerned may, of course, be
legitimately questioned. But why not try, even if it
seems difficult to break men's habit of doing without
the will? If it is good, it is worth trying.

Thus Satyagraha appeals to us because it is based
upon the appreciation of the active instead of the
passive elements in human character.

This is so far as our points of agreement and difference are concerned. There is only one more point

to which, I shall unwillingly make a reference. In our first article we spoke about a certain faith we have in Gandhi. Mr. Kulkarni has characterized this as a blind faith in the 'infallibility of Mr. Gandhi'. That is hardly doing justice to us. For it is not true that our faith in non-violence is there because we have faith in Gandhiji. It is just because we do not see how violence can end violence, but rather believe that non-violence alone has the power to end violence, and also because we have observed that Gandhiji's actions have been consistently inspired by non-violence, and that for him complete non-violence means the complete extinction of all forms of exploitation, that we still retain faith in him.

Mr. Kulkarni will probably say that Gandhi has betrayed the working classes, diverted or channelled their rising tide of rebellion into useless paths and thus become an ally of capitalism which is completely violent. But here we do not agree. He may have had to retreat now and then; but we still do not doubt that his object is to convert the people of the world into a band of labourers having no room for idlers or exploiters. In it, every man will have to perform bread-labour, and no one will possess anything which others cannot also possess if they need it.

Thus our differences with Mr. Kulkarni lie not merely in certain fundamental beliefs but also with regard to our opinion about facts. As time progresses, we shall perhaps approach nearer one another

so far as facts and opinions based on them are concerned ; but with regard to fundamentals, we shall
evidently remain far away from one another. Further discussion will hardly be of any use, we shall
not be able to help each other in that way.

THE QUINTESSENCE OF GANDHISM

The Realization of God

The foundation of Mahatma Gandhi's life is formed by his firm faith in God. He looks upon God as that Universal Being which encompasses everything and of which humanity is one small part. God is also the Law working behind all that manifests itself to us through the senses ; for the Law and the Law-maker are not distinguishable from one another. It is not possible for us to comprehend the fullness of God on account of the limitation of our senses. But it is possible to form a conception of the working of the Law, even if imperfectly, if we make a diligent effort for that purpose. The highest aim of human life is to try to discover the Law, and while so doing to purify every act of our life in conformity with the Law, in so far as it has been revealed to us by enquiry.

As soon as we try to move along the path outlined above, we discover that the chief obstacle to the realization comes finally from the narrownesses of our personal self. Selfishness and cruelty in a subtle form, laziness and the pride that we are already in possession of all truth, are the greatest obstacles in our path. Our lives should accordingly be an unremitting exercise of self-purification, so that truth may shine clearly upon it. Our activity should also be as unwearied as that of the 'drop of water in the ocean.' And if such is the grace of God, this

22

tireless pursuit may, one day, bring us within reach of a happiness, the like of which can never be experienced in any other way. All other happinesses are false or transient.

In course of his life's varied experiences, Gandhi has reached the conclusion that just as his own path must lie through the service of oppressed humanity, so for others it may be otherwise. There may be many roads to the same goal ; and, personally, he would feel happy if every one tirelessly pursues the path which lies before him, and never lays down the burden which he has been appointed to carry. Of one thing, he feels certain : whatever may be the path which one chooses, its sincere pursuit is sure to uplift the quality of character in the seeker after truth. In such a man, continuous exercise not only brightens the vision of Truth, but his heart also becomes filled with an abundance of human love. In other words, his charity and toleration increase.

Satyagraha

This forms the core of Gandhi's philosophy of life ; all that he does or preaches by example springs finally from this basic attitude towards Truth. The use of Satyagraha as a social instrument is only the above law of individual spiritual life projected into the sphere of mass action. Collective Satyagraha is, for Gandhi, the same discipline for realizing the truth of human unity as the individual's private effort in that direction may be. Thus Swaraj becomes synonymous with that undefinable, yet limitless term *Moksha* or emancipation, while economic and political freedom turn out to be necessary, but lower rungs in the ladder which leads up to the individual's highest emancipation.

Samskaras

The adove ideas of Mahatma Gandhi do not, however, exhaust the whole of his mental make-up. He has certain personal likes and dislikes, derived either from life's early experiences or from the masters whom he has acknowledged as his own ; and it is through these *samskaras* that his universal ideas find expression. Of such ideas, we can readily think of two, one derived from ancient Hindu culture and the other, apparently, from Christianity. His predilection for forms or institutions which have endured through ages, in other words, the recognition of permanency as a quality of Truth, has obviously been derived from his traditional social equipment. This has led him to a very mild form of conservatism, but which has the redeeming feature of being always subjected to the final tests of reason and universal morality. In spite of this, the thin strain of conservatism makes Gandhi a shade more receptive of old ideas than of those which have not yet been tested by the hand of time.

The other *samskara* which may have resulted from a reaction in his own life against childhood's married experiences, or from his early Christian associations, is his concept of sin and the special attitude which he bears towards sensual purity. Some observers have compared this to that of mediaeval Christian saints. But, whatever may be the origin of these *samskaras*, they have to be taken into account when we try to form an estimate of Gandhi's real greatness, which consists in the magnitude of his realized ideals.

Economic Idealism

A further study of Gandhi's writings reveals the strong influence exercised upon him by thinkers like Ruskin and Tolstoy. This gives a meaning to his intense dislike for industrialism with its inseparable centralization of power and control. With Tolstoy, Gandhi believes that the root of the present distress lies in man's selfishness and his predatory habit of living upon the toils of others, a habit which has been encouraged rather than restrained under the influence of modern civilization. In that civilization selfish men have starved others of wealth as well as of power, and turned everything to the advantage of their own class, and thus been the cause of much human misery which could otherwise have been avoided. They have not only ruined the lives of others, but also been degraded themselves as a result of the act of exploitation. The first law of economic morality should therefore be that everyone, who does so, should get off other people's backs, and live according to the law of bread-labour, which is a true consequence of the Christian law that man should live by the sweat of his brow.

In the free society of the future, Gandhi holds that incomes from all socially necessary forms of labour should be equal. All men should be in a position to satisfy their natural wants without encroaching upon similar satisfaction in others. Natural inequalities will remain till the end of time, and will not be suppressed on any account. But the talented persons will be persuaded by the force of enlightened public opinion to place their talents at the service of humanity. Their gain will be the pleasure which they derive from a due exercise of their native abilities.

Non-resistance

The question is, how can such a society be brought into being in the face of the opposition of those in enjoyment of power today, and interested in the maintenance of their existing privileges. Tolstoy prescribed the Christian law of non-resistance ; he gave it a new meaning. According to him, the only moral form of dealing with evil was to return it by good. For if we return evil by evil, we really co-operate with evil. The correct way, therefore, is to non-co-operate with evil by developing that which is its opposite. Thus non-resistance or non-violent resistance, is not a negative process, but is an intensely active and positive process in which evil is countered by good for the sake of its liquidation.

Gandhi imbibed his first lesson in non-resistance during his boyhood days from the poem of a Vaishnava saint and from the stories he heard of Prahlad and Harischandra. But his reading of the *Sermon on the Mount*, of Tolstoy's *The Kingdom of God is within you*, and the *Bhagabadgita* helped him to add deeper meaning to the law of non-resistance. Consistent with the rule of matching evil by good,

there can be only one form of revolution. And it
has been in the discovery and development of this
means that Gandhi's genius has found highest
expression. Instead of discovering details about the
form of future society, Gandhi has devoted all his
talents to the elaboration of a way of resistance by
means of which common men and women, who are
otherwise considered defenceless because unarmed,
may develop the strength to fight against the
heaviest odds in pursuit of their goal. Let us see
how Gandhi proposes to do that.

The Law of Suffering

According to him, the institutions of the present
world are there because both the exploiters as well as
the exploited co-operate in its maintenance ; they do
so either in a direct or in an indirect way. If both
could be persuaded to dissociate themselves from
the existing system, the present order would go
to pieces in a moment. But how can this conversion
take place ? Gandhi has found the way in the law
of suffering. He thinks that an appeal to the head
of those who are in enjoyment of power is of no avail
unless it is backed by the shock which comes from a
view of the courageous suffering of those who are
bent on non-co-operating with it. The latter should,
first of all, refuse to derive any advantage from the
present system, and also withdraw their co-operation
from it. In so doing, they will draw upon themselves
the wrath of those whose interest is thus endangered.
If their suffering is adequate, the heart of the
opponents is sure to be touched by a sense of

surprise, respect for the Satyagrahi taking the place of anger against him, and a way opened for human reconciliation on a higher plane. It is a law of Satyagraha that the nobler the object, the higher should be the price paid for it in terms of suffering. This suffering may come directly in the form of punishment induced by non-co-operation, or in the form of intense labour necessary to build up the social order according to one's own ideal.

Some have imagined that non-violent non-co-operation means the 'minimum suffering of the maximum number.' But, Gandhi personally feels that Satyagraha can never succeed unless one is prepared to pay the highest price of which one is capable. The Satyagrahi may not actually be called upon to lay down his life for his goal ; but unless he is mentally prepared in the fullest measure for such sacrifice, the goal may never be reached. Moreover, in order to hasten the desired consummation, it is necessary that during the process of non-co-operation, the heart of the civil resister must ever remain bright with the spirit of human brotherhood, and his hand held back by an infinitude of patience. It is only love of this kind which can work miracles.

Gandhi's Originality

Someone asked Gandhi whether non-co-operation was not a process of seizure of power. Gandhi said, no. It was meant to transform the relationship between human beings, which would ultimately lead to a peaceful transfer of power from the erstwhile exploiter to both, who now share the power and become equal in toil. Now, this process may seem long and arduous to many. Some may even feel that the aim of converting the mind of the upholders of a system is irrelevant when we are out to destroy the system itself. But Gandhi is clearly of opinion that it is only by a conversion of our opponent, and by gaining his co-operation in the making of the new system that we can build for permanency. Such a process of revolution is indeed the shortest one, because it is also the surest. A good social order, when imposed by force from above, cannot root out the evil which lies hidden within. Good based upon authority is ultimately no good at all. Freedom alone is the prime condition of human growth.

In the last analysis, therefore, Gandhi does not hold forth any tempting ideal which can draw men along a difficult path. He is more concerned in discovering the way for himself and in avoiding the pitfalls which he may encounter in course of the journey. He has the hope that his pursuit of Truth has the power to evoke in other men a similar courage to face the hardships of the Road. Truth, he believes, has in it the seeds of its own propagation. Perhaps the way that he has chosen is an old one, perhaps many have successfully treaded it before. But it is Gandhi who has rescued it from the world's private armoury and fashioned out of it a first class instrument of wide social application.

GANDHI AND LENIN

In the midst of the gloom which encircles mankind on all sides, there are always men who struggle with the surrounding darkness and succeed in saving their souls from its oppressive influence. Of such men in the present age, we can think of two who carry the marks of having successfully fought the battle, and whose lives bear testimony to the enormity of the suffering through which they have had to pass. Lenin and Gandhi. Both these men resemble one another in their tireless pursuit of Truth, as well as in their great passion for the poor and the oppressed portion of humanity. Yet in the matter of their inner convictions and attitudes, they differ as widely from one another as possible.

According to both Lenin and Gandhi, the world's suffering is mostly caused by the existence of an unjust social system which allows one class of men to live upon the toils of another. The system not only blights the lives of those who are exploited, but also degrades those who live upon the toil of others. It has therefore to be destroyed if we want men to gain the opportunity of free and full exercise of their talents. In this, both Gandhi and Lenin agree. But it is with regard to the means, as well as the mental attitudes which they bring to bear upon their task that the two drift completely away from one another.

Lenin was of opinion that the unjust social and economic system exists today because the exploiters hold the power of the State in their hands. If that power can be transferred to the exploited by means of a revolution, then they can so build society anew that a repetition of the present wrongs becomes impossible. All his endeavours were therefore directed towards securing such a revolution as would bring the State under the dictatorship of the proletariat. Under that dictatorship, property relations will be entirely recast, men's entire outlook on life would be reshaped by education, and no scope left anywhere for the exercise of the former desire to exploit.

Gandhi however holds quite another view. He is opposed fundamentally to the coercive centralization involved in Lenin's scheme. He is of opinion that such coercion will only perpetuate the passive aspect of human character on which the structure of capitalism itself has been reared today. He believes that the root of the problem does not lie in the authority of the State, but in the character of the individual which has made the existence of the State possible. Those who rule, do so because others are afraid of violence all the time. Therefore, we can enjoy the right of freedom only if we cast the fear which lies buried in our hearts, and, at the same time, labour with our hands for the production of our daily bread. All his efforts are therefore directed towards bringing about the necessary change in individual character; and this he proposes to do by his constructive economic and social programme, on the one hand, and by non-violent non-co-operation, which advances by progressive stages, on the other.

But what will be the shape of things when labouring humanity succeeds in reorganizing socia llife completely by means of its own effort and the help of those who cast in their lot with the former ? Gandhi has said that inequalities of wealth, power and position will be equalized to the utmost extent possible. But even when man-made inequalities have been completely reduced, their will remain over certain inequalities due to nature. These should not be interfered with; only they should not be made the basis for the formation of privileged classes. To prevent exploitation arising out of natural inequalities, it is necessary to do something more. Every man should be inspired with the idea that whatever his special talents may be, they should be turned to social use and not to personal advantage. This is true of individuals as much as of nations ; every one should place his resources and his abilities at the service of humanity taken as a whole. The aim of those who employ Satyagraha to convert either individuals or communities, should be to convert them into this ideal of common possession and of trusteeship.

The wide divergence between Lenin and Gandhi with regard to the means, as set forth above, springs ultimately from a fundamental difference in their opinion regarding the role played by the individual in human history. Lenin held that, in spite of rare exceptions, men are mostly creatures of circumstance ; so that if they are to be made moral, they should be placed under circumstances which render a particular moral code imperative. His principal endeavour was

therefore to build up an architectural system of the
necessary kind. But Gandhi has little faith in good
life based principally upon compulsion or habit, if
it is blind. Such morality, in his opinion, fails to
develop the best which lies dormant in the human
personality. Really fruitful change can only come
from within ; and the principal object of social change
should therefore be to bring it into being through
change already wrought in human individuals.
All change in outward form should be an expression,
as well as a measure, of the degree of inner progress
attained. We may describe the difference between
Lenin and Gandhi by saying that the former builds
his plans on man as he actually is today, while
the latter bases his upon what it is possible or
desirable for him to be.

Lenin was like a mighty warrior who held aloft
a great hope for mankind, while his soul was steeped
in the dream of a millenium when no man would
live in cruelty and idleness but in love, and actively
employ his talents for the service of mankind. With
his strong taste for reality, he turned to History for
a sanction of the hope which swelled within his
bosom ; and there he discovered the finger of Fate
pointing towards such fulfilment as he desired for
mankind. It was because of the fatalistic nature
of this belief that Lenin could employ the most
ruthless weapons of destruction in order to overcome
the obstacles which came in his way. The path,
he thought, may lie today through violence and
hatred, but the day will surely dawn when it will be
time to lay down the sword, or perhaps melt it for

building the plough, for then man will have no reason to hate man. But until that day arrives, our path must lie through violence and bloodshed, for that is the inevitable law of History. Lenin was like a workman, passionately hammering away at the anvil at night, in the glow of the lamp which he had lighted out of his heart's desire, while he was oblivious of the dark sky which hung over his head. And in that sky, the cold stars shone with a glitter which knew no compassion for the love or the hate which alternately burned within the bosom of the workman.

But Gandhi, the pilgrim soul, is ceaselessly on the march in a journey which seems to be without end. With the staff of the traveller in his hand, he moves towards a distant light which guides him inexorably towards itself. Hope burns in his bosom, and he yields to its impulse, for there is nothing more for him to do. In the inner depth of his being, he knows it is not his business to enquire if ever the millenium will come or not. All that he is called upon to do is to submit, at the present moment, to the forces of his purified nature and thus fulfil the task for which he was appointed by God. It is his ideal 'to become merely like a lump of clay in the Potter's divine hands.' And this is also the reason why he can say in true humility that his task is the 'service of God and therefore of humanity.'

Gandhi believes that God never admits us into the design of the future. He has given us no control over the end, and only a limited one over the means ;

and the means is love. And Gandhi claims that he has discovered the secret whereby love can be employed to transform one's environment and free human life from the oppression which weighs down upon it from all sides. That secret is to love the oppressors of mankind as oneself, even when we are opposing them by militant non-co-operation in order to end the system which has so far been based on injustice. We seek to transform the mutual relationship between the exploiter and the exploited, and this will eventually lead to the extinction of the present system by common effort, and the creation of a new order based upon the transformed social relationship. It is a terribly difficult adventure to which Gandhi invites us, to oppose a tyrant while bearing no malice, but positive love and respect for his personality in our hearts. But as this is the noblest way, Gandhi asks us to spare no pains in following it to perfection. All his genius is exercised in discovering this path of non-violent non-co-operation in order to remedy wrongs ; the results he leaves in the keeping of God.

But weak as we are, our strength fails us when we are confronted by the heights to which we are expected to raise ourselves. We find that Gandhi's absolute insistence upon the means often leaves us despairing of our own weaknesses. So we turn to him and ask him if it is wrong to be intoxicated with a dream and a hope when darkness presses upon our soul from all around. Gandhi answers : Indeed you should believe in the promise of the day when man shall disdain to enrich himself at the cost of his neighbour, but live instead by means of Work and Love. In the meanwhile, he asks us to take care of the means, to guide our next step in accordance with our own strength, with single-mindedness in the direction of universal good and of complete human brotherhood.

Secretly, to the chosen few who can bear it, he whispers a less luring truth. To them Gandhi says that the promise of the dawn is but the bait with which God tempts His creatures to action, along paths which He chooses. And if He so wills, He may anyday sweep aside all our hopes and joys and hurl us into the depths of unutterable misery, for He is above all the greatest Tyrant ever known. Our business is to toil unceasingly at our appointed task and throw ourselves against every obstacle which oppresses human life, without regard to consequences. We belong to the gang of workmen employed to keep the road ready for God's chariot to pass by. Even with regard to his mother-land, he says that it is true that he wants his countrymen to enjoy political freedom, he wants food and raiment for the hungry millions, but these are only the things with which India will clothe herself before she is called upon, in the interest of humanity, to embrace death as her divine bridegroom. 'My idea of nationalism is that my country may become free that, if need be, the whole country may die so that the human races may live.'

These are indeed awful words. But Gandhi consoles us by saying that the powers of patience which reside within the human soul are also of unlimited measure. If we throw aside all attachment to the flesh, which is the root of all fear, and have our being in God who is the repository of all strength, we shall never lack in the necessary strength to bear His message of love in our lives.

This is the prospect which Gandhi holds out to his comrades ; no vision of any distant millenium, but only a vision of the thorns which we shall encounter in our pilgrim's march. He shows us only the way, even while seeking it himself whereby we can lay down our lives so that humanity may live. And in that path, God Himself is transformed into the Flaming Sword which leaps and plays over the road of thorns. The sole aim of our existence is to surrender ourselves to that Almighty Being. Our own joys and sorrows sink into the uttermost insignificance, while life and death are transformed into so many milestones in our lonesome march.

This ultimate acceptance of the permanent nature of that which we call sorrow and suffering, and from which we shrink instinctively, does not spring in Gandhi from any inner morbidness of spirit. It comes from a recognition of the fact that both light and darkness, life and death, are parts of one Universal Being which we may not accept in fragments. It is this aspect of Gandhi, with its apotheosis of labour and of suffering, which drew forth the instinctive repulsion of the poet Tagore, whose admirable temper was now and then ruffled by the prospect of a flood of morbidity overcoming the land in the wake of Gandhi's political movement of 'non-co-operation.' But in Gandhi himself, there is not the least trace of morbidness ; for his whole soul has been bathed clean by the tears of humble admission of weakness before God. Love of man has given him the strength to bless all sufferings which come in his way ; indeed it is the same kind of heroism which a mother displays when her child is torn out her being.

If that be the character of Gandhi's philosophy, devoid of hope, of romance, how is it, one may ask, that men follow him in thousands even when he calls upon them to proceed to the portals of death ? The secret lies in the character and personality of the man, in which his philosophy has clothed itself, rather than in any direct appeal which lies in that philosophy. And here perhaps we reach the inner truth of the present revolution in India, as we also do of all those great movements which have affected human societies to their depths. Russia today is inexplicable except in terms of Lenin, the movement of Christ except with reference to the personality of Jesus, while India's Satyagraha is likewise understandable only with reference to the character of the man who stands at the head of the movement today.

A lone man marching with set purpose upon the road of God ; whose heart beats in unison with every sorrow in the human breast ; determined to share all human suffering and degradation, and ready to sacrifice himself in the effort to lift all that oppresses

23

human life ; but who is never prepared to betray the sacred trust of human unity even for the sake of temporary gain ; such a character holds an appeal and an encouragement far greater than the cold star of truth towards which the pilgrim may be marching himself. It is only when the light of the stars shines forth through the life of a man that we can feel its glow and light our own life's path by means of its radiance.

It is good to live at a time when such men are born on earth ; for their living testimony to the might of the human spirit restores to us faith and gives us the strength to hope afresh and try to build the world anew.

INDEX

ABBREVIATIONS

Auto—The Story of My Experiments with Truth. Navajivan Press, Ahmedabad. Second Edition, May 1940.

CB—Congress Bulletin issued by the All India Congress Committee. Swaraj Bhawan, Allahabad.

CP—Constructive Programme : Its Meaning and Place by M. K. Gandhi. Navajivan Publishing House, Ahmedabad. December, 1945.

Ceylon—With Gandhiji in Ceylon by Mahadev Desai. S. Ganesan, Triplicane, Madras. 1928.

Doke—M. K. Gandhi by Joseph J. Doke. First Indian Edition, G. A. Natesan & Co. Madras. Originally published in 1907.

Gandhiji—Gandhiji : His Life and Work. Published on his 75th Birthday, October 2, 1944. Karnatak Publishing House, Bombay.

GC—Gandhiji's Correspondence with the Government 1942-44. Navajivan Publishing House, Ahmedabad. Second Edition, September 1945.

H—Harijan, 1934 onwards.

HC—The History of the Indian National Congress, Volume I (1885-1935) and Volume II (1935-1947) by Dr. Pattabhi Sitaramayya. Padma Publications, Bombay. 1947.

HS—*Hindusthan Standard*, Calcutta.

IAR—The Indian Annual Register, published by N. N. Mitra. Annual Register Office, Sibpur, Calcutta.

IHR—Hind Swaraj or Indian Home Rule by M. K. Gandhi. Published by the Navajivan Publishing House, Ahmedabad. 1944.

IID—Is India Different ?, published by the Communist Party of Great Britain. December, 1927.

IV—Gandhiji in Indian Villages by Mahadev Desai. S. Ganesan, Triplicane, Madras. 1927.

NV—The Nation's Voice. Navajivan Press, Ahmedabad. 1932.

PU—Punjab Unrest : Before and After, published by the Annual Register Office, Sibpur, Calcutta. April 1920.

Natesan—Speeches and Writings of Mahatma Gandhi, Fourth Edition. G. A. Natesan & Co., Madras.

SA—Satyagraha in South Africa by M. K. Gandhi. S. Ganesan, Triplicane, Madras. 1928.

YI—Young India, 1919-1932.

YI, Tagore—1919-1922. Tagore & Co., Madras, 1922.